D1716620

KANSAS
The Prairie Spirit - History People Stories

By Phyllis Griekspoor and Beccy Tanner

A Publication of
The Grace Dangberg Foundation, Inc.

A Dangberg Historical Publication

The Grace Dangberg Foundation, Inc.
David Thompson, President
Denise Dangberg, Vice-President
James H. Bean, Sec./Treasurer & Director

The Grace Dangberg Foundation was established in 1982 by the late Grace Dangberg, a distinguished Nevada historian and granddaughter of Carson Valley pioneers. The Foundation was created to improve the study of history by young people through the publication of books.

Publisher: The Grace Dangberg Foundation, Inc.

Writers: Phyllis Griekspoor and Beccy Tanner

Editors: Don Lynch and James H. Bean

Editorial Assistant & Book Layout: Susan Bean

Title: Kansas: The Prairie Spirit – History, People, Stories

Library of Congress Catalog Number: 99-80186

ISBN: 0-193205-26-5

Printed by Automated Graphic Systems

The cover art is by Jose Cruzpagan. The back cover quilt is courtesy of The Kansas State Historical Society.

Acknowledgments

The Board of Trustees of The Grace Dangberg Foundation wishes to thank those who helped in any way towards the completion of this history of Kansas, its people, and their stories.

Without the writers, Phyllis Griekspoor and Beccy Tanner, this book would not have been written for the people of Kansas. The Trustees thank them for their long days and nights of hard work.

Consultants Stan R. Harder and Michael Kelly gave generously of their time, knowledge, and skill to provide the illustrations and photos which best tell the story of Kansas. Consultants Harder and Kelly also conducted research for items of information needed by the writers.

A very special thanks to local Kansas artist, Jose Cruzpagan, who produced the colorful cover art and the colorful chapter dividers just for this book.

The Trustees have appreciated the work of Editor/Writer Don Lynch for over fifteen years. Don has written books for the Foundation and he edited most of this Kansas history book and did some re-writing where needed. Don died on January 6, 2000 at the age of 84. We will miss him.

Reviewers and readers were most valuable in keeping the writers on track as they wrote their overview of many events in the Kansas story. Among these wonderful readers were Mary Ann Thompson who pointed to the fine points of specific events. Dave Loder, Foundation reader, assisted by reviewing several chapters. Joan Cline of Garfield, Darla Mallein of Emporia, Deanna Nech of Kensington, Marsha Parry of Olathe, Tina Sayler of Hutchinson, Kyle Shively of Monument, and Dave Wutke of Girard read chapters and provided needed comments as to possible student reactions to the text. The writing team and the Foundation staff welcomed their astute comments, which saved much time and many pages of work. The Teacher readers provided valuable understanding as to what was appropriate that belonged in the book as well as what was not appropriate and did not belong in the book. For their time and help we are most appreciative.

The Trustees gratefully acknowledge the services of the Kansas Historical Society, Wichita State University Special Collections; Wichita-Sedgwick County Historical Museum; Mennonite Library and Archives at Bethel College; Kaufman Museum at Bethel College; Boeing Commercial Airplane Group; Cessna Aircraft

Company; High Plains Museum; Reno County Museum; Leonard H. Axe Library Pittsburg State University; Finney County Historical Society; Barton County Historical Society; Kansas State University; The University of Kansas; Russell County Historical Society; Old Cowtown Museum; Kansas Aviation Museum; the Karen P. Newforth Collection; the Kansas 4-H Foundation, Inc.; and the Santa Fe Trail Center, and The Wichita Eagle and Beacon Publishing Company and its staff for any assistance given to the writers and for photo and story assistance from their newspaper archives.

A special appreciation for help provided by Carl E. Parry, CEO, Utilities Service Alliance for his research and information on the Wolf Creek Generating Station. He also assisted with teacher meetings and facilities.

A hearty thank you to John Avery and Avery Postcards for allowing the use of their postcards which brought wonderful photography and color to the book.

A special appreciation to Steve Hawley for giving some of his busy time, for an interview just prior to his July 1999 Columbia flight and a "thank you" to NASA for arranging the interview and photos.

The writers and researchers acknowledge the help, advice, and support of Scott Price, Fort Riley historian for sharing his knowledge and resources; Bob Pickett and Jami Frazier Tracty; John Thiesen; Dr. Rachel Pannabecker; and Nancy Sherbert and staff, The Kansas State Historical Society.

Appreciation to Jaclyn Jacobs for handwriting most of the postcards used in the book.

There are always others who have contributed to such an effort. We sincerely appreciate their help and assistance in producing, *KANSAS: The Prairie Spirit – History, People, Stories*.

J. H. Bean
Trustee and Director, The Grace Dangberg Foundation, Inc.

Table of Contents

Historical Events

1541 - Conquistadors led by Coronado comes to Kansas

1803 - The Louisiana Purchase

1804 - The Lewis and Clark Expedition

1806 - The Pike Expedition

1819 - Adams-Onis Treaty with Spain

1819-1820 - The Long Expedition

1830 - Congress passed The Indian Removal Act

1839 - Epidemic of Smallpox and Cholera

1846 - U. S. and Mexico goes to war

1854 - Congress passed The Kansas-Nebraska Act

CRUZ PAGAN 99

Chapter 1

The Indians and The Explorers

CHAPTER 1

The Indians and The Explorers

When European explorers first came to the land that would be Kansas, there were four main tribes of people already living there. These were the first people of historic times. The Quivira (later called the Wichita), the Pawnee, the Osage, and the Kaw (Kanza). There were also tribes of Comanche, Kiowa, Southern Cheyenne, and western Plain Apache.

Earlier people in Kansas left their stories in the rocks, not as fossils, but as carvings, drawings or figures made by laying out stones in a pattern. Even before people learned how to write, they told stories with shapes and drawings. They left us clues about their lives and the things they made for tools and weapons.

There are about 4,000 archaeological sites that have been documented in Western Kansas alone. Of those, nearly 100 are on the National Register of Historic Places.

All of those things found, and the written stories and objects of the more recent residents, make up the history of Kansas. It is a history full of changes, violence, growth and ideas, jam-packed with drama and action. Like all history, it is about people and their decisions and how those decisions changed the world.

As the first explorers came to the New World, there were no maps to guide them. The maps they used to travel across the oceans weren't even close to the actual shapes of the land or the distance across the land. The information on the map he had was 13 centuries old. It showed Europe and Asia covering as much as half of the world!

The new land was vast. It had all the resources the Indians needed to live and be happy. There was plenty of clean water, elk, deer, and other game. The rivers were full of fish. The great grassy plains were home to enormous herds of bison (buffalo).

What happened to the native Indians when Europeans intruded upon their way of life is a story to be told.

The First People

It is believed that in prehistoric times, this bridge of land and ice was used by ancient ancestors of the American Indians to migrate from Siberia to North America. At some time later, rising oceans covered the land bridge.

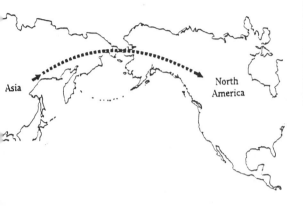

The Arrival of the Conquistadors

After 1492, the simple hunting, gathering and farming life of the tribal people of the Americas was drastically changed.

When Christopher Columbus sailed west across the Atlantic Ocean in search of a new trade route to Asia, he discovered a new land. He claimed the land for Spain. Soon other Spanish explorers came. They wanted to find more land to claim. They hoped they would find gold and other treasures, too. These explorers were called conquistadors, which means one who conquers.

With the conquistadors came another type of Spanish explorer -- the missionaries. They wanted to spread the word of God to the native people.

Five Periods of Early Civilization

Scientists divide early civilization into five periods. Evidence of people who lived as long as 10,000 years ago have been found in Kansas.

Bones and teeth of huge mammals can be found in the Arkansas River Valley and the Walnut River Valley. A hunting site where early people killed bison has been found in Logan County.

* **The Paleo-Indian Period,** about 11,000 to 7,000 B.C. People were nomadic hunters and gatherers. They followed herds of big animals such as the bison and mammoth. These people also ate berries, seeds, roots, and small animals. They used spears tipped with large chipped stone projectile points. These points have been found in all parts of Kansas.

* **The Archaic Period,** about 7,000 B.C. to 1 A. D. Big herd animals declined. People planted foods and hunted small game. They began to grind seeds and to make pottery.

* **The Woodland Period,** 1 A. D. to about 1000 A.D. Chipped stone tools became smaller and the bow and arrow replaced the spear. Homes became more permanent. The dead were buried with ceremonies. Ancient burial sites are still found in northern and eastern Kansas.

* **The Village Garden Period,** 1000 A.D. to 1500 A. D. Indians hunted bison and grew corn, squash, and beans. They were skilled with bows and arrows. They developed a trade route with the Pueblo Indians of the Southwest.

* **The Protohistoric Period,** 1500 A. D. to 1800 A. D. These people were the ancestors of the today's tribes: Pawnee, Kanza, Wichita, and Apache.

The Mapmakers

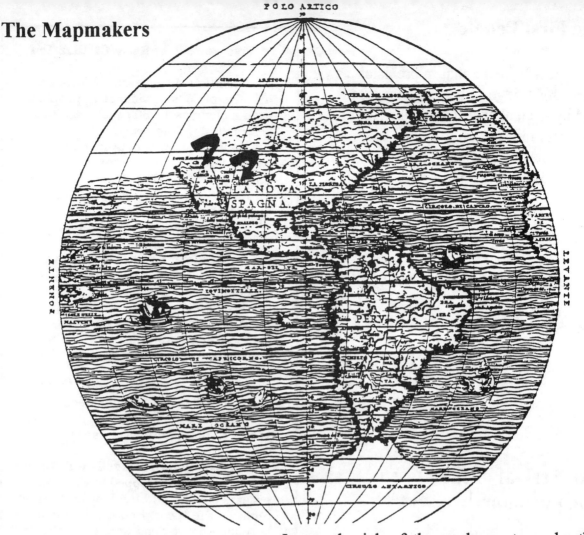

This 1556 Spanish map is the first to show Quivira in the west of the known land. Find Quivira near the arrow placed on the map. Also note Cibola. Note how little the Spanish knew of the West at this time.
Map courtesy of Wichita State University Special Collections

Star Chart
The Pawnee Indians of Kansas were skilled in the making of star charts. They painted their charts on elk skins and used them as a guide to cross the Plains at night. Their system was much like the one sailors used to find their way across the ocean by the stars.

It was the job of the explorers to make the maps as they went. Map making earlier than 1569, was crude and distorted, until Mercator made a more accurate projection.

But as exploration of the New World began efforts were made to show the actual features of the land. Scales were also developed to show distances between places.

The Spanish maps of the New World pointed to the likely locations of gold and silver mines.

The French later made maps marking places where they met with Indians to trade.

Much later, when American explorers began to map the land, they marked places that may be good places for people to live.

Their maps showed which rivers were deep enough for boats or barges to carry people and goods. They marked the trails to settlements of the Southwest

Greed Comes to Kansas

Francisco Vasquez de Coronado was one of the most famous of the Spanish conquistadors. He had conquered a lot of territory in Mexico before he came to Pueblo, in what is now New Mexico. He was looking for riches. He had been told there were "Seven Cities of Cebola" with untold riches. He found only poor Indian villages.

In Pueblo, Coronado met a Quiviran Indian who had been captured and was being forced to work as a slave among the Pueblo Indians. Coronado called this man "El Turco" (The Turk) because he resembled someone from Turkey.

The Pueblos didn't like the Spanish conquistadors and they wanted to find a way to make them leave. They had already tried an armed revolt, but their primitive weapons were no match for the conquistadors' armor. They were defeated and brutally slaughtered.

El Turco decided to make up a story that would lead Coronado and his army far away from the village into the desert (Western Kansas) where, he hoped, the

The petroglyph at Palmer's Cave in Ellsworth County depicts a ladder and several figures, some carrying shields. Archaeologists believe ancient people drew on the walls of sandstone to tell a story.
Photo courtesy of The Kansas State Historical Society

bert T. Reid's painting shows what the artist imagined Don Francisco Vasquez de Coronado's arrival may have oked like. It was painted somed 350 years after Coronado's arrival. In the early part of this century, Reid was a litical illustrator for the Kansas City Star.
oto courtesy of The Kansas State Historical Society

Spanish would lose their directions, become lost, star[v]
and die. He would then make his way home.

Knowing how his enemies hungered for gold, [?]
Turco told them that the land he came from, Quivir[a?]
was rich, splendid, and wonderful.

He told them: *"In my land there is a great
king named Tatarrax, who takes his naps under
trees filled with tinkling, golden bells and eats
his food from plates made of gold and silver."*

There were seven cities of pure gold, he sai[d]
and the people walked on streets paved with gold.

He offered to lead them there. Th[e]
Spanish were all too willing [to]
believe El Turco's stories.

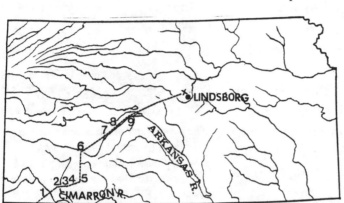

*1541, Don Francisco Vasquez de
Coronado's journey.*
1. Liberal, 2. Plains, 3. Meade,
4. Fowler, 5. Minneloa, 6. Dodge,
7. Kingsley, 8. Larned, 9. Great Bend.
Map courtesy of The Dangberg Foundation.

The March Northward

In April of 1541, Coronad[o]
following El Turco, set out with a[n]
impressive array of almost 1,00[0]
people. There were conquistadors dressed in full arm[or]
with horsemen and footmen at their sides.

There were settlers and Indians they ha[d]
brought along as slaves and servants. They broug[ht]
cattle, sheep, and hogs to slaughter for food along t[he]
way. Imagine the sight they must have been for t[he]
Plains Indians who had never seen a horse before, [let]
alone shining men riding astride strange creatures.

Not far into the march, Coronado decided th[at]
the land was so empty and dry that his entire expediti[on]
could not complete the journey.

He sent most of his men back to New Mexic[o.]
Coronado selected about 30 men to press on [and]
find the Seven Cities of Gold. He told El Tur[co]
to lead the way. Coronado's march include[d]
much of what is today Texas and the Oklaho[ma]
panhandle. He entered Kansas near what is no[w]
Liberal. He passed near the areas of Plain[s,]
Meade, Fowler, and Minneola before crossi[ng]
the Arkansas River near where Dodge City [is]
today. The expedition encountered son[?]
Quivira/Wichita Indians near present da[y]
Kinsley and Larned.

Photo by Douglas Oplinger, courtesy of The Dangberg
Foundation

Close to Great Bend, Coronado's party found a cluster of Quivira villages. The Turk, foiled in his plan to lose the Spanish in the desert, tried to get the Indians to attack the Spaniards. Coronado's men discovered his plan. They had him put in chains. Later, he was strangled.

Artifacts left behind by Coronado's march are still being found today along the path he took. Some artifacts are on display in the museum at Lyons.

No Gold, but Pleasing Land

The Spanish did not find gold in the land of Quivira. There had never been gold in Kansas. Apparently they did find land that they liked very well. Coronado's chronicler, Jaramillo said otherwise.

He wrote of Kansas:

"The country has a fine appearance - the like of which I have never seen anywhere in our Spain, Italy, or part of France....it is not a hilly country, but one with mesa's, plains, and charming rivers with fine waters and it pleased me indeed."

Coronado left Kansas in August of 1541 and made his way back to the Rio Grande valley (New Mexico) where he rejoined his original group. He had found no riches.

The Early Missionary Effort

There were, however, lasting effects on the Plains Indians from the Spanish intrusion. Juan De Padilla, a Franciscan priest wanted to introduce Christianity to the natives. He was part of the original group of 30 and he got along well with the Quivira. Next spring, he returned to Quivira land. He hoped to teach Christianity to more Indians. He had with him a few assistants and servants. Padilla was described as young, energetic, and devoted. He was a humble man and did not try to impress the Indians with his power and ability. The soldiers had worn armor and rode horses. Father Padilla wore simple

Padilla Monument erected 1950.
Photo by Doug Oplinger, courtesy of The Dangberg Foundation

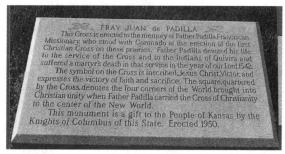

FRAY JUAN de PADILLA
This Cross is erected to the memory of Father Padilla Franciscan. Missionary who stood with Coronado at the erection of the first Christian Cross on these prairies. Father Padilla devoted his life to the service of the Cross and to the Indians of Quivira and suffered a martyr's death in that service in the year of our Lord 1542.
The symbol on the Cross is inscribed, Jesus Christ, Victor, and expresses the victory of faith and sacrifice. The square, quartered by the Cross, denotes the four corners of the World brought into Christian unity when Father Padilla carried the Cross of Christianity to the center of the New World.
This monument is a gift to the People of Kansas by the Knights of Columbus of this State. Erected 1950.

robes and he walked instead of riding.

When he returned to the Indian village, Father Padilla was pleased to find that the cross he had built the year before had been kept and cared for. He was encouraged by his converting the people to the Christian faith.

He announced he was going on to other tribes to spread his message there.

The Quivira liked Padilla and did not want him to leave to go to other Indians. To keep him from leaving, they killed him. This made Padilla the first Christian martyr to be killed on Kansas soil. Memorials to Padilla have been erected at both Council Grove and near the town of Lyons.

Despite Coronado's failure to find riches and the fate of Father Padilla, the Spanish continued to believe there was gold in Kansas. Over the next century they made several expeditions to search for gold. They found the native people were turning bitterly hostile. This was partly because they feared disease that the Europeans had brought with them. Gold was never found and the later expeditions had little lasting impact.

The French Explorers

Beginning in the mid-1600s, the French were seeing the need to make explorations into Kansas. Spain was gaining influence in the world.

The French also were lured by the promise of gold and silver.

But like the Spanish, the French never found gold. They settled instead for selling the furs they aquired by trade with the Indians. In 1724, Ethienne Veniard de Bourgmont led a French expedition as far west as Saline and Ellsworth counties and met with the Plains Apache. His idea was to make friends with the Indians and open the way for more trade.

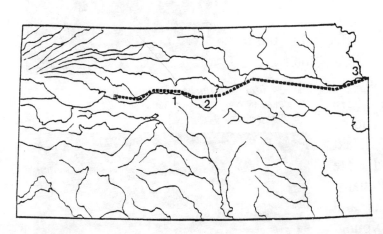

1724 Route by Ethienne Veniard de Bourgmont.
1. Ellsworth County area. 2. Saline County area. 3. Fort de Cavagnial.
Map courtesy of The Dangberg Foundation

The French built Fort Cavagnial in 1744 at a ...aw Indian village near where Fort Leavenworth is ...day. The fort was built both as a place to station ...ldiers and as a trading post. It soon became a ...mmercial and military center for much of Kansas, ...issouri, and Nebraska. The fort became the first ...sting European outpost in Kansas.

ensions Grow

As the French gained a stronghold in the fur ...ade, they found themselves in direct conflict with an ...cient rival, the British. Tensions grew as the French ...ilt forts all along the frontier to protect their fur ...ade. In 1754, those tensions led to hostilities which ...rew into war. Both the French and the British hired ...dians to fight with their soldiers. The conflict came ... be known as "The French and Indian War."

France was also at war with Spain. In the end, ...ey both lost battles. In 1763, France gave all its land ...eld west of the Mississippi River to Spain. Almost all ...e rest of its holdings in the New World went to Great ...ritain.

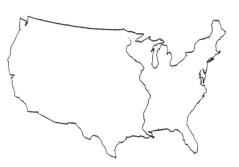

One great highway was the Mississippi River. The people of the United States needed a way to transport trade goods to markets.
Map courtesy of The Dangberg Foundation

At the same time, a conflict was beginning in ...merica. The colonists wanted to be free of British ...le. They declared themselves an independent nation ...d in a revolution that followed, the country of ...merica was born.

The new country needed to use the Mississippi ... transport trade goods to New Orleans. There they ...uld be shipped across the ocean to Europe. Spain ...so let the Americans store their goods in New ...rleans while they waited to load them on freighters.

Then, the balance of power in Europe shifted ...;ain. Napoleon Bonaparte led France to a return to ...ilitary power. Napoleon having a strong Army forced ...ing Charles IV of Spain to give Louisiana back to the ...rench. This included control of the traffic on the ...ississippi River and the Port of New Orleans.

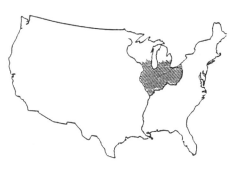

After 1776, the people of the new United States quickly settled all the land between the Ohio River and the Mississippi River.
Map courtesy of The Dangberg Foundation

The Louisiana Purchase

United States President Thomas Jefferson wa afraid the French would charge America to use th river or the port. He sent Robert Livingston to France He told him to buy New Orleans.

There was no Kansas when this map was published in London in 1782 in a book called "North America, Agreeable to Most Approved Maps and Charts," by Thomas Conder. The area that was to become Kansas is shown as an area labeled "Louisiana" some land which belonged to France and some land belonged to Spain. That area became part of the United States 21 years later when the United States bought it from France.
Map courtesy of Wichita State University Special Collections

Livingston could not get the French leaders t talk to him. To get their attention, Livingston started rumor that America might return to an alliance wit England. France wanted no part of more war wit England. Napoleon, short of money and militar people, offered America a deal. He would sell th French holdings in the New World to the Americans fc $15 million. The area included the whole watershed c the Mississippi River. Jefferson bought the land whic came to be called "The Louisiana Purchase." With th purchase, the United States had doubled in size.

All of what is now the states of Louisian Missouri, Iowa, Arkansas, North and South Dakot Nebraska, and Oklahoma were part of the Louisiar Territory. So was what is now Kansas, Colorad Wyoming, Montana, and Minnesota.

1803, The Louisiana Purchase, showing the future Kansas.
Map courtesy of The Dangberg Foundation

Exploring the New Territory

The truth was Jefferson had no idea exactly what he had bought.

There wasn't even a written agreement as to how far west of the Mississippi the territory actually went. The wording of the sale set the western boundary as "as far westward as is habitable." It was years later, in 1818 and 1819, that the United States signed formal treaties with both Spain and Great Britain to establish boundaries.

The northern boundary was set at the forty-ninth parallel between Lake of the Woods and the Rocky Mountains in a convention with Great Britain in 1818. A year later, Secretary of State John Quincy Adams and the Spanish minister Luis Onis signed a treaty establishing the border between the United States and Spanish territories. The Adams-Onis Treaty set the Sabine River, the Red River, the 100th meridian, the Arkansas River, and a line from the source of the river to the forty-second parallel for the boundary. With the treaty, about 7,500 square miles of what would have been Kansas were returned to Spanish territory.

Jefferson didn't know what the land was like or how many native tribes lived there. But he was already thinking that the new land might prove useful as a new homeland for the Indians who were living in the settled United States.

Tribal leaders east of the new territory had sold as much land as they would willingly give up. Jefferson could see that soon they would refuse to sell any more. He, thought, the new land might be suitable to offer in exchange for their land.

He sent a secret message to Congress, asking for $2,500 to pay for a journey of exploration. He told Congress that he needed to send explorers into the new Louisiana Territory to determine if it would be a good place to move the Indians.

1819, Adams-Onis Treaty with Spain, map showing future Kansas. The United States gave to Spain the western states of Colorado, the Oklahoma panhandle, the northern part of Texas, and part of Wyoming. Also included was the lower southwest corner of Kansas.
Map courtesy of The Dangberg Foundation

President Thomas Jefferson, served from 1801 to 1809.
Photo courtesy of Wichita State University Special Collections

Lewis and Clark

Jefferson chose a military officer, Meriwether Lewis to lead a mapping expedition into the Louisiana Territory. Jefferson wanted to discover more about the land he had bought. Lewis chose William Clark to accompany him.

Just how little was really known about the Louisiana Territory is revealed in President Jefferson's instructions to Lewis for the trip.

"The object of your mission," he wrote, "is to explore the Missouri River and such principal stream of it, as by its course and communication with the water of the Pacific Ocean may offer the most direct and practicable water communication across the continent, for the purposes of commerce."

Meriwether Lewis
Illustration courtesy of Wichita State University Special Collections

He thought that boats might be able to go all the way to the Pacific Ocean on the Missouri River or on some other river that could be reached by traveling up the Missouri. Many people of the time believed that a "Northwest Passage" to the Pacific Ocean could be found.

President Jefferson also told Lewis to find everything he could about the people who lived in the new territory. He also wanted to know about the land and whether or not it would be suitable for farming.

He told Lewis to learn:

"...the names of the nations and their numbers; the extent and limits of their possessions; their relations with other tribes or nations; their language, traditions, monuments; their ordinary occupations in fishing, hunting, war, arts and the implements for these; their food, clothing, domestic accommodations (houses); the diseases prevalent among them and the remedies they use."

William Clark
Illustration courtesy of Wichita State University Special Collections

He also wanted Lewis to pay attention to any items of trade they might find useful.

Jefferson went on to tell Lewis to write down all sorts of notes about the soil, the climate, minerals he might find, locations of salt or mineral waters and what kind of plants, animals, and insects he saw.

Jefferson told Lewis to show friendship to the Indians.

"If a few of their influential chiefs, within practicable distance, wish to visit us, arrange such a visit with them...at the public expense," he wrote.

"If any of them should wish to have some of their young people brought up with us and taught such arts as may be useful to them, we will receive, instruct and take care of them."

He also told Lewis:

"...carry with you some matter of the kinepox (cowpox), inform those of men with whom you may be of its efficacy as a preservative from the smallpox; and instruct and encourage them in the use of it."

There is no indication in Lewis' journal or in later history to show this last directive was carried out or even attempted.

By the time of Lewis' visit to eastern Kansas, thousands of Indians had already died of smallpox, cholera, diphtheria, and other diseases to which they had no immunity. Thousands more would die in the years ahead.

The expedition of Lewis and Clark started on May 14, 1804.

The explorers canoed on the well-traveled Missouri River portion of Kansas and spent the Fourth of July holiday near what is Atchison today. To celebrate the holiday, they fired a small cannon from the keel of their boat. They named the two nearby creeks: one Fourth of July Creek and the other Independence Creek.

1804-1806, Lewis and Clark mapped a land route all the way from St. Joseph to the Pacific Ocean. They did not find the waterway that Jefferson had hoped was there.

Map courtesy of The Dangberg Foundation

The Pike Expedition

Meanwhile, another army officer, Lieutenant Zebulon M. Pike was commissioned to explore the southern portion of the Louisiana Purchase.

He entered Kansas in September of 1806 near what is now Fort Scott. He explored the Neosho and Verdigris Rivers. He camped on the Cottonwood River in what is now Chase County. He then moved on to the Smoky Hill, Saline, and Solomon Rivers.

Pike liked eastern Kansas because of the Flint

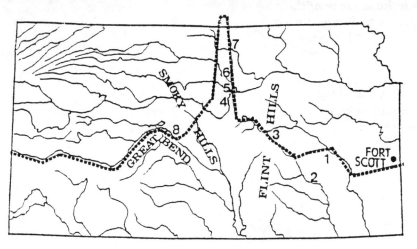

1806, Lieutenant Zebulon M. Pike. 1. Neosho River.
2. Verdigris River.
3. Cottonwood River.
4. Smoky Hill River. 5. Saline River. 6. Solomon River.
7. Republican River.
8. Arkansas River.
Map courtesy of The Dangberg Foundation

Hills and the abundance of wildlife. He noted it would make great pasture land and indeed, it has been just that for close to two centuries. The Flint Hills today covers 1 counties and 3.9 million acres in Kansas. It is considered the finest grazing land in the world.

Pike went up into the north central portion of the state near the Republican River. He went on into Nebraska where the Pawnee Indians who claimed most of the land of northern Kansas were camped. They had recently been visited by the Spanish and had kept a Spanish flag as a gift. Pike told them that they could not have two "father" nations and persuaded them to raise an American flag instead.

Pike then traveled south to the Arkansas River. He followed a trail used by the Pawnees.

When he arrived at the "Great Bend" of the river, he followed it west into what is now Colorado. He saw the Rocky Mountain peak that would be named after him. He did not climb the peak.

Pike was much less impressed with the potential of western Kansas than he was with the eastern portions of the state. He reported that he found it unsuitable for farming and compared it to the sandy deserts of Africa.

The Long Expedition

Reinforcing Pike's opinion of Kansas was another American explorer, Major Stephen H. Long, who led an expedition into the west in 1819 and 1820.

Detachments from his expedition, led by Thomas Say and Lt. John R. Bell, reported on the land that is now Kansas. Say visited a Kaw village on the Blue River in 1819. Bell followed the Arkansas River from the west.

Prairie Spirit

The first important scientist to visit Kansas was Thomas Say. He arrived in the area in 1819 with the Lt. Col. Stephen Long Expedition. While Say was meeting with Kansa Indians, he captured a beetle — which turned out to be a never-before-discovered species.

Long, who was a military officer, was assigned to explore the western frontier. His job was to gather scientific information about the area.

Long found the territory dry and sandy when he made the trip. He was the first to call the western territory, "The Great American Desert."

Others soon picked up this name for western Kansas.

Long's report was merely the first to start leaders talking about the best use for the land of western Kansas. Other explorers and visitors to the area would add their comments. Kansas, the land that for millions of years was an ocean, was now called the Great American Desert. In Washington, politicians had been told that the land was virtually worthless and that the only thing "out there" was Indians.

Congress decided that Kansas should be designated "Indian Territory." Then, as white settlements moved west, the Indians should be relocated.

Thus, the stage was set for the clash of two civilizations.

1819-1820, Major Stephen H. Long expedition and detachments.
1. Thomas Say visited Kaw Village.
2. Ft. Calhoun. 3. Long's Peak.
4. Pike's Peak. 5. Bell Springs.
6. Lt. Bell visits Great Bend.
7. Ft. Osage. 8. Ft. Smith
Map courtesy of The Dangberg Foundation

June 17, 1820 watercolor of a Longhorn Antelope by T. R. Peal, a member of Major Long's exploration to gather scientific information on the western frontier.
Illustration courtesy of The American Philosophical Society

The Hunger for the Land

Great changes had already been caused in th future Kansas by the growing population of the Unite States. This began before the first white settlers cam to Kansas. The changes were caused by the tribes c Indians moving to the west, out of the way of the whit settlers. The settlers took over the native homeland from the East Coast to the Mississippi River.

As the eastern Indians moved west, they foun other tribes of Indians already living in Kansas. B many of the newcomer Indians had guns and iro weapons they had obtained from the European settler They easily drove the native Kansas Indians from the lands and forced them to move to other locations.

The Osage

The Osage were well-known to the French. Th French explored the Louisiana territory mo extensively than the Americans or Spanish.

The French had found silver and lead on Osag land in Missouri and the French had mines there. Th Osage were the first Indians to trade with the Frencl They obtained guns, powder, and metal cookin implements as well as beads and decorative items fro the traders. In exchange, they gave the French som pelts, furs, and sometimes slaves they had captur from other tribes. The Osage often served as guides f French visits to other tribes.

The Osage had special ceremonies for li events, war, peace, and the naming of their children.

Most marriages were arranged by the parent The father of the bride gave many gifts to the groo and his family. At this time as in the past many Indi men had several wives. It was the duty of the men marry the sisters of their wives when the sister husbands died or were killed.

The women were trained in domestic tasks su as taking care of the gardens. The gardens were hug The women and children harvested beans, corn, ar squash. In the Spring and the Fall, the whole tril would leave to hunt bison for meat. They would the turn to the same homes they had left behind.

The Osage population was more than 6,200 in 1750, but the French, like other Europeans, brought them more than guns and trade goods. They also brought alcohol and disease.

In 1806 and 1807, the American explorer Zebulon Pike was on a mission to find the headwaters of the Arkansas River. He made a census of all three bands of the Osage.

In the band of the Great Osage, led by Chief White Hair, he counted 1,694 people. The Little Osage, who also followed White Hair, were counted at 824 people. The Arkansa band led by Chief Cashesegra or Clermont, had 1,500 people, mostly young men.

This would indicate that almost a third of the Osage had died or been killed in the 50 years between the two counts. It was not a loss that really bothered the French, who were far more concerned with riches than with what happened to the Indians. After hearing of the losses to the fur trade because the Indians were dying of smallpox, an angry French official wrote his country's leaders in America and asked, "How could it happen that the small pox among the Indians cost the French king a million francs?"

Little White Bear, a warrior of the Kaw tribe.
Illustration courtesy of The Kansas State Historical Society

The Kaw, also called the Kanza or Kansa

It is from the Kansa Indians, whose name means "People of the South Wind," that the Kansas territory and later the state of Kansas got its name.

(To have less confusion among the names of Kansa or Kanza and Kansas, we will use Kaw.)

The Kaw lived in what is now northeast Kansas. Their land stretched along the Missouri, Kansas, and Osage Rivers, then south to the Arkansas River.

The Kaw had a language and customs similar to that of the Osage. They dominated the plains west of

This early 1800s prairie scene depicts life along the Arkansas River.
Illustration courtesy of Wichita State University Special Collections

Mo-hong-go was an Osage woman who was kidnapped and put on display in Europe for a time. The peace medal she wears may have been given to her husband, Little Chief, who died of smallpox on the voyage to Europe. Peace medals were given to the Indians as friendly goodwill tokens.
Illustration courtesy of Wichita State University Special Collections

Chief White Plume of the Kaw, visited *Washington in 1825.*
Illustration courtesy of Wichita State University Special Collections

of the Missouri and called themselves simply "the people."

Like the Osage, the food they grew was important to the Kaw. They not only grew corn, beans and squash, but they hunted for berries and nuts which were used to supplement their diet and to season their food.

In 1702, the Kaw were estimated to have about 5,000 people. But war with the Pawnees, who lived near them and contact with European diseases killed large number of the Kaw.

When Pike visited them in 1806 he counted 46 men, 500 women, and 600 children.

The Kaw people had very strong families. Marriages were arranged by parents and gifts were given. Young Kaw girls were trained to work hard. French military men saw girls only eight to ten years old carrying as much as 100 pound loads for several miles.

Young boys were encouraged to seek spiritual communication. A boy was also supposed to look inside himself and develop a strong spirit. Sometimes boys hurt themselves as a way to prepare to be strong in battle.

The Kaw farmed and went on hunts twice a year. Their homes in their permanent villages were made of poles, covered by bark, branches, and twigs. The lower walls were made of sod. Some houses were laid out as rectangles and some were circles. The big houses had as many as three to five families living in them.

When the Kaw left to go hunting, they took poles to put up tepees and hides to cover them.

Part of Pike's job was to try to make friends with any tribes he met. He met with the Osage and the Kaw at the main village of the Pawnee on the Republican River. He told them that the "great white father, the President of the United States" wanted them to make peace with one another. On September 2, 1806, the Kaw and the Osage agreed to make peace.

The Kaw and the Osage saw a great deal of benefit in being friends. Both tribes had lost a lot of people to war and disease. Together, they were better able to defend their land. They signed the peace treaty

either tribe ever broke
at treaty. Instead, they
ined forces against the
awnee and later against
e white man who
ossed their land.

*This is the first known engraving
ade of the Kaw tribe. It depicts
e ritual of the "Dog Dance." It
as drawn by a member of the
ong expedition in 1819. Long sent
detachment led by Thomas Say to
sit the Kaw on the Blue River.*
ustration courtesy of The Kansas State
storical Society

The Kaw *lived in sturdy bark houses that they sealed with mud and sod.
Inside, they elevated the beds on platforms around the walls and made
racks to store their possessions.*
Photo courtesy of Wichita State University Special Collections

he Pawnee

The Pawnee had their homes along the
epublican and Platte Rivers and ranged across the
entral plains to hunt, from Nebraska to the Arkansas
iver.

They were aggressive warriors. They were a
ge powerful nation of 25,000 people. They fought
hen others ventured into their territory. They
tacked traders who tried crossing into Kansas to get

The Indians and The Explorers   19

The Pawnee built permanent homes that offered protection from the weather and shelter for a fire for cooking and warmth.
Photo courtesy of Wichita State University Special Collections

Shar-i-tar-ish or White Wolf, was principal chief of the Grand Pawnee, one of the tribal divisions of the Pawnee. He was visited by Zebulon Pike in 1806. Chief White Wolf arranged for the young men of the tribe to entertain Pike and his company with traditional Pawnee dances.
Photo courtesy of Wichita State University Special Collections

into Spanish territory in New Mexico.

Many scholars believed that the Pawnee ha well-traveled trails that went from their main camps Northern Kansas and Southern Nebraska to the Grea Bend of the Arkansas River. Then the trails went sout to Santa Fe where they traded with the Pueblo Indian

They studied the stars and realized that the could be used as a guide through strange territor They drew charts on elk hides. The journals of man explorers, including Pike, indicate that they took th Pawnee Trail to cross Kansas.

The Pawnee lived in well-developed village They left during the summer to hunt the buffal returning home again when it became cold. The homes were round and made of earth and sod. The dug out a circle two or three feet deep and built the home with a structure of poles made from small tre trunks and covered with sod.

They also hunted bison for food, but the bison to them had an additional significance. They believe that they needed to offer bison meat during religious ceremonies. If they did not, the Great Spirit would b offended and their crops would fail.

Like the Osage and the Kaw their tribe was hard hit by smallpox and other diseases. In 1831, their agent, John Dougherty wrote this in his yearly report:

"Their misery defies all description. I am fully persuaded that one-half of the whole number will be carried off by this frightful distemper (smallpox).... They were dying so fast, and taken down at once in such large numbers that they had ceased to bury their dead, whose bodies were to be seen in every direction lying in the river, lodged on the sand-bars, in the weeds around the villages, and in their own corn caches."

This photo of an Eagle Chief of the Pawnee was made in 1866. Each piece of decoration on his leggings has a special meaning to his tribe. Note that he wears a "peace medallion" coin.
Photo courtesy of Wichita State University Special Collections

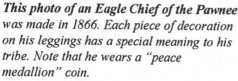

The Quivira, also later called The Wichita

The Quivira occupied the territory that is now south central Kansas. In spite of what the Spanish conquistador Coronado was told, there was no gold in the land of Quivira.

The Wichita was a peaceful tribe. They lived in sturdy grass-covered huts, planted gardens and spent the summers following the bison herds. Some of their lodges were very large. As many as 15 people lived in the larger lodges. There were platforms along the sides for beds and racks for storing clothing and utensils.

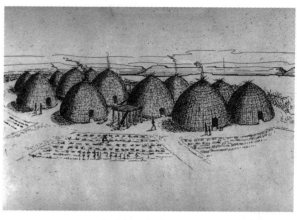

Quivira Indians, later called the Wichita, lived in well-developed villages. They built thatched or grass homes. They also planted extensive gardens and processed meat for storage.
Illustration courtesy of The Kansas State Historical Society

Sometimes, the men went on hunts for smaller animals when meat was in short supply. The women and children remained in the village.

Archaeological digs indicate that the Wichita traded with the Pueblo and other tribes to the southwest. At the time of first contact with Europeans, there were between 38,000 and 50,000 Wichita in what is now Kansas. The Spanish visited one of their larger cities, built near the junction of the Walnut and Arkansas Rivers, that today is Arkansas City. The remains of that village is one of the finest archaeological sites in Kansas. As more Indian tribes from other areas poured into Kansas, the Wichita were crowded out. They left their lands in Kansas and moved southwest into northern Texas.

The Plains Indians

Many tribes shared the hunting grounds of the western plains of Kansas. They included the Comanche, Kiowa, Arapahoe, Southern Cheyenne, Cuartelejo Apache, and the Kiowa Apache.

The plains tribes were nomadic hunters who followed the bison herds all year long. They depended heavily on the bison to proved hides for their tepees, clothing, and for meat to eat. They made tools and utensils from the bones and teeth.

The Plains Indians planted fewer a[nd] smaller gardens, but they did harvest w[ild] herbs, roots, and leaves to flavor their fo[od] or make medicine.

They were excellent horsemen. The[re] was a warrior society, where fighters we[re] honored. While they did not speak t[he] same languages, they had a sign langua[ge] that allowed them to communicate. Th[eir] weapons, methods of fighting and even t[he] way their horse's hooves were trimm[ed] allowed members of one tribe to tell wh[en] friends or enemies were near or had recently traveled the same area.

Plains Indians used horses to help them in the hunt for bison and in many other ways.
Illustration courtesy of Wichita State University Special Collections

Treaties and lost land

The plan to move eastern tribes to the n[ew] Louisiana Territory meant that the two tribes whi[ch] held much of the described land -- the Osage and [the] Kaw -- had to be moved to smaller areas.

The government used treaties to obtain the la[nd] from the Indians. The Osage made three treaties, [one] in 1808, another in 1818 and a final one in 1825 givi[ng] up first their land in Missouri, then some of the land [in] southeast Kansas. The Osage still owned a vast porti[on] of southern Kansas with an undefined weste[rn] boundary.

The Kaw owned most of the northern half [of] what is now Kansas. They were a powerful tri[be] especially in alliance with the Osage and were thou[ght] to be reluctant to make the needed treaties.

President James Monroe had the Kaw ch[ief]

A Wichita Village.
Photo courtesy of Wichita State University Special Collections

hite Plume, escorted to Washington in
321. He wanted White Plume to see
ow powerful the white people were and
ow many of them lived in America.
lso to realize that getting out of the
ay of the whites was best for his
eople.

White Plume was convinced.
hen he came home, he told his people
at they faced a threat of being wiped
ut. They could not move west, because
at was the land of the Pawnee. White
vilization was crowding them from the
st. Game was getting scarce. He told
s tribe that only by dealing with the
hites could they survive.

In June of 1825, the Kaw signed
eaties to give up their land. They were
ven a reservation near present-day
peka. They were to receive $3,500
ch year in either money or
erchandise and provisions or domestic animals.
ey were also to be given cattle, hogs, and farming
ols and taught how to farm.

White buffalos were thought to be
*sacred to the Plains Indians. This
statue is by artist L. M. Winter.*
Photo courtesy of Avery Postcards and The
Pawnee Indian Village Museum

HORSES CHANGE LIFE

When the Spanish conquistadors explored the plains
tates, the Indians were in awe of the horses. They viewed
he horse as a mystical and god-like creature. Historians
elieve that horses may have made their way to the Plains
hen they broke loose from their corrals. Perhaps they
ere left to wander after their riders died or were killed.
n time, those horses made their way into the way into the
ands of the Indians and had a profound effect on their
ves.

With horses, the Indians were able to travel farther and
aster. They could pile the poles, skins, and utensils they
eeded on a travois, which could then be pulled by a horse
nstead of by people. Horses enabled them to hunt over a
ider area and to chase down bison.

Tribes with horses had a big warfare advantage over the
ibes who did not. The Comanches and the Apaches
specially became excellent riders and trainers of horses.

The first agency was near present day Kansas City. Daniel Morgan Boone, grandson of the famous pioneer, was their first farming teacher. His son Napoleon was recorded as the first white child born in Kansas Territory.

Santa Fe Trail opens the southwest to Trade

In 1821, something happened far away that would have great consequences for the Indians of Kansas. After ten years of fighting, Mexico won its independence from Spain. The town of Santa Fe became a Mexican territory, not Spanish. The Mexicans welcomed traders.

In the same year, William Becknell, a Missouri trader made a trip from Franklin, Missouri to Santa Fe. That trip gave Becknell the credit for "discovering" the Santa Fe Trail.

The trail Becknell discovered was one that had been used earlier by the native tribes, especially the Pawnee. Now it became an "American" trail.

Hundreds of traders now made the trip across Kansas. The Santa Fe Trail became a great commercial highway of America. Mexican and American traders made up to 500 percent profit on a single trip. For the Indians, whose hunting and trapping grounds lay in the path of the trail, it was a disaster.

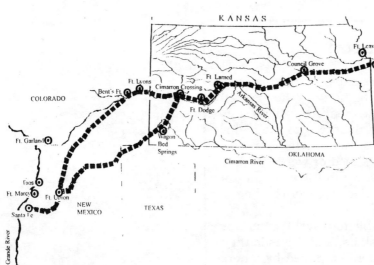

Santa Fe Trail. *In Western Kansas travelers chose between two routes, the western mountain route into Colorado and one to the southwest, a dry route into the western desert.*
Map courtesy of The Dangberg Foundation

Soldiers arrive

By the end of the 1820s, traffic on the Santa Fe Trail was intense. Wagons full of trade goods made their way westward and returned with items bought in Santa Fe.

Sometimes they brought silver and gold as well. These wagon trains were targets for Indian tribes who wanted the goods they carried. The government responded by building forts where they would station soldiers who would ride with the teamsters and wagon trains to protect them.

In 1842, the government established Fort Scott. Its soldiers helped the exploration of the west and had the mission of guarding the "permanent" Indian frontier.

Promises of 'Forever'

In May of 1830, Congress passed a law known as the "Indian Removal Act." All of the tribes living in the states already admitted to the Union were removed, by force if necessary, to Indian territory in the west. They were promised this move to what is now Kansas would be their last.

It would be theirs *"as long as the grass grows and the water flows."*

The Shawnees of Missouri gave up their lands in southeast Missouri in a treaty signed on November 7, 1825 and they came to the Kansas Indian Territory.

They were followed by more than 10,000 Indians from other tribes including Delawares, Kickapoos, Wyandots, Miamis, Sac and Fox, Potawatomis, Ottawas, and Senecas.

All of them were given reservation land that had once belonged to the Kaw and the Osage. Many of them did not want to be neighbors.

Their hunting grounds overlapped. Soon, there were conflicts, especially between the Kaw and the Shawnees; Shawnee and Delawares; and the Delawares and the Kaw.

Delegates of the Indian tribes meet with the Commissioner of Indian Affairs in Washington, D.C. Photo courtesy of Wichita State University Special Collections

> **Prairie Spirit**
>
> Jedediah Smith, an explorer and fur trader, was called "half-grizzly" and "half-preacher" by his friends because of his ability to read the Bible and sing hymns along the rugged trails. He became one of the West's best known trail-blazers and was the first white man to travel overland from the Rocky Mountains to California. He met his demise in Kansas along the Santa Fe Trail when his wagon train ran out of water and Indians ambushed him.

Speaking for the Indians

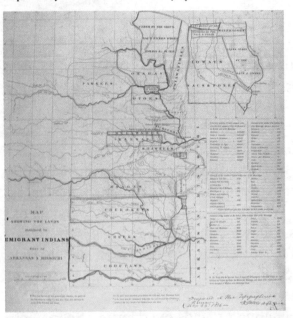

There were two groups of people primari[ly] responsible for looking out for the interests of t[he] Indians, who were entitled to trade goods and annu[al] payments and other treaty promises. One group w[as] Indian Agents appointed by the government. The oth[er] was missionaries who came to try to help the India[ns] adjust to white culture and to teach them abo[ut] Christianity.

Some of the agents who were placed in char[ge] of helping the Indians adjust worked very hard. The[y] tried to help government leaders understand how ha[rd] life was for the Indians. They also tried to make su[re] that the Indians got the money and goods they h[ad] coming.

One such agent was the Reverend Issac McC[oy,] a Baptist missionary, who was very much in favor [of] moving the Indians in the eastern states to the west. [He] led an expedition to check out land and determine if [it] would be suitable.

Potawatomi Chief Metea, was orator, warrior, and a tribal leader. The Potawatomie were not native to Kansas but were removed to the land that had once belonged to the Kaw and the Pawnee after the Indian Removal Act of 1830. Today, they are one of only four tribes that have land in Kansas.
Illustration courtesy of Wichita State University Special Collections

1836 Area Map.
Map courtesy of Wichita State University Special Collections

expressed his thoughts this way:

"We are going to look for a home for a homeless people who once were lords of all the Continent of America and whose just claims have never been acknowledged by others, nor conveyed by themselves...we are limited to the regions west of the Arkansas territory, and Missouri State. Should the inhospitableness of that country deny them a place there, they will be left destitute."

But much more of the time, the agents seemed be taking care of themselves first. It was rumored at some of the money paid every year for ad found its way into some agents' ckets. Some reports sent to Washington ay not have been accurate and truthful as e rumors went.

The missionaries that came to insas with the resettled Indians wanted establish churches, win converts, and t up schools. Denominations competed the right to control tribal missions. ly one church was assigned to each be. The church that had the mission t money from the government for hools and often for agriculture agents well.

None of the religious efforts could called a success. The Indians clung to ir tribal beliefs.

Members of the Indian tribes are depicted here in conference with the Commissioner of Indian Affairs.
Photo courtesy of The Kansas State Historical Society

he Seth Hays Story

Seth Hays was neither an agent nor a ssionary. He was a pioneer and a merchant, the indson of Daniel Boone and a cousin to famed sterner Kit Carson. He came to Kansas to help run ading post near the Kaw Methodist Mission in 1844. liked the Kaw and they liked him.

When cousin Albert Boone, another grandson of niel, wanted to open a new trading post on the new w reservation near Council Grove, they asked Seth ys to run it.

Seth Hays. His trading post at Council Grove has been restored and can still be visited today.
Illustration courtesy of The Kansas State Historical Society

He built the trading post and small log cabin. The Santa Fe Tra[il] passed in front of his cabin.

The Hays House and othe[r] landmarks associated with his busines[s] in Council Grove, are still there today. There is a museum in the Kaw Missio[n] Schoolhouse where missionaries worke[d] at teaching the Kaw children the ways o[f] the white man.

The Kanza Indian Mission at Council Grove served as an acency, a mission, and a boarding school. It has been restored and is used today as a museum and gift shop.
Photo courtesy of The Kansas State Historical Society

The Toll of Disease

Just as the arrival of French and Spanish trade[rs] had introduced disease, the explosion of travel on th[e] Santa Fe Trail increased its spread.

In 1827, the Kaw came to the city of Westport [to] collect they money owed by the Treaty of 1825. Whi[le] there, many of them became sick and as many as 200 died of a disease that is presumed to [be] smallpox. Before the epidemic ran its course, mo[re] than two-thirds of the tribe had been infected. Th[ey] were so weak they couldn't even make their annu[al] bison hunt that fall.

In 1839, there was an epidemic of "ragi[ng] fever" that may have been either smallpox or chole[ra.] Another 100 of the Kaw people died during th[e] epidemic. That same epidemic killed hundreds [of] Pawnee. The summer of 1849 brought a territ[le] outbreak of cholera.

Jotham Meeker, the missionary who ran t[he] Ottawa Baptist Mission reported it this way:

> "30 of the Sauk (Sac) & Fox have just died with Cholera besides women and children...about 100 Kaws (Kansa) and many Osages and Pawnees have also just died."

The Osage agent reported the tribes we[re] infected in June. They separated into small bands a[nd] wandered the plains looking for a place to escape u[ntil] August. Travelers on the Santa Fe Trail repor[ted] seeing about 4,000 Cheyenne, Arapahoes, Kiowas, a[nd] Comanches all infected with cholera.

Travelers Were not Spared

The white settlers who traveled the Santa Fe Trail were not spared from the same diseases that killed the Indians.

There were stories of Indian massacres on the Trail and there were incidents to give them a ring of truth; however, far more pioneers died of smallpox, cholera, and diphtheria. The most vulnerable were children. Marion Russell writes of her first journey as a seven-year old child:

Wagons leave Fort Leavenworth, making the steep climb up the hill. So many wagons made this climb that the ruts they wore can still be seen today.
Illustration courtesy of The Kansas State Historical Society

"Gradually, however, we came to know that every one in the waiting wagon train was torn between joy at making the great overland trip and terror of the Indians. Tales of frightful Indian atrocities were told without number. The dread cholera was raging in Fort Leavenworth," the day they left, she writes: *"Tar barrels were burning in the streets of Fort Leavenworth to ward off the cholera and clouds of black smoke drifted over us as we pulled out."*

Even for a child, death was a fact of life on the Trail. Russell wrote of the family that buried a dead child beneath a tree they would recognize again so they could return and visit his grave.

Pressures on the Indians

Events in the late 1840s came together one after the other to add to the pressure for Indian removal.

In the spring of 1844, devastating floods on the Republican and Kansas rivers wiped out nearly all the crops planted by the Kaw and the Pawnees.

When Texas became a state in 1845, settlers poured in from all parts east. Efforts to establish reservations for the Indians did not work because settlers took over the land.

Prairie Spirit

Christopher "Kit" Carson's name is almost synonymous with the Old West. Carson was a fur trader, scout, soldier and Indian agent during much of the time the west was being settled. He spent several years trapping fur from the Rocky Mountains to California. In the 1840s he served as a guide for John Fremont. He also was active along the Santa Fe Trail . He was one of the signers of the Little River Peace Treaty in 1865 and served as a mediator in the conference between the United States government and the Indian nations. He died in 1868 from an aneurysm at Fort Lyon, Colo.

Comanches and the Plains Apaches fled to Kansas.

In 1846, the United States and Mexico went war. Troops headed for battles crossed Kansas. February of 1848, the Mexican War ended. The term of the peace agreement gave the United States ne land. But Indian Territory lay between that land a the established United States.

May of 1848, gold was discovered by Jam Marshall in California. The California Gold Ru began and more than 50,000 gold hunters headed f the gold in California. Many of them took the Oreg Trail, others took more direct routes across Kans Westport, St. Joseph, Council Grove, and Topeka did thriving business. Indian agencies were anxious to g business from the gold seekers traveling west.

By 1850, California was demanding feder help in building a railroad across the United States. 1853, the government began working on making th happen.

Agreements for peace

In 1853, the Plains tribes of Kansas agreed stop taking hostages along the Santa Fe Trail exchange for being allowed to hunt on the land south the Arkansas River.

It was an agreement much like the one reach two years earlier in Wyoming with the northern Plai tribes, who promised not to disturb trail traffic and allow the railroad to build.

Congress passed the Kansas-Nebraska Act a in 1854 Kansas became a United States territo Land-hungry settlers came pouring in. They broug their own conflicts over the question of slavery. It w not until 1867, after the Civil War and statehood, tha new treaty for peace was reached with the Southe Plains tribes.

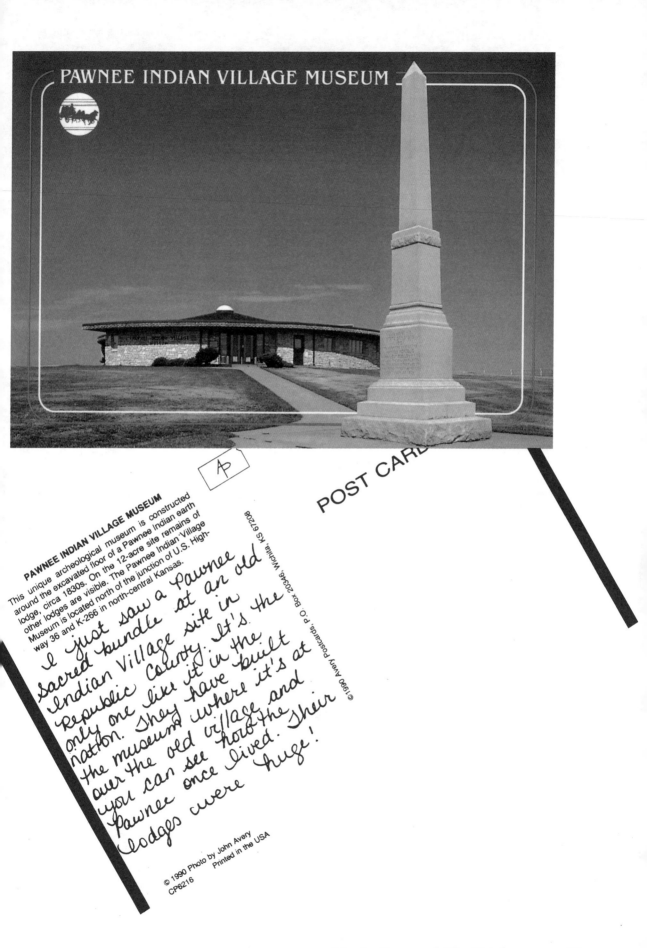

PAWNEE INDIAN VILLAGE MUSEUM

PAWNEE INDIAN VILLAGE MUSEUM
This unique archeological museum is constructed around the excavated floor of a Pawnee Indian earth lodge, circa 1830s. On the 12-acre site remains of other lodges are visible. The Pawnee Indian Village Museum is located north of the junction of U.S. Highway 36 and K-266 in north-central Kansas.

POST CARD

A

I just saw a Pawnee sacred bundle at an old Indian Village site in Republic County. It's the only one like it in the nation. They have built the museum where it's at over the old village and you can see how the Pawnee once lived. Their lodges were huge!

© 1990 Avery Postcards, P.O. Box 20344, Wichita, KS 67208

© 1990 Photo by John Avery Printed in the USA
CP6216

Historical Events

1820 - Missouri Compromise

1854 - KS 1st Territorial Capital built

1856 - John Brown leds a raid in Franklin County

1858 - Marais des Cygnes Massacre

1861 - Kansas becomes a state

Chapter 2

Bleeding Kansas

CRUZ PAGAN 99

Chapter 2

Bleeding Kansas

The people came with dreams and ambition.

From all parts of Europe and Asia and from other places in the new land of America they came, hoping to claim land, find work, and discover riches.

The Kansas territory in 1854 was a tough, rugged place to start a home and raise a family. Summers were hot and dry, winters were bitter cold with harsh winds.

But the greatest threat to life and peace came from the struggle to find the answer to just one question: should Kansas allow slavery?

Opinions were strong and tempers were hot on both sides of the question. Arguments often turned violent. Bloodshed happened so often that the time was nicknamed, "Bleeding Kansas."

Set-up for Conflict

Slavery was a problem that the United States government had tried to solve since the beginning of the country. The country was already divided into slave states in the South and free states in the North by the Mason Dixon Line.

There was agreement on a new dividing line between slave states and free states in 1820. That agreement, called the Missouri Compromise, stated that Missouri would be admitted as a slave state. At the same time, Maine would be admitted as a free state. This would keep the balance of free and slave states. The Missouri Compromise also said that no slavery would be allowed in the new western territories.

The first bill to form a new territory, was introduced by Senator A. C. Dodge of Iowa. He proposed a Nebraska Territory that would have included all of present day Nebraska, Kansas and part of Colorado. It lay north of the 1820 Missouri Compromise Line. According to the Missouri Compromise, the proposed Nebraska Territory would have been free. If Dodge's bill had been adopted, much bloodshed in Kansas might have been avoided.

Dodge's bill, however, did not pass unchanged 1820.

Thirty years later in 1850, California had been admitted as a free state and the count of free states vs slave states stood at 16 free and 15 slave. Kansas as a slave state would have evened the score.

In January of 1854, Senator Stephen A. Douglas of Illinois, came up with a new bill that did pass.

Douglas's bill formed two new territories; one be called Nebraska and the other Kansas. It included the idea of "popular sovereignty." It said that the people who lived in a new territory would vote to decide whether it would be slave or free.

People who felt strongly on both sides of the question of slavery saw opportunity. Kansas shared its

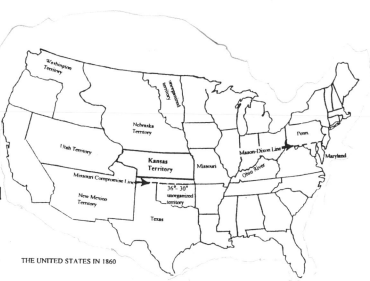

THE UNITED STATES IN 1860

The Mason-Dixon Line was used, as a generally accepted boundary between slave and free states, 1770 to 1780. This line was the boundary between Pennsylvania and Maryland surveyed by English astronomers Charles Mason and Jeremiah Dixon between 1763-67. The Missouri Compromise, reached by Congress in 1820, provided that all the new territories north of a line at 36 degrees and 30 minutes north latitude would be free. Notice where that line crosses the United States. Today it is generally accepted that the 36 degree-30 minute line, all of Missouri and the Ohio River to Pennsylvania may be used as the boundary between the North and South when regarding slave states.

Map courtesy of The Dangberg Foundation

James Lane was among the many people who came to Kansas to fight slavery. He had served as lieutenant-governor of Indiana. A House of Representatives member when Stephen A. Douglas introduced the Kansas-Nebraska bill, Lane voted in favor of the bill.

He was an exciting speaker who often emphasized his speeches by peeling off articles of his clothing and waving them at his audience.

Illustration courtesy of The Kansas State Historical Society

entire eastern border with Missouri. The Pro-slavery supporters thought they had a good chance to win vote for slavery in the new territory.

Pro-Slavery Settlements

Many of the first settlers came from western Missouri. They built the towns of Atchison, Leavenworth, Doniphan, and Kickapoo. Southern organizations were called "Buford's Men" and "The Blue Lodges of Missouri." Both tried to find people who were willing to move to the Kansas territory and vote to make it a slave state. They looked for people who were leaders who supported slavery. One such person was Samuel Jones, who later became sheriff of Douglas County. Another was Wilson Shannon, who became the second governor of the territories.

Free-State Supporters

In the north, people who opposed slavery found others of the same belief to move into the new territory

An 1856 daugerrotype shows a Free State cannon crew. The Free State Hotel in Lawrence was used to hide a cannon from the pro-slavery forces. That was one reason the hotel was later destroyed in a raid on Lawrence.
Photo courtesy of The Kansas State Historical Society

Those settlers created the towns of Topeka, Lawrence, Osawatomie, and Oskaloosa. An organization called, The New England Emigrant Aid Company helped people who wanted to move to Kansas to vote against slavery. Leaders of that organization helped them buy important businesses such as sawmills and newspapers. They told the new Kansans to build hotels so there would be places for more emigrants to stay when they came to Kansas.

Some of the people who came believed very strongly that slavery was wrong and should be abolished. They were called abolitionists. They believed in helping slaves escape from their owners. One such abolitionist was John Brown, who came to Kansas from Ohio.

The First Government

The first territorial governor appointed by Congress, was a slavery supporter named Andrew Reeder. He called for an election in November of 1854 to choose a territorial delegate to Congress. On election day, huge numbers of people came from Missouri to vote and a Pro-slavery representative was elected. Four months later, Reeder called for an election to choose Kansas legislators. Again, large numbers of people crossed the border just to vote. Because of that, the Kansas legislature had a majority of members who supported slavery.

Governor Reeder pushed for a capital to be built in the small town of Pawnee near Fort Riley. The legislature met only one time there. It quickly passed laws that created severe penalties for anyone who freed slaves or spoke out against slaveholding. Other laws ordered the death penalty for anyone who helped a slave escape or who wrote, printed, or circulated any document that would make slaves want to rebel against their owner.

That government was recognized as official by the United States even though many people in Kansas protested the illegal voters from Missouri and the laws passed by the first legislature.

They called them "Bogus Laws."

Kansas's First Territorial Capital

When Governor Andrew Reeder called for the territory's first legislative session, he picked the town of Pawnee near Fort Riley to be the capital. Reeder, who owned the land in Pawnee, was hoping the capitol would help the small town. The town had only 15 to 20 residents. By the end of the year the town's population had increased to 500 citizens.

The capitol building was still being built and the west end of the building wasn't finished when the legislature first met. Blankets were hung over the hole to kept the prairie dust from blowing in and disturbing them.

One legislator was walking into the building when a floorboard that had not been nailed yet flew up and hit him in the back of the head.

The legislature met for only five days and moved the capital to Shawnee Mission.

The building was donated to The Kansas State Historical Society in the 1920s.

Photo courtesy of The Kansas State Historical Society

A Governor in Trouble

Territorial Governor Reeder was soon in troubl with all the political factions. The Free-sta supporters were angry about the illegal elections an the Pro-slavery laws. The Pro-slavery people wel angry because Reeder had overturned the election i some districts. But his worst trouble came over th hastily chosen capital of Pawnee. Reeder had made lot of money selling land after he spread the word th Pawnee would be the capital. But it turned out that th town was actually inside the boundaries of Fort Rile The land belonged to the federal government. Th sales were illegal.

Worse still, the legislature voted in its fir session to move the capital from Pawnee to Shawne Mission.

In July of 1855, the United States Preside Franklin Pierce fired Reeder. Reeder had to fl Kansas to avoid being killed by his enemies.

Before Kansas became a state, Reeder wou have a lot of company as an ex-governor. In the s years between 1854 and 1860, Kansas had s governors and four temporary governors. None serve more than a few months.

Pawnee land sell bill.
Courtesy of The Kansas State Historical Society

Andrew Reeder was appointed governor of the Kansas Territory by President Pierce in 1854. His actions as governor made people so angry that he had to disguise himself as a woodcutter and fled the state.
Illustration courtesy of The Kansas State Historical Society

A Confusing Time

The government of the United States st recognized the Pro-slavery constitution written by th first legislature as the legal government of Kansa William Shannon, another slavery supporter w appointed to replace Reeder.

But the people of Kansas were so divided I this time that there were two separate governments. went so far that both sides elected representatives Congress. Both men showed up to claim the Kans seat in Washington, D.C. Congress decided to pa them for their travel to Washington, but not to give seat to either one of them. So Kansas had r representative in Congress at all for that session.

Outside of Politics

Some of the new citizens who came to Kansas did not care whether Kansas was a slave state or a free state.

For whatever reason they came, many found the struggle was almost unbearable. The climate of Kansas was harsh. The people weren't ready for the hardships they faced. Crops didn't grow because there wasn't enough rain and the winter was bitter cold. Many people became ill and others were very homesick.

Kansas Bleeds

Those who wanted to win control of Kansas when it became a state did more than talk at conventions. They also took action and even took up arms.

The terms "Jayhawker," "red-legs," "border ruffians," and "bushwhackers" all originated in the early days of the Kansas Territory. During this time fighting, killing, and burning of homes and crops were commonplace. While most of the fighting was over slavery, the conflict provided a perfect cover for hoodlums who were simply bent on violence.

Missourians gave the Kansas raiders the name "Jayhawkers" after a mythical bird from Ireland which, it is said, worried its prey to death.

The Kansas militia also wore uniforms that had tight-fitting red trousers and bright blue coats, a combination that many Missourians commented made them look like bluejays.

They said those birds were known for their habit of raiding the nests of other birds, a trait they felt the Kansans shared. The name "red-legs" also came from those early uniforms.

The Missourians who rode into Kansas territory were referred to as border ruffians because of their

Border Ruffians.
Photo courtesy of The Kansas State Historical Society

> ## Ann Shatteo
> Another resident came only to be free. Ann Shatteo had been a slave but had bought her own freedom for $450. She was talented, strong and resourceful. She worked as a cook for the wagon trains passing through Kansas. She saved up enough money to buy a 100-acre farm near present day Topeka.
>
> Shatteo had more land than many white people of her time. She had to be both smart and stubborn to survive and remain free in Kansas' most violent time.

rough tactics and lack of manners. They were als
called bushwhackers because they often literally be
the bushes looking for Kansans who were hiding.

Six years before the Civil War engulfed the re
of the nation, Kansas was already at war.

The Wakarusa War

John Geary.
Photo courtesy of The Kansas State Historical
Society

One incident illustrates how quickly a situatic
grew to become a threat of major conflict. It was calle
the Wakarusa War and began on November 21, 185
about 10 miles south of Lawrence along the Wakaru:
River.

A Free-state supporter, Charles W. Dow, g
into an argument with his Pro-slavery neighbc
Franklin Coleman. They argued over their opposi
viewpoints and their land claims. The fiery-tempere
Coleman shot and killed Dow, who was unarmed.

Pro-slavery supporters arrested Jacob Branso
a friend of Dow's, because they had seen him at
protest meeting earlier.

Branson's friends soon caught up to the gro
and tried to rescue him. S. N. Woods, a member
Branson's rescue party, said that the Free State gro
called to Branson to come on over and join them. H
captors warned that if he moved he'd be shot.

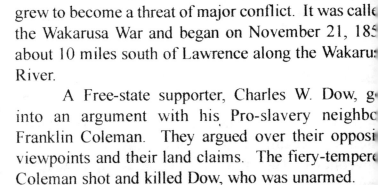

Governor John Geary

John Geary of Lecompton was one of the first political victims, of Bleeding Kansas, whe
he tried without success, to stop corruption in the court system.

Geary had been the first mayor of San Francisco before President Franklin Pierce appointe
him to be the territorial governor of Kansas in 1856.

He objected to Free Staters being arrested and held without trial and to a man charged
with murder being granted bail.

Geary talked to Chief Justice Samuel Lecompte and threatened to establish military
courts if the situation was not fixed.

Lecompte responded by leaving Lecompton and returned to Leavenworth where he set
court dates for the Free-Staters far into the future.

Geary tried, but failed, to get Lecompte replaced. He had no better luck at stopping the
violence that tore Kansas apart.

In 1857, Geary was fired by President James Buchanan because he had failed to bring
peace to Bleeding Kansas. There were threats against his life. He slipped out of the state
in the night and went home to Pennsylvania. During the Civil War, he commanded the 28
Pennsylvania Infantry and advanced to the rank of Brigadier General. After the war, he
served as a military governor in Savannah, Georgia. He was elected Pennsylvania's governe
in 1866. Geary County, where Fort Riley is located is named in his honor.

The Situation Escalates

Woods said the Free-State group replied with a threat of their own:

"*Gentlemen,*" Woods reportedly said, "*shoot and not a man of you shall stay alive.*" Branson was freed and the rescue party rode into Lawrence. When they told their story, the residents expected the Border Ruffians to attack the town.

The Pro-slavery group accused the residents of Lawrence of helping criminals because they sheltered Branson.

Samuel Jones, the sheriff of Douglas County, was a Missourian and a slavery supporter. He appealed to the governor, Wilson Shannon, another Missourian, for help. Shannon allowed Jones to use the state militia. In turn, the governor asked the U. S. military for help. No soldiers came.

Governor Shannon finally sent a letter to Sheriff Jones, ordering him to disband his group. Jones protested he was just trying to do his job. After a week Governor Shannon negotiated a truce, and the two factions went home.

Beecher's Bibles

Lawrence residents and their supporters stayed ready for battle. A New England preacher named Henry Beecher sent them Sharps rifles in crates labeled "Bibles." They formed an army that drilled with the rifles, which they called "Beecher's Bibles."

Newspapers outside the Kansas Territory fired off editorials and stories about the "war." Lawrence remained one of the most-watched towns because it was a headquarters for the Free-State movement.

Even though the Wakarusa War did not erupt into shooting, violence did follow. In the spring of 1856, Sheriff Jones raided Lawrence and burned the town. Pro-slavery newspapers bragged about the conquest of Lawrence. They called it a victory and ran several stories about the sacking.

Samuel J. Jones, was not happy with the governor's solution to the Wakarusa War. He later returned to take his revenge on the Free-State town.
Photo courtesy of The Kansas State Historical Society

Governor Reacts

Governor Shannon warned he would not send militia to another such incident as the Wakarusa War.

"*If the citizens submit themselves to the territorial laws, and aid and assist the Marshal and Sheriff in the execution of process in their hands, as all good citizens are bound to do when called on, they, or all such, will entitle themselves to the protection of the law. But so long as they keep up a military or armed organization to resist the territorial laws...I shall not interpose to save them from the legitimate consequences of their illegal acts.*"

Free State supporters did not consider their acts illegal. They said the only laws violated were the "bogus laws."

Sheriff Jones raided Lawrence in the spring of 1856, burning the town. *Pro-slavery newspapers bragged about the "conquest" of the free-state stronghold of Kansas.*
Illustration courtesy of The Kansas State Historical Society

John Brown

John Brown. He came to Kansas in 1855 as a surveyor.
Photo courtesy of The Kansas State Historical Society

John Brown was a radical abolitionist. H believed slavery was evil and that any amount of for or violence was all right if it helped to end slavery.

He was born May 9, 1800 in Torringto Connecticut and moved to Ohio with his family wh he was five years old. When he was 34, he moved t Pennsylvania and started a project to teach ex-slaves

He came to Kansas in 1855, not because wanted to be here to fight slavery but because his so sent for him. Five of them had come to Kansas a settled near Osawatomie in an area they call "Brownsville." Soon they were having problems w claim jumpers and Pro-slavery supporters. They wro their father and asked him to come and bring rifl Brown helped his sons build their log cabins, but nev took a claim as his own. He chose instead to live w his half-sister, Florella and her husband, the Revere Samuel Adair.

Brown became very angry when he hea Lawrence had been sacked. He vowed to get even. the night of May 24, 1856, Brown, four of his sons a three other Free Staters took action. He led a raid o settlement near Dutch Henry's Crossing

ottawatomie Creek in Franklin County. Until this
oint, all the fighting had been in daylight, one-on-one
etween men. On Pottawatomie Creek Brown attacked
night, going to each man's home, calling him by
me and then murdering him. The men's bodies were
opped by short broadswords that Brown and his sons
ought with them from Ohio. The remains of the men
ere strewn along the road or thrown into the creek.

People in the Kansas territory and across the
tion were revolted by this brutality.

But Brown said:

*"It is better that the guilty pro-slavery men should
die than that one free-state man should be driven out.
God is my judge; we were justified, the people of
Kansas will yet justify my course. I knew all good
men who loved freedom, when they were acquainted
with the facts connected with the case would approve
of it."*

Pro-slavery forces were determined to find
rown and arrest him. If Brown did not surrender, they
id, they would shoot him.

From then on, John Brown became a fugitive
ding in the brush, sleeping alone and keeping a gun
ways within his reach.

*ollowing the Wakarusa War and the destruction of Lawrence in 1856, Free Staters fought pro-slavery forces at
ickory Point. One man was killed and nine wounded in the "out for revenge" battle that was typical of the
eeding Kansas period of history.*
ustration courtesy of The Kansas State Historical Society

Revenge Fighting

Among the people seeking revenge again[st] Brown was a Virginian, Captain H. C. Pate. He h[ad] himself appointed deputy marshal. He organized [a] group of about 50 men and went looking for Brown.

He found Brown and his men, a group of on[ly] about 25, near Baldwin City. Brown and his men we[re] good at hiding and fighting, a style of war call[ed] guerrilla fighting. They overcame Pate's forces a[nd] took them prisoner.

When word of the fighting reached Washingto[n] the U.S. government sent dragoons under the comma[nd] of Col. J. T. L. Preston, to hunt down Brown's can[d] and set Pate and his men free. Preston was told to se[nd] everyone home and to stop the fighting. He fou[nd] Brown's camp and freed Pate's troop. But nobo[dy] could stop the fighting.

Dr. John Doy *and his rescuers are* *shown in this daugerrotype. Doy was* *kidnapped in Kansas in Jan. of 1859* *and put in a Weston, Missouri jail. In* *June, he was convicted of stealing* *slaves so he could free them. He was* *sentenced to serve 5 years in a* *Missouri prison. He was rescued by 10* *of his friends from Lawrence, led by* *James Abbott.*
Photo courtesy of The Kansas State Historical Society

Fuel on the Fire

Newspapers in the east helped to keep tempe[rs] hot and emotions high. Editorial writers coined t[he] phrase "Bleeding Kansas" and wrote about what w[as] happening in Kansas.

The stories encouraged people who felt strong[ly] on both sides of the slavery issue to come to Kans[as] and join the fighting.

he Adair Cabin sits on a 20-acre park in Osawatomie.

The Adair Cabin

The cabin was dedicated as a historical site by President Theodore Roosevelt in 910. This cabin is where abolitionist John Brown stayed with his sister and rother-in-law, Florella and Samuel Adair, while leading his raids. The cabin was uilt from logs and the raw wood was whitewashed on the inside. The interior of the abin is now furnished with many of the things the Adair family used, including a airror, a table, a trivet, plates, bowls, coffee mill, irons, and much more.

In December of 1995, the cabin was broken into, looted and set on fire. There vas almost $160,000 in damage to the building and historic collections. The egislative Heritage Trust Fund and federal money helped supplement funds raised y local and state preservationists to restore the cabin and pay for new exhibits. It eopened to visitors in August of 1998.

The Raid on Harper's Ferry

By 1856, Brown had come up with a plan to fr[ee] slaves by armed force. He wanted to build a safe pla[ce] for slaves who were running away into the mountai[ns] of Virginia. On October 16, 1859, with "18 men, so[me] of whom were his sons," he seized the U. S. Arsenal [at] Harper's Ferry, Virginia. He thought all the slaves [in] the area would rebel against their owners and suppo[rt] him.

The next day a company of U. S. Marines led [by] Colonel Robert E. Lee, overtook Brown. In the batt[le] that followed, 10 of Brown's men, including two of h[is] sons, were killed. Brown was wounded and forced [to] surrender. He was arrested and charged with treas[on] and murder, among the crimes. He was found guil[ty] and was hung on December 2, 1859 at Charlestow[n], Virginia.

Years after his death, Brown was regarded [by] abolitionists as a martyr. He became the subject o[f a] famous song, "John Brown's Body," sung to the tune [of] the popular "Battle Hymn of the Republic." Its fi[rst] line is "John Brown's body lies a-mouldering in t[he] grave."

For a time, Brown was a hero to Kansas. Fr[ee] state supporters believed he saved Kansas fro[m] becoming a slave state.

The Underground Railroad

During the 1850s and 1860s, people in 30 sta[tes] all across the United States helped slaves escape. Th[ey] operated what was called the Underground Railro[ad]. Colonel John Ritchie built a cellar in his home a[nd] used it to hide runaway slaves. He once shot and kil[led] a Pro-slavery deputy marshal who came to his home [to] arrest him for his anti-slavery actions.

John Brown and Jim Lane also provided sa[fe] places for people to hide. Such places were cal[led] "depots" or "stations." The people who helped sla[ves] find their way from place to place were cal[led] "conductors." Depots included fields where runawa[ys] hid, trees they slept in, streams they crossed, a[nd]

...uses, barns, and buildings where they stayed. Slaves ...ld stories or sang songs about escapes.

Nearly 50 sites in Kansas have been ...ocumented as stations on the railroad. Seven are ...cognized as "significant."

Colonel John Ritchie

Col. John Ritchie of Topeka was among the ...any Free State supporters who came to Kansas in the ...rly years. His support for human rights went beyond ...e issue of slavery. When African-Americans began ...oving to Topeka in large numbers following the Civil ...ar, Ritchie was one of the few whites to welcome ...em, giving them lots for houses and donating a ...rtion of his land for their cemetery.

He supported rights for women as well. His ...ife, Mary Jane, started Topeka's first Women ...uffrage Association, holding meetings in their home. ...hen suffrage leaders Susan B. Anthony and Elizabeth ...dy Stanton came to Kansas in 1867, Ritchie shared ...e podium with them in Topeka.

In addition, Ritchie was a promoter of education ...d became one of the founders of Washburn ...niversity in Topeka.

His home at 116 S. E. Madison in Topeka, is that ...y's oldest surviving structure. It is listed on the ...gister of Historic Kansas Places.

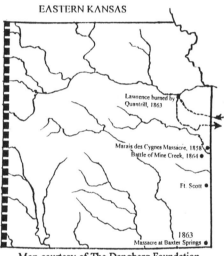

EASTERN KANSAS

Lawrence burned by Quantrill, 1863

Marais des Cygnes Massacre, 1858
Battle of Mine Creek, 1864

Ft. Scott

1863
Massacre at Baxter Springs

Map courtesy of The Dangberg Foundation

The Marais des Cygnes Massacre

Violence in Linn County ...out four miles northeast of ...ading Post did much to bring ...tional attention to the struggle ... Kansas.

They had first taken the ...en prisoners then shot them ...wn in cold blood.

Five men were killed and four wounded in what became known as the "Marais des Cygnes Massacre."
Illustration courtesy of Wichita State University Special Collections

The Kansas Weekly Herald of Leavenwor[t]
called the killings a "cowardly proceeding" and [a]
"disgrace to a civilized country," saying that "n[o]
excuse can be offered in justification."

After this incident, however, things settle[d]
down in the territory. People were looking for ways [to]
settle political differences without violence.

It was in this era of relative calm that a ne[w]
convention to try to frame a state constitution wa[s]
called. This time, both pro-slavery and Free Sta[te]
delegates came to a convention at Wyandotte.

Establishing Boundaries

One of the first jobs of the convention was [to]
establish boundaries for the new state.

The territory's western boundary was ne[ar]
Denver and included much of the gold mining territo[ry]
in what is now Colorado. In fact, the city of Denv[er]
was named for Kansas's fifth territorial govern[or]
James W. Denver.

Free staters were concerned, however, that the[y]
could never settle that large a territory with free-sta[te]
supporters. So they voted to move the boundary farth[er]
east to where it is today. They chose the line that mar[ks]
the 25th longitude as the western border.

Constitution at Wyandotte

The Free Staters attending the constitutio[nal]
convention backed the national Republican Party. [Its]
members wanted to build a railroad from coast to co[ast]
and to give free land to people willing to settle in ne[w]
territories. It also said that Congress had a duty [to]
forbid slavery in new territories.

The Pro-slavery people were divided betwe[en]
the Northern Democrats who wanted popular cont[rol]
and the Southern Democrats who wanted legal slave[ry.]

The Underground Railroad

* Quindaro Ruins, near Kansas City. From 1857 to 1862, runaway slaves crossed the Missouri River to find haven in Quindaro.
* Joel Grover's Barn, Lawrence. The barn, built in 1858, was used as a station for runaways.
* Quantrill Trail Historical Marker, Lawrence. This site was a crossing point for runaway slaves.
* Capt. John E. Stewart's Log Fort, Lawrence. The fort offered protection for runaway slaves.
* Robert Miller House and Barn, Lawrence. A smokehouse served as shelter.
* The community of Wabaunsee. The runaway slaves took refuge with residents.
* The Adair Cabin, Osawatomie. John Brown brought slaves from Missouri on Christmas Eve, 1858.

The convention adopted a constitution that outlawed slavery. But delegates rejected a provision that would have outlawed African-Americans in the state. They also discussed and rejected prohibiting liquor sales.

In September of 1859, the voters of Kansas approved the new constitution.

It was signed by President James Buchanan on January 29, 1861 and the free state of Kansas was admitted to the United States.

Clarina Nichols

One of the most noteworthy people among those who attended the Wyandotte convention was prohibited from speaking as a condition of being allowed to attend.

She was Clarina Nichols, a nationally known 19th century women's rights supporter, teacher, and journalist.

She was the only woman at the convention. She sat, listened, and knitted. And each time the meetings recessed, Nichols put down her knitting needles and met with the delegates.

Because of her efforts, women in the new state of Kansas were given rights of custody of children. When The University of Kansas opened its doors in 1866, the law required that women be given the same right to schooling as men.

Nichols also was able to persuade men at the Wyandotte Convention to allow Kansas women a chance to vote in school district elections - nearly half a century before the 19th Amendment to the nation's constitution, granting women the right to vote, was passed.

In noting the women's rights movement in Kansas, *The New York Times* reported on July 29, 1859:

"It is not at all impossible that Kansas may set a brilliant example to the rest of the world."

Clarina Nichols. Kansas women can credit Miss Nichols for making sure the state's constitution included rights for women.
Photo courtesy of The Kansas State Historical Society

Getting Organized

The Wyandotte Convention also had anothe[r] important decision. Where to locate the state capita[l?] After considerable debate, Topeka was chosen.

In the state's first election, Charles Robinso[n] who had served as the leader of the Free Sta[te] government, was elected governor. James Lane an[d] Samuel Pomeroy were chosen as the state's first Unite[d] States Senators.

Kansas had much work to do. The state ha[d] undergone a prolonged drought and thousands [of] residents had left the state for their homes in the eas[t.] Others were saved only by relief efforts. A new capit[ol] building had to be planned and built.

But there was not much time for the ne[w] government to get to work. Only months aft[er] statehood came the Civil War. Everything else had [to] wait while the state answered a call to arms with th[e] rest of the nation.

David Atchison.
Photo courtesy of The Kansas State Historical Society

Atchison, 1860.
Photo courtesy of The Kansas State Historical Society

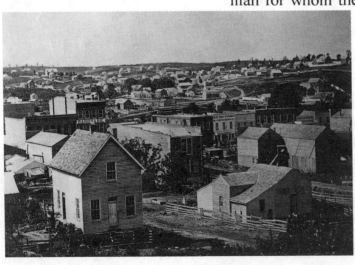

President for One Day

When he was only 42 years old, David Atchis[on] became President of the United States.

Granted, it was for only 23 1/2 hours. But th[e] man for whom the town of Atchison is named, is st[ill] considered the first President wi[th] Kansas ties.

Atchison was elected to t[he] Senate from Missouri in 1843 a[nd] served as President Pro Tempo[re] from August, 1846 to Novemb[er] 1854.

His presidential "hour[s"] took place on Sunday, March [4,] 1849. Polk's administrati[on] ended at noon that day and t[he] new president, Zachary Tayl[or] refused to take office on [a] Sunday.

The law provided that [in] the event both the offices

esident and vice-president were vacant, the President o Tempore of the Senate would assume the job.

Later, Atchison would call the event "this cidental dignity." He is said to have slept through ost of it.

Atchison's ties to Kansas are immense. He was notorious leader of the Missouri "border ruffians" ading hordes of pro-slavery Missourians to the ansas polls. He helped pass the Kansas-Nebraska bill d also helped to form the pro-slavery town of tchison in 1854.

Little Girl's Opinion Matters

In 1860, when Lincoln ran for President, Grace edell was an 11-year old living in Westfield, New ork. She liked him but thought his face could use me improvement.

So she wrote to him before the election, telling m to grow a beard.

"You would look a great deal better for your face is so thin. All the ladies like whiskers and they would tease their husbands to vote for you."

Lincoln wrote the little girl back, thanking her. nd he grew the beard. By the time he became esident, he had a full beard and was the nation's first arded president.

When Bedell grew up, she married and came to ttle in Kansas. Among her belongings was Lincoln's tter. She stored it in a bank vault in Delphos. When ople found out about it, they offered her huge sums money, as much as $5,000. She turned them all wn.

After she died in 1936, a television producer ught the letter for $20,000.

Samuel Adair and Family.
Photo courtesy of The Kansas State
Historical Society

***Another bloody attack on
Lawrence,*** *confirming the
nickname "Bleeding Kansas*
Photo courtesy of The Kansas Sta
Historical Society

JOHN BROWN MUSEUM

The John Brown Museum, located at Tenth and Main streets in Osawatomie, KS, houses the Adair Cabin, one of half a dozen territorial homes left in the state. The noted abolitionist used the house of his brother-in-law as his headquarters during the 1855-1858 struggle to make Kansas a free state.

© 1990 Avery Postcards, P.O. Box 20346, Wichita, KS 67208

I have stood in the same cabin that John Brown once visited and lived in. What's really strange is that the cabin was set on fire during the 1990s and has been restored. But you can still see the smoke marks from that fire! It's weird!

POST CARD

Historical Events

1860 - Topeka established as permanent capital of Kansas

1861 - The Battle of Wilson's Creek

1862 - African-Americans become   soldiers

1863 - Quantrill raids Lawrence

1863 - The Baxter Springs Massacre

1864 - The Battle of Westport

1864 - The Battle of Mine Creek

1865 - The Civil War ends

Chapter 3

Kansas and The Civil War

Chapter 3

Kansas and The Civil War

Kansas was at war.

The same questions that tore Kansans apart during her territorial days were now tugging at the hearts of people across the nation.

At the forefront was slavery.

Kansas had found its answer. But the rest of the country had not.

When Fort Sumter surrendered on April 14, 1861, Lincoln called for 75,000 volunteers to fight in defense in the Union.

Kansans immediately began forming military companies.

Kansans Sign Up

Most of the volunteers who joined the Union army were farmers with families or merchants just starting their businesses.

Jim Lane, now a United States senator, formed the Frontier Guard. It was a political group, made up mostly of people who wanted jobs in Washington.

These Kansans traveled to Washington specifically to guard the president and the White House. The Frontier Guard remained in the capital for three weeks. By that time, Washington was full of federal troops. There appeared to be no danger of an attack.

One reason Kansas men organized so quickly may have been because of a major drought in the state. Crops were failing and many of the early settlers were simply packing up and heading back to their homes on the East Coast. The Kansas Relief Committee helped distribute food, clothing, and medicine, and seeds to hundreds of people. Many farmers may have felt that after a few months at war, the weather would change in Kansas and they could start their farms again.

Wilson's Creek

Kansas troops saw their first action at The Battle of Wilson's Creek near Springfield, Missouri on August 10, 1861. It was the first major battle of the war in the West. Union General Nathaniel Lyon, who lost his life in the battle, was outnumbered by Confederate forces, led by General Sterling Price. The battle was a defeat for the Union.

The Battle of Wilson's Creek introduced Kansas troops to the war.
Illustration courtesy of The Kansas State Historical Society

An engraving from the book Pictorial War Record, published in 1882 showed this version of Kansas "Jayhawkers" stealing horses from pro-slavery farmers.
Illustration courtesy of The Kansas State Historical Society

Along the Missouri bord the official war simply ga raiders on both sides a ne way to continue the o fighting.

Kansas troops crossed t border to raid Missouri town The Seventh Kansas Caval was especially known for "Jayhawking" skills. Troo often stole cattle, horses, a other property from settlers.

The Kansans slept cornfields while men wi binoculars kept watch night and day for the Misso Confederates to attack. T two sides did not engage often in official battl however, their raids were brutal attacks on civilia and soldiers.

Jennison's Jayhawkers

Some of the most ruthless fighting done Kansans against Missourians occurred with the Kansas Volunteer Cavalry Regime nicknamed "Jennison's Jayhawkers" a the organizer and first commandi officer, Charles Jennison.

The regiment had its roots in "Bleed Kansas." It was organized in October 1861, and drew soldiers and officers fr the ranks of Free Staters and abolitioni Arnold Schofield at the Fort Sc National Historic Site said of the outfit

"This regiment was bad to the bone. Wi they would go into Missouri they were robbing and pillaging. There was murd and mayhem. What they did was nas

The regimental battle flag of "Jennison's Jayhawkers."
Photo courtesy of Brian Corn for The Dangberg Foundation

It was, he said, the essence of border warfare:

"The borders of Kansas and Missouri suffered greatly, more than any other area of the Civil War. This was hard guerrilla fighting out here. It was a different war. It was nasty and dirty. It was what the Civil War was all about."

The regiment was transferred to the South in ne of 1862 and won honor for its fighting record.

utlaws Join the Fight

American outlaw Jesse James and his brother, ank, gained much of their early experience on raids o Kansas. The two brothers from Clay County, issouri joined the guerrilla forces of William aantrill. Quantrill was raiding the border towns of issouri and Kansas that were sympathetic to the nion. The James brothers later became infamous as tlaws after the War. Jesse James was shot by his usin, Bob Ford, in Missouri in 1882. His cousin llected the $10,000 reward offered by the governor Missouri.

William Quantrill led guerrilla raids along the Missouri-Kansas border during the entire "Bleeding Kansas" period.
Photo courtesy of The Kansas State Historical Society

frican-Americans Become Soldiers

Former slaves and freed African-Americans in ansas contributed to the war effort. In the beginning, any of them worked as laborers and teamsters. But in ugust of 1862, a novel experiment, led by Senator n Lane, began in Kansas.

The 1st Kansas Colored Volunteer Infantry giment was the first regiment of African-Americans fight for the U. S. Army and the first to serve ongside whites. Five officers and 173 enlisted men ere killed in action. One officer and 165 enlisted men ed of disease, the highest casualty rate of any Kansas giment.

Between July, 1862 and October, 1863, the 1st d 2nd Kansas Colored Volunteer Infantry Regiments ere recruited in eastern Kansas and almost 2,000 men ere mustered into the Union Army at Fort Scott and rt Leavenworth. The first four of the six companies

Confederate guerrilla "Bloody Bill" Anderson was among Quantrill's men when they raided Lawrence. He was known for his ruthlessness. Looks like a pirate, doesn't he?
Photo courtesy of The Kansas State Historical Society

Kansas and The Civil War   59

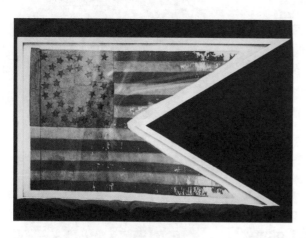

The 1st Kansas Colored Volunteer Infantry Regiment carried this flag into battle.
Photo courtesy of Brian Corn for The Dangberg Foundation

Battles Involving Kansas Black Troops

1. Honey Springs, Indian Territory, July 16, 1863
2. Poison Springs, Arkansas, April 16-18, 1864
3. Flat Rock Creek, Indian Territory, September 16,1864
4. Timber Hills, Indian Territory, November 19, 1864

---

were inducted at Fort Scott. Th
1st and 2nd Kansas Colored
campaigns included battles
Kansas, Missouri, Arkansa
and the Indian Territory, no
Oklahoma. Washington officia
resisted the idea of black troop
But the Kansas regimen
proved themselves again ar
again.

The Battle at Island Moun
near Butler, Missouri c
October 27, 1862, was the fir
time the 1st Regiment lost me
and the first time that Kansas blacks in blue uniforn
died in the Civil War.

After the battle at Island Mound, the Kans:
troops went back to Fort Scott where they remaine
during the winter, cutting hay and building a telegraj
line from Fort Scott to Fort Leavenworth. This ups
the regimental commander, Colonel James William
who wrote letters to Army officials encouraging the
to use his men for fighting. He also wanted the Arn
to pay his men salaries equal to wages paid whi
soldiers and give them proper supplies.

His letters worked. On May 18, 1863, th
regiment went into action, meeting the Southe
soldiers at Reeder Farm near Carthage, Missouri. Aft
the July 1-2 Battle of Cabin Creek in Indian Territor
they chased rebel troops deep into the territory.

The regimental commander, Colonel William
is quoted as saying:

> *"The officers and men all evinced the most heroic spirit, and those that fell died the death of a true soldier."*

Indians Become Refugees

Indians also were forced to take sides when th
Civil War broke out. Many of the Indians who ha
been removed to Indian Territory in the West ha
loyalties based on the location of their old home
Some southern tribes even had slave owners amor
their members. Other tribes were loyal to the Unio

nd some were divided. Tribal warfare was the result.

In 1861, Creek Chief Opothleyahola learned of Confederate attack on Indians and Texans. He cided to align with the Union. But his territory in esent-day Oklahoma was surrounded by tribes who vored the South. He had to flee Indian Territory.

With Confederate troops chasing him, pothleyahola marched his tribe as well as a number of eminoles, Cherokees toward Kansas. His force mbered 800 to 1,200 warriors. They fought their ay northward in a six-week campaign that involved ree battles.

Poorly fed and poorly clothed for winter, they ally reached a camp on Fall River about 60 miles est of Humboldt in late December of 1861.

A government record says:

"Dotting the trail for 300 miles behind them lay the bodies of their dead and the bloody tracks of the barefooted."

Their conditions shocked Union officials. An rmy Surgeon, Archibald B. Campbell reported:

"They greatly need medical assistance; many have their toes frozen off, others have feet wounded by sharp ice or branches of trees lying on the snow; but few have shoes or moccasins. They suffer with inflammatory diseases of the chest, throat, and eyes."

During the first two months after their arrival, 0 Creeks died of exposure or starvation. Doctors nputated more than 100 frozen limbs.

Other loyalist Indians also were driven from the dian Territory into Kansas that season. They cluded members of the Quapaw, Seneca, Shawnee, d Wichita tribes.

To care for the thousands of Indians who were uring into Kansas, the superintendent of Indian ffairs, William Coffin, gathered them near the erdigris River and the Neosho Valley.

By spring of 1862, more than 7,000 Indians ere refugees in Kansas. An average of three to seven dians in the encampment died daily. More than 200 y sick with frostbite, smallpox, measles, mumps, phtheria, and pneumonia.

Groups wanting the Indians out of Kansas

1. The Indians themselves wanted to go back to the Territory from which they had come.

2. The Department of Interior/Bureau of Indian Affairs, which was paying to feed and clothe them.

3. Kansas politicians.

4. The Union Army, which wanted them to take control of the Territory away from the Confederates.

Lane Has an Idea

Kansas Senator Jim Lane offered a solution. H
proposed making soldiers of the Indian refugees.

Three regiments of Indian Home Guards we
formed. One was based at Leroy. Another was at B
Mile Creek, about 15 miles south of Humboldt. Th
third was at Carthage, Missouri.

To avoid starvation for themselves and the
families, many of the warriors became soldier
Records show that more than 3,000 warriors served a
soldiers.

Lawrence is Burned Again

Kansas received its hardest blow of the Civ
War on August 21, 1863, when William Quantri
raided Lawrence. He had raided border settlemen
throughout the Bleeding Kansas era. The Union ha
declared him an outlaw. Now he was a captain in th
Confederate Army.

The spark for the raid came in midsummer
1863 from an incident that was largely an accident.

Federal soldiers had arrested friends an
relatives of known or suspected Confederate guerrilla
They put them in jail in Kansas City, Missouri.
August, the makeshift jailhouse collapsed, killing fiv
prisoners.

In retaliation, Quantrill organized 300 men
ride with him from Missouri into Lawrence. The
arrived at dawn. They shot every man they saw. The
fired into windows as they rode by. They loote
burned as many buildings and houses as they could.

The raiders killed 150 people, all of them mer
Some of them escaped by hiding under buildings,
wells, in outhouses or in a cornfield at the edge
town.

In the National Spotlight

The raid put Kansas once again in the nation
spotlight and drew the wrath of newspaper edito

ross the country:

The New York Times wrote:

"Quantrill's (sic) massacre...is almost enough to curdle the blood with horror. In the history of the war thus far...there has been no such diabolical work as this indiscriminate slaughter of peaceful villagers...It is a calamity of the most heartrending kind an atrocity of unspeakable character."

The Chicago Tribune wrote:
"What pen can depict the horrors...fiends

e nation was outraged *by the bloodiness of William Quantrill's raid on Lawrence, August 21, 1863.*
tration courtesy of The Kansas State Historical Society

incarnate...shooting down unarmed citizens... butchering them with wives and mothers clinging to them and begging for mercy."

The Leavenworth Conservative printed:
"Shot down like dogs...No fighting, no re- stistance - cold blooded murder."

he Love Story of Elizabeth Fisher

Elizabeth Fisher and her husband, Hugh lived in wrence. Hugh was sick on the day of Quantrill's d. With a baby in her arms and a toddler at her side, zabeth saved him. She hid him in the family's cellar d told Quantrill's men he wasn't home.

They set fire to the house. Elizabeth raced to th
well and filled buckets, pans and tubs with water t
douse the flames -- particularly on the kitchen flo
above where her husband lay in the cellar.

In his book, *"Bloody Dawn,"* Thomas Goodric
gives this account of Elizabeth:

> *"A neighbor woman, as mystified as the
> bushwackers, asked her why she was trying to
> save a piece of the floor when her entire world
> was burning. 'A memento,' she yelled back
> above the roar."*

As the fire and debris fell into the kitchen, Hug
had to be moved. He crept out the cellar door and sh
threw her dress over him. She lifted a heavy carpet fo
him to duck under. Then, with him crawling as clos
to her as he could, she pulled the rug out into the yar
The guerrillas still watched as she ran back an
grabbed chairs, bedding, and other items.

So moved were Quantrill's men in watching h
efforts to save the family heirlooms, they helped h
move a divan, desk, and a piano from the fire -- nev
suspecting that her husband lay a few feet away.

Elizabeth Fisher
Hugh Dunn Fisher
Photos courtesy of The Kansas State Historical
Society

Women Were Never the Same

Historians say that Elizabeth Fisher's actio
during Quantrill's raid illustrate a defining moment f
Kansas women. Just as she was forced to move beyo
standing by helplessly in a time of battle, the w
forced women from their traditional protected lives.

As their men went off to war, Kansas wom
had to do the heavy field work of planting, cultivati
and harvesting crops. It was Kansas women w
repaired the houses, mended the barns, fed t
livestock, rebuilt the fences and took care of
children.

Never again would frontier women be judged
frail. They had become hardened by battle.

The Other Side of the Picture

Kansas guerrillas were also guilty of raiding and burning towns in Missouri.

Modern United States Army historian Major Scott Price writes:

"It is all too easy to forget when we mourn the dead who were killed when Bill Quantrill and his men burned Lawrence in 1863, that it was Kansans who initiated the practice of burning undefended civilian towns and murdering noncombatants in 1861. While Col. James Mulligan and his Federal Irish Brigade were fighting for their lives during the siege of Lexington Mo., in September, 1861, Kansas troops, who might well have raised the siege of Osceola, Missouri. The men lynched there following their so-called "court-martial" were considered by their families to be the victims of cold blooded murder."

The Massacre at Baxter Springs

Quantrill made several more raids into Kansas. One of them was what came to be known as the Baxter Springs Massacre of October 6, 1863.

Lt. James Pond and 95 of his Union soldiers were encamped at the springs. The guerrillas caught the camp by surprise and intense firing followed. Pond managed to load and fire a howitzer cannon and Quantrill pulled back.

Pond had saved the camp, but the fight prevented him from going to help another Union unit.

General James Blunt, about 100 of his men, a wagon train, and the regimental band were on their way from Fort Scott to Fort Gibson. They were near Pond's camp. When Blunt spotted riders in blue, he thought Pond had sent an honor guard to welcome him. He was wrong. Several hundred of Quantrill's men were dressed in shades of blue. The guerrillas opened fire on the surprised column.

Quantrill had more guns and more men. Often, each guerrilla carried four six-shot revolvers, a single shot carbine, a saber and a bowie knife. A Union soldier carried only one saber, one six-shot revolver, and a carbine.

Union General James G. Blunt.
Photo courtesy of The Kansas State Historical Society

That day, the Union lost 101 soldiers, Quantr
lost two men.

Blunt never made it to Fort Gibson. Instead
returned to Fort Scott with the remnants of his army
recover and reorganize.

The Battle of Westport

In the fall of 1864, the w
was going badly for the Sou
The Confederates launched
all-out, last-ditch offensive.

General Sterling Price l
the Confederates toward Kan
City and Leavenworth. The Pri
campaign numbered nea
15,000 men and 14 pieces
heavy artillery and stretched c
for miles.

*Andrew Reeder, a watercolor artist
and Kansas pioneer, was in the Kansas
Militia during The Civil War and made
paintings of the things he saw. This
picture, made in 1865, depicts an
incident in 1864 when the Confederate
General Sterling Price led a raid into
the Kansas City area. The Confederate
flag with its crescent moon and circle
of stars, is on the right side of the
picture.*
Painting courtesy of The Kansas State Historical
Society

As the Price column approached Kansas
October 6, 1864, Governor Thomas Carney sen
telegram to Major General Samuel Curtis, w
commanded Union troops in Kansas, Nebras
Colorado, and the Indian Territory:

*"The State is in peril! Price and his rebel hosts
threaten it with invasion. Kansas must be ready to
hurl them back at any cost..."*

Curtis met price with two divisions along
Blue River near Kansas City, Missouri. Three days
fighting ended in The Battle of Westport, which I
been called the last-full scale battle of The Civil Wa
the West.

On the morning of October 24, a defeated Pr
began a retreat southward.

The Battle of Mine Creek

On the night of October 24, the Confeder
camped to rest at Trading Post, six miles north of M
Creek.

lose by, Union troops stood beside their mounts in the
in all night, waiting for orders to attack the camp.
he order came just before dawn.

The rebels were quickly driven from high
ound around Trading Post and pushed back to Mine
reek. Price was forced to halt there because his
agons became bogged down in the mud. After the
ng night of rain, trying to climb the river bank was
ke walking up a hill made of molasses. Confederate
orses, mules, wagons, and soldiers slipped and
ecame trapped in the mud as they tried to climb.

Price tried once to turn back and fight. But his
oops took the full force of a Union cavalry charge.
anic broke out. The Confederates broke ranks and
ed back across the creek.

Lt. General Sterling Price.
Photo courtesy of The Kansas State Historical
Society

Kansan Barbara Jane Dolson, who helped nurse
e wounded at the battle would later say:

> *"Here...was a sickening scene. Some wore their*
> *pain without a murmur, some groaning, some crying,*
> *some praying, and some dying...I certainly have no*
> *desire to see such a sight again."*

Confederate Private Henry Luttrell of the 10th
lissouri Cavalry described the battle this way:

> *"Cavalry horses are breaking from the*
> *enemy's line and are running riderless across*
> *the prairie...About this time Charley Howard*
> *catches a bullet in the fleshy part of his leg. He*
> *slings his gun, takes out a handkerchief and*
> *binds the wound, then goes on firing again, as*
> *he remarks that 'It is better to catch 'em in the*
> *leg than in the head.'"*

More than 500 Confederates were captured and
rice's army barely missed being wiped out. Fewer
an 100 Union men were wounded or killed.

The threat of a rebel invasion of Kansas was
ded.

Enlisted men of Company E, Eighth
Kansas Infantry, which took part in
heavy fighting at Chickamauga.
Photo courtesy of The Kansas State Historical
Society

Other Engagements

Several Kansas volunteer regiments became a
art of the Union army fighting in the South during the
ar. Three regiments and an artillery battery made up
 all-Kansas brigade which saw action in Kentucky,

Tennessee, and Mississippi. Several other units wer in the Indian Territory to control tribes sympathetic t the Confederate cause. General U. S. Grant used som Kansans to fight in the Vicksburg campaign of 186 and the Eighth Kansas Infantry took part in heav fighting at Chickamauga. A monument honoring th Eighth for its gallantry stands on Missionary Ridge high above Chattanooga, Tennessee.

During the course of the war, Kansas sent 2 regiments and four artillery batteries to fight for th Union, more than 20,000 men, two-thirds of all th adult males in the state. Of those, nearly 8,500 die giving Kansas the highest death rate of any state in th Union.

A Kansan Influences the Reconstruction

After the war ended on April 9, 1865, man Union veterans moved to Kansas seeking land whei they could settle down and raise their families. Man were Republicans who had very strong opinions on th issue of slavery.

James Lane was re-elected to the Senate afte the war ended. He had raised an army to fight again: slavery. His views had strongly influenced the state constitutional convention at Wyandotte. He had see his choice of candidates elected to state office. But, i July, 1866, facing poor health, he left office.

His successor in the United States Senate wi Edmund G. Ross, a Lawrence newspaper editor wh had come to Kansas in 1856.

Kansan Edmund G. Ross.
Photo courtesy of The Kansas State Historical Society

Ross took his seat in turbulent times. Preside Abraham Lincoln was assassinated just days after th surrender of the South at Appomatax Courthouse i Virginia. His successor, Andrew Johnson, a Democra was not popular with radical Republicans. The radica wanted to see the South punished. Johnson wanted see it rebuilt. He was soon at odds with members of h own cabinet, especially Secretary of War Edward N Stanton.

When Johnson attempted to fire Stanton, the United States House of Representatives voted Articles of Impeachment. And the junior senator from Kansas found himself a juror in the trial that followed. Most of the senators were quick to reveal how they would vote. But Ross said he would wait until he had heard all the evidence before deciding.

When the roll was called, Ross held the deciding vote. He voted "not guilty." Andrew Johnson remained president and many of his more lenient policies toward reconstruction prevailed.

Ross would later write of that one vote he cast:

"I almost literally looked down into my grave. Friendships, position, fortune, everything that makes the world desirable to an ambitious man were about to be swept away by the breath of my mouth, perhaps forever."

When the next election came, Kansas Republicans voted Ross out of the Senate. He returned to the newspaper business, opening a paper in Coffeyville, only to see his building destroyed by a tornado. He moved to New Mexico where he was appointed territorial governor in 1855.

Relative Calm

Post-war Kansas became relatively quiet in the nation's eyes, but its strongly anti-slavery and pro-rights majority still showed its leadership as Kansas became the first state to ratify the 15th Amendment to the United States Constitution, giving African-Americans the right to vote.

During the late 1860s, construction began on the state capitol in Topeka and by the end of 1869 the east wing was complete and the state government had moved into its new offices.

Kansas was now prepared to grow.

Prairie Spirit

The man who shot and killed John Wilkes Booth, Abraham Lincoln's assassin, may have been none other than Kansan, **Boston Corbett.** After President Lincoln was assassinated on April 14, 1865, Corbett was in a group of volunteers from the 16th New York Cavalry who were to capture Booth. They tracked him to a barn in Virginia. On the morning of April 26, 1865, the soldiers surrounded the barn and set fire to it. As they waited for Booth to come out, a shot was heard and when the soldiers opened the doors of the barn, found Booth dying from a wound in the neck. . After he was discharged from the Army he eventually came to Kansas and homesteaded near Concordia

Construction got started on a new state capitol building shortly after the war ended in 1866.
Photo courtesy of The Kansas State Historical Society

Building a capitol building

Topeka was voted the site for a tempora[ ] capital at the Wyandotte convention in 1859. In t[ ] general election of 1860, it was made the permane[ ] capital of Kansas.

The 20-acre capital square was given to the sta[ ] by the Topeka Town Association.

Construction began in 1866, but the $3.2 milli[ ] project was not finished until 1903.

Crews put the finishing touches on the State Capitol Building in Topeka, which was finally completed in 1903.
Photo courtesy of The Kansas State Historical Society

KANSAS STATE CAPITOL

The Kansas State Capitol in Topeka, constructed over a period of 37 years from 1866 to 1903, cost a total of $3.2 million. The French Renaissance style is constructed of native limestone and is considered one of the most beautiful state capitols.

POST CARD

SPACE BELOW RESERVED FOR U.S. POSTAL SERVICE

We visited the state
Capitol today.
The museum inside has
lots of neat stuff.
The painting of John Brown
is stunning.
His eyes are really
wild!!

Historical Events

1862 - The Homestead Act Passed

1865 - Fort Dodge established

1865 - Peace Treaty of the Little Arkansas

1867 - Treaty at Medicine Lodge

1867 - First Texas longhorns shipped from Abilene

1868 - Atchison, Topeka, and Santa Fe Railroad built

1874 - Buffalo hunting becomes a popular sport

1875 - After Newton, Ellsworth, Caldwell & Wichita
          Dodge City became a cowtown

CRUZ PAGAN 99

Chapter 4

The Frontier After The War

Chapter 4

The Frontier After The War

The people who moved west during the years after the Civil War were looking for cheap land. Many felt it was their future, to move on west and to settle down. If enough people moved west and settled at places along the way, there would one day be people from sea to sea, Atlantic Ocean to Pacific Ocean. The government believed it, too. They made it happen by passing a land act. They called this idea, of what was meant to be, our "Manifest Destiny."

Kansas was a new state. But much of its land was still Indian Territory. Homesteads were available; however, the state remained more a place to cross than one in which to stay. Railroads crossed the lands. Stagecoaches crossed the land in places where railroads were not built. Hundreds of freight wagons traveled the Santa Fe, Oregon, Smoky Hills and other trails to the west. Millions of cattle were herded up the Chisholm and other trails to the railheads.

It was a violent time on a rough and hostile land.

People fought storms and disease, insects and poisonous snakes. In times of drought, they fought the lack of water and the lack of food. Most of all, they fought each other. They fought over which town would get the railroads. They fought over who would have cattle markets. They fought over land claims. They also fought over women and gambling debts.

ettling the Land

America needed people to tame the West, the nd west of the Missouri and Mississippi Rivers. And e elected officials knew just what it would take to ake people risk the move to the frontier land.

In 1862, Congress passed a law called, The omestead Act. It opened plenty of land for new ttlers. It offered 160 acres of land, virtually free, to yone who would stay and live there.

Even as the Civil War raged, people began oving to Kansas to claim land. In 1863, the vernment agreed to help pay for the building of a ilroad from coast to coast, right across the heart of insas. The Homestead Act combined with the velopment of the railroad made Kansas seem like an eal land. There was space, freedom, and plenty of tile land for farming.

Much of unclaimed land was in the western o-thirds of the state. The fact that this was the same id promised to the tribes of the Indian Territory for rmanent hunting grounds was ignored. There was o the problem of a long drought in the land that ephen Long once called "The Great American esert."

Another problem was that much of Kansas was l Indian Territory. To the white settlers, it appeared Indians were wasting the land because they did thing on it but hunt and fish. The settlers wanted to ild farms and cities. This would be a better way to the land. The government apparently thought so,).

Also in 1863, Congress and President Lincoln irked together to find a way to move all the Indians t of Kansas. Lincoln wanted to make room for them land taken from the "Five Civilized Tribes" in lian Territory what is now Oklahoma. Those tribes re being punished for supporting the Confederacy in Civil War.

The Homestead Act

Land was offered under these conditions:

* Any person, male or female, who is 21 years old or the head of a family and
* Who is a U. S. citizen or promises to become one and
* A $10 filing fee is paid and
* Who promises to live on the land for five years and
* Some improvements, such as building a house, barn, or corral, or planting a garden.

Little Chief, his wife, and daughter are shown in a studio portrait. They were members of the Potawatomie tribe.
Photo courtesy of The Kansas State Historical Society

Four Tribes Left in Eastern Kansas

Of the tribes in the most settled land in east Kansas, only four were left on reservations by the e of the Civil War. The Prairie Band of the Potawatom the Vermillion Band of the Kickapoo, the Sac and F and the Iowas held on to some portions of their la Those four tribes still own some land in Kansas to t day.

The preferred method of moving the India was to get them to agree to treaties and to mc peaceably to reservations in Indian Territc (Oklahoma).

If a chief did not agree to a treaty, he could replaced by a "government chief." A government ch was an Indian who the government agents spoke instead of the true chief. After awhile, the tribe beg to listen to the "Government Chief." He was the c who could be persuaded to sell the land and tl moving was best for his people. When this approa did not succeed, force was an alternative that could applied.

The Forts

The government's policy after the Civil V was simple to apply. Keep the Indians away from white settlers. In western Kansas this was hard to The railroads, stagelines, and trails crossed Ind

hunting grounds. The trib responded to intrusion w attacks on wagon trains, railrc building crews and settlers. clashes happened more oft more forts were built. Soldi assigned to a fort, they we responsible for building it. Th used whatever local materi. they could find. Kansas fo generally had no protecti outside walls because there v little danger of direct attack.

Fort Leavenworth was well established by the time Kansas became a territory.
Photo courtesy of The Kansas State Historical Society

They built barracks, stables, and warehouses. The headquarters buildings were built in a square around an open center parade field.

Fort Leavenworth was the first of the Kansas forts. It was built in 1827 near the site of an old French trading and military post, Cavanaugh. It was near enough to Westport (which later became Kansas City) to act as a supply station for the westward journey.

Hundreds of wagons gathered at Leavenworth, waiting until leaders thought they had enough people to make a safe trip across Kansas Indian territory.

Earlier, troops during the Mexican War were mustered across Kansas to fight. Soldiers from Ft. Leavenworth patrolled the Missouri border in the days of "Bleeding Kansas." Later, during the Civil War, Leavenworth became an arsenal and a training camp.

Fort Scott in the southeastern part of the state was built in 1842. It was to protect the "permanent Indian frontier." This was in the days when it was believed that much of Kansas would always be Indian territory. The fort was used to supply troops for the Mexican War and as a staging station for explorations of the territory to the west.

Fort Riley was recommended as early as 1852, and was built as "Camp Center" in 1855. Materials to build it were shipped by boat to Fort Leavenworth and then hauled by wagon train to the new post.

Before the Civil War, most of the officers stationed there were southerners. "Jeb" Stuart and Lewis Armistead, later to be Confederate generals, were

Fort Scott has preserved the officer's quarters building so visitors can see how the fort once looked.
Photo courtesy of The Kansas State Historical Society

Fort Riley. This is how the frontier outpost looked in 1860.
Photo courtesy of The Kansas State Historical Society

Fort Larned. Soldiers stationed here made notes in their diaries about being able to see the flag pole for miles on the prairie. This sketch was done by Harper's Weekly artist T. R. Davis in June of 1867.
Photo courtesy of Wichita State University Special Collections

A burned village and a price to pay

In the spring of 1867, Gen. Winfield S. Hancock decided to make a show of force in Kansas. He marched 1,400 men to Ft. Larned to meet with tribal leaders. But there was a blizzard and the Indians did not come. He marched on the where the Cheyenne and Sioux were camped. When they saw the massive column of soldiers coming, the Indians fled. Hancock reasoned they must be "hostiles." He burned the village and sent George Armstrong Custer to hunt down the runaways. It was a summer of fighting made worse by anger over the burning of the village.

Fort Harker.
Photo courtesy of The Kansas State Historical Society

among the fort's commanders. The main job intend for Fort Riley was protecting wagon trains from Indi raiders.

After the Civil War, Fort Riley became a cava outpost. It was home to some famous Indian fighte including the 7th Cavalry, led by Mexican War veter Andrew J. Smith in command with Col. George Custer as second in command.

The 7th was sometimes called "The Gar Owens" because that was the name of its official sor The band played the lively Irish tune during battles a it was the last music heard by Custer and his men wh they left for the Battle of Little Big Horn.

Fort Larned was first established as a camp soldiers on the Santa Fe Trail at the Pawnee Fork of t Arkansas River. Later, it was called "Camp Ale because its residents needed to be constantly on t alert against Indian attacks. The main job of t original fort was guarding the mail as it traveled wagon and stagecoach across the trails. The garris started out with only one company of infantry and g troops from Fort Riley when needed. It was renam Fort Larned in 1860.

During the Civil War, Fort Larned was not w staffed and the Plains Indians increased their attacks trail traffic. On July 17, 1864, the Kiowas raided Fc Larned and stole 172 army animals.

Fort Harker was established near today's tov of Kanopolis in June of 1864. It was founded as Fc Ellsworth with the primary mission of serving as home station of the Butterfield Overland Stage. T road which stretched 592 miles from Atchison Denver along the Smoky Hill River, came to be kno as the "Smoky Hill Route."

In November of 1866, it was renamed Fc Harker and moved about one mile northeast of t original site. When the Union Pacific Railroad reach the fort in 1867, the fort became an outfitting depot f troops stationed in the west.

Fort Harker was home to the 10th Cavalry, t famed "Buffalo Soldiers." In June and July of 18 these troops were given the assignment of escorti stages and wagon trains traveling the Smoky Hill an

nta Fe trails.   Also to protect the
ews working on the railroads.

That same summer, cholera
ruck the post. In all 892 people --
ldiers, civilian workers, and settlers
came ill and 46 died. This outbreak
d the post's surgeon general, Dr.
eorge M. Sternberg, to become a
ading authority on communicable
seases.

As the Indian Wars escalated,
rt Harker became the home to seven
ops of the 5th Cavalry under the command of
eneral Philip Sheridan. In 1870, Harker was ordered
join Fort Hays in providing men as needed for
eneral George Custer's fight against the Indians.

When the railroad finally reached Denver in
70, Fort Harker's role diminished greatly. By 1872,
th the Indian wars largely over, Harker was
andoned. In 1880, the military reservation was
ened to settlement.

Fort Hays was called Fort Fletcher when it
ened in 1865 with a mission of protecting the
litary roads, the Smoky Hill trail, and guarding the
il. Its soldiers were assigned to defend and protect
e crews building the Union Pacific Railroad.

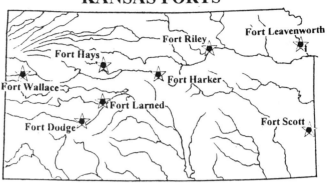

KANSAS FORTS

Map courtesy of The Dangberg Foundation

The main mission of the soldiers
posted at Kansas forts was protecting
the travelers heading west. This train
of freight wagons is camped on Big
Timber near Hays in 1869.
Photo courtesy of The Kansas State Historical
Society

lian attacks on freight caravans, settlers, and lone riders like messengers were reported frequently on the
ins at the time this illustration was printed in Harper's Weekly in January of 1866. Tension between
lers and Indians increased dramatically after the end of the Civil War when homesteaders came to Kansas
earch of new land and new lives.
tration courtesy of Wichita State University Special Collections

Photo courtesy of The Kansas State Historical Society

Famed Indian Fighter George Custer had a hard time living without his wife, "Libby" nearby. She came with him when he was assigned to the frontier to fight the Indian Wars. In 1867, the Custers were stationed at Fort Hays.

In 1866, he was ordered to hunt down Indians who fled a camp near Fort Harker. The Custers were to be reunited at Ft. Wallace. But instead of going to Ft. Wallace, Libby went to Ft. Riley. When George got to Ft. Wallace, his wife wasn't there. So, he took three officers and 75 men and went to Ft. Hays and then to Ft. Riley looking for her.

He was court-martialed for leaving his command without proper authority. He was suspended for a year without pay.

Custer and "Libby" having breakfast *in a tent in Ellis County, 1867.*
Photo courtesy of The Kansas State Historical Society

It served as a supply depot for troops on the move in the territory. Among the men who spent time at Fort Hays were Gen. Custer, William "Wild Bill" Hickok, Buffalo Bill Cody, and Gen. Philip Sheridan.

Fort Hays was closed in 1889 and the land was used for the construction of a university. Fort Hays State University still stands on the land today.

Fort Dodge began as a supply depot and operations base for the western frontier in 1865. The first buildings were made of sod and adobe, with some of the soldiers living in dugouts.

Fort Wallace in 1879, the final outpost in Kansas, this was one of busier forts. This shows the typical layout of a Kansas fort with the parade ground in the center and with buildings surrounding it.
Photo courtesy of The Kansas State Historical Society

In 1866, lumber was brought by wagon train to build a permanent fort; and, at the height of its operations, Fort Dodge had four companies of infantry.

Fort Wallace was one of the busiest of western forts. It was further west than any other outpost and its soldiers guarded the travelers on the Smoky Hill trail. Many of them were headed to the Colorado gold fields. It was abandoned in 1882.

Life At The Fort

Life at a fort in Kansas was hard. When forts were new, soldiers had to live in tents until they built their own quarters. Cutting timber, hauling wood, operating a sawmill and constructing buildings were all on the duty list. Sunday was the only day of leisure and even Sunday included guard duty and stable work.

After a fort was established, married officers could bring their wives. Enlisted men lived in barracks and were not allowed to bring their families to the fort. However, many families moved to the frontier towns near the older forts like Leavenworth, Riley and Larned.

Usually, the only women at the fort besides wives of officers were the women who did laundry and cleaning for the soldiers. Laundresses, who made as much as $2 a month for each soldier's laundry, were often better paid than the lower ranking soldiers. Privates made $13 a month. Non-commissioned officers earned $30 a month and officers were paid $150 a month.

It was quite common for the women, who were often orphaned or widowed immigrants, to marry the enlisted soldiers.

Disease was the deadliest enemy of people at the forts. Cholera epidemics raged in 1849 and again in 1867. At the time, the soldiers did not know that drinking water from the river could make them sick. They took barrels of water from the river because they thought it was cleaner than the wells, which produced

A Day in A Soldier's Life

Daybreak: Reveille
7:10 am : Sick Call
7:30 am : Breakfast
8:00 am : Fatigue (duty) Call
12:05 pm: Mess Call
1:00 pm : Fatigue Call
Sunset: Retreat
6:30 pm : Evening Mess
9:30 pm : TAPS

In their non-working hours, officers spent time with their families or enjoyed time in the "officer's room" where they could drink, play cards, shoot billiards or visit with one another.

There was also an "enlisted room" for the lower-ranking soldiers.

Plains tribes met with officials at Medicine Lodge and signed a peace treaty in October of 1867.
Photo courtesy of The Kansas State Historical Society

water that tasted of the limestone rock in the soil.

They dumped sewage into the rivers, believir that running water was purified as it flowed. At Fo Riley and Fort Larned, the latrines (outdo bathrooms) for the houses were built above the level the river, allowing human waste to flow into the wate

The prairie no longer smelled of fresh flowe and rain-washed grasses. It smelled horrible with th stench of human sewage, garbage, horse manure ar hundreds of people living in close quarters.

There were not a lot of treatments for diseas except to hope people got well. Becoming sick or hu was a dreaded thing. Wounds became infected ar limbs and lives were lost.

Living in close quarters caused disease to spre quickly, poor ventilation and bathing facilities caus breathing problems and skin diseases. Injuries we common too. Cavalrymen were hurt by their hors and soldiers were injured by accidental gunsh wounds or in fights with each other, or with civilians Indians.

The Peace Treaty of the Little Arkansas

In October of 1865, the Kiowa, Comanch Cheyenne, Arapaho, Apache and Wichita met wi government leaders on the banks of the Little Arkans River at what is today Wichita. The treaty propos would allow the Indians to hunt if they stayed south the Arkansas River.

Indian leaders protested that it was unfair. Black Kettle said:

> *"Your young soldiers, I don't think they listen to you. You bring presents and when I come to get them, I am afraid they will strike me before I get away."*

New Treaty at Medicine Lodge

When the treaty was signed, *the Indians were given the rations that had been brought to Medicine Lodge.*
Photo courtesy of The Kansas State Historical Society

Two years later, the same tribes met again w the government at Medicine Lodge. For days, the ta went on. There were hundreds of soldiers, wagonloa of gifts and dozens of promises.

In the end, the Indians ave in. They were promised oney every year for 30 years. hey were to be given clothing, d food, and taught how to rm. They agreed to move to e new Indian Territory where ey were promised land and hools for their children.

But again, many leaders ere not present. The treaty eated peace on paper but in al life, war went on.

The Cheyenne, Kiowa, omanches, and Arapaho killed ttlers in the Smoky Hill and line River valleys and stole eir property.

ast Tribes Removed

Three tribes of Indians mained in Kansas after the edicine Lodge treaty.

The Osage fought a long ttle with the railroad and the vernment over the best price r their land. They finally sold d moved to a reservation in klahoma in 1872. In later ars, oil was discovered on sage land in Oklahoma and ses of mineral rights made e Osage nation the richest in e world.

The Kaw began their st forced migration in 1873. ey had agreed to give up all e land in the territory that re their name.

During the 17 days June, they left Kansas d moved to a new home

Custer's men attack the Cheyenne Camp, 1868.
Photo courtesy of The Kansas Historical Society

A Final Battle

In the fall of 1868, Gen. Philip Sheridan took action to bring Col. Custer back to Kansas. His one-year suspension was not ended, but Sheridan said he needed him for this winter campaign against the Plains tribes. Custer and a unit of the 7th Cavalry followed the trail of Indian raiders to a camp in the Washita Valley in present day Oklahoma. Chief Black Kettle, who had helped lead the raid was there.

Custer's men attacked the camp and killed 103 Indians, including Black Kettle. The following spring, Gen. Sheridan reported that the raid succeeded where talks failed.

All of the nomadic tribes of Kansas were now confined to reservations in Indian Territory.

Custer marches his prisoners back to the fort.
Photo courtesy of The Kansas State Historical Society

in Oklahoma. That fall, with special permission from government officials, they conducted their last buffalo hunt. It was a success.

The Wichita did not have land claims. They had been moved back to the area around the Big and Little Arkansas Rivers because of the fighting in Indian Territory during the Civil War.

The Osage, on whose land they lived, wanted them gone. The Wichita didn't want to go. They said their crops had been planted and they wanted to wait until harvest. They also said they were afraid of the war still going on in Indian Territory.

After all, they reminded the government, they had fought for the Union. Many of the tribes in Indian Territory had supported the Confederacy and they might not be welcome.

They were sent anyway. The trip was awful.

Prairie fires had burned the land along the trail and there was no food. They had few blankets and many of their horses had been stolen by the Osage. At their first camp, 85 horses were killed when a prairie fire overtook them. Later, Chisholm Trail cattle headers would name a nearby small stream, "Skeleton Creek" because of all the bleached bones that lined it. The bones were those of the Wichita people who died on the march and were left unburied.

William "Buffalo Bill" Cody earned his nickname for his skill at killing buffalo.
Photo courtesy of Wichita State University Special Collections

A huge pile of bones lies ready to be gathered up and shipped east. The bones were ground up and used for fertilizer.
Photo courtesy of The Wichita-Sedgwick County Historical Museum

The End of the Buffalo

Buffalo hunting and the profit to be made from the sale of hides brought many early adventure-seekers to Kansas.

Buffalo meat and hides sold for a tidy profit for the hunters. Tanners in New York discovered buffalo hides made excellent leather and the demand for the hides grew at a rate that made hunters rich.

Dodge City was originally named "Buffalo City." Long before it became a cowtown, it was a major buffalo hide shipping point. The hide hunters usually left the meat to rot, saying it wasted too much time. They wanted to kill and skin more animals.

Later, when the bones were discovered to be good for fertilizer, whole rail cars full of bones were shipped east. Skulls were left intact because they were popular ornaments.

or the Thrill of It

Some buffalo hunters came just for the thrill of hunting and killing the big beasts. "Shoots" were organized so people could enjoy the sport of killing the animals.

Hunters would ride out onto the prairie looking for herds. When they found them, they would just shoot until they got tired.

One such hunt, organized to entertain the Grand Duke Alexis of Russia, visiting in 1872, included both George Custer and Philip Sheridan in the shooting party and Buffalo Bill Cody was the leader. The party killed about 90 buffalo in a two-day outing and reported that it made a "nice celebration" of the Grand Duke's twenty-second birthday.

Sometimes, the hunters took the train. A correspondent for Frank Leslie's Illustrated Newspaper wrote an account of trip by train to kill buffalo in 1868:

"In an instant a hundred car windows were thrown up, and the left of our train bristled with 200 guns. The engine screamed and spectators shouted.....the mass were too quick for us, but three immense bulls were cut off."

Buffalo hides purchased by R. M. Wright are shown in a pile in Dodge City in 1874. There are about 25,000 hides shown here.
Photo courtesy of The Kansas State Historical Society

Well-known western artist Frederic Remington spent a summer on a ranch in Kansas. This painting "Downing the Nigh Leader" was printed as an illustration for a work of fiction in Collier's Magazine on April 20, 1903.
Illustration courtesy of Wichita State University Special Collections

An 1867 freight bill, showing goods purchased.
Photo courtesy of Wichita State University Special Collections.

By 1873, passengers on the same railroad sa "few live ones but whole catacombs of dead." Railro conductor, J. H., Hilton said this of the scene:

"One could have journeyed more than 100 miles along the railroad right of way, without stepping off the carcass of a slaughtered bison."

By the mid 1870s, there were no buffalo her left in Kansas. Hunters moved into Indian Territor they violated the Medicine Lodge Treaty by killing c the herds living on land reserved for Indian hunting.

Later, the hide hunters would say they provid a service by removing the buffalo from the rangela so cattle could thrive. They also served the nation, th said, because killing the buffalo removed the fo supply of the Indians and made them more "subdued

By 1876, the great hide market in Dodge Ci stood empty. The herds which had provided the Indi with all his needs for centuries, were destroyed.

Trading with the Indians

The end of the buffalo opened the door greater profits for one group of people in particular the traders.

Even before the Civil War, a trader named Mosley had a trading post in Indian Territory. He a a partner whose name is recorded only as "Moxle reportedly had a thriving business.

He was associated with Jesse Chisholm, a h Cherokee/half Scottish trader who had originally co to the junction of the Arkansas and Little Arkans Rivers looking for gold.

Chisholm did not find gold, but he did find ideal location for doing business and he got on qu well with the Kaw and Osage Indians. The travel rou he took to Indian Territory south of Kansas was to fi fame of its own in years to come.

The Civil War years were hard on the trade Moxley drowned after stealing livestock intended the Confederate Army and Mosley moved to t Medicine Lodge area. He was killed in an Indi attack and his trading post was burned to the ground

he Railroads

Of all the symbols of progress of the Old West, ilroads are perhaps the best known. They contributed settlement, to business and to the end of the buffalo d the Indian.

Railroads were sometimes referred to by cknames that indicated power such as "iron horse" or at emphasized their role in civilization such as "the el Nile."

Railroads in Kansas began as early as 1857 nen the Elwood and Marysville Railroad was ganized. Track was laid from Elwood, just across the issouri River from St. Joseph, Missouri and Wathena. a April 28, 1860, the Albany, the Elwood, and arysville's first locomotive, was ferried across the er and set on the tracks.

Other lines were quick to get charters, including e Atchison and Topeka, the Chicago, Kansas and braska, the Union Pacific, Eastern Division, which

Painting by Jose Cruzpagan for The Grace Dangberg Foundation, Inc.

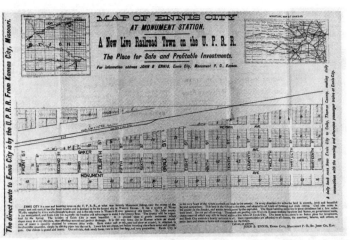

The Union Pacific Railroad offered lots for sale in the city of "Ennis City" in 1870. Ennis City was never built.
Photo courtesy of Wichita State University Special Collections

Prairie Spirit

Kansas Citian **Octave Chanute** became one of the most popular civil engineers in the 19th century. He came to Kansas City in 1867 and designed and built the first bridge across the Missouri River. He built four railroad lines in Kansas along with several bridges for the Atchison, Topeka and Santa Fe. The town of Chanute is named after him.

later became the Kansas Pacific

The years of the Civil W brought a slowdown in railroa development but it also broug federal money to lines that we in a position to serve the militar

On July 1, 1862, Preside Abraham Lincoln signed a b designed to encourage t construction of telegraph lin and railroads from the Missou River to the Pacific Ocean.

This created huge lan grants for the railroads. The were allowed to sell half of the land to settlers. T builders could also get government loans of $16,000 mile to lay track. Three companies were formed, t Union Pacific, the Central Pacific, and the Kans Pacific. The hope was they would build track to allo travel between military posts during the war. Railroa were also seen as a way to promote development aff the war.

It took seven years to build the railroad. T Kansas Pacific built the line from the mouth of t Kansas River through Manhattan, Junction Ci Salina, and Denver and connected to the Union Paci at Cheyenne, Wyoming.

On May 10, 1869, the "Golden Spik connecting the rails all the way across America w driven at Promontory Point, Utah and the telegra sent out a single-word message, *"Done!"*

In Kansas, the single second largest proj began in 1868 when the Atchison and Topeka becar the Atchison, Topeka & Santa Fe. The railroad beg building a line that covered about the same route as old Santa Fe Trail.

By 1882, Kansas had 3,855 miles of railroa and by 1905, it had 8,905 miles. Railroad traf dwindled when competition from automobil highways, and trucking arrived.

Kansas had eight main railroad lines: the tchison, Topeka & Santa Fe, Union Pacific, Missouri acific, Chicago Rock Island and Pacific, St. Louis & an Francisco, Chicago Great Western, Missouri-ansas-Texas, and Kansas City Southern.

ailroad Kings

All the Indian tribes had signed treaties omising to let the railroad cross their land and to low settlers to travel through Kansas.

But the railroads did not just bring the travelers. hey also brought people who wanted to stay. Because e workers building the railroad needed protection, ore forts were built all across the state. The trains' aring, smoking steam engines scared away the wild me the Indians depended on for food. And the cars ere loaded with "sportsmen" who killed the buffalo the millions.

The railroads were given vast tracks of land in yment for building the lines that built the towns. alf of that land was immediately made available for le to settlers. The railroad companies believed pulation in the new land was their key to success. ey placed advertisements in eastern newspapers and cruited people to come to Kansas to live.

Men who owned or controlled the railroads came extremely rich. Cyrus K. Holliday, who came Kansas looking for his fortune found it in the chison, Topeka and Santa Fe Railroad, a link tween the oldest cities of Kansas and the busy trade the southwest.

Other men became rich by building business at served the railroads and the people who built them. ed Harvey realized that people traveling to the "end the track" would want a nice place to stay and good d to eat. He built a chain of hotels called "Harvey uses" to satisfy that need.

It was Holliday, perhaps without realizing it, at wrote a unique chapter in the state's history, when encouraged the Russian Mennonites to come to nsas. They brought with them the seed of Turkey d Winter Wheat, a crop that thrived on the Great

Cyrus K. Holliday, first president of the Atchison, Topeka and Santa Fe Railroad.
Photo courtesy of Wichita State University Special Collections

Plains and that has given Kansas the nicknam "breadbasket of the nation."

The railroads helped play a role in removing th Indians from the state by offering to buy land fro them at higher prices than the government offere They could then sell both the land they were given t the government and the Indian lands to white settlers

Having railroads meant people could come Kansas much easier and faster than they could come wagons. Families with children could travel to t towns where the railroads ran and have only a short tr to their new homes.

As the railroads became the method of settlin new towns, a need grew to extend "branches" "spurs" off the main lines to supply smaller towns wi rail service.

Among the most famous railroads in Kans were the Union Pacific and the Atchison, Topeka Santa Fe. But in those early years, the big rail prof were often made by the smaller companies who we paid lots of money to bring a rail line to a specif town.

Great Bend, 1879.
Photo courtesy of The Kansas State Historical Society

Cow Trails and Cowtowns

Nothing is more symbolic of the W West than the "cowboy time," a period th lasted only about 20 years, but gave America endless romantic legacy. Tales that live today were generally created by easte newspapers and by the writers of "dir novels." They used the colorful cowtowns the backdrop for their fiction. Sometimes th wrote about real people but greatly exaggerat their deeds and misdeeds.

There is no doubt that life in the west v very different than it was in the east. Cowbo wore big hats, boots, spurs, and carried gu

Cowboys gather at the chuckwagon for dinner.
Photo courtesy of Wichita State University Special Collections

They lived in the outdoors and made their living horseback. They made great heroes for novels and t writers made them larger than life.

In the business world, the era of the cowtown was created by a high demand for beef in the northern states and a big supply of cattle in Texas.

The northern states had used up their cattle to feed the Army during the Civil War. But the wild Texas longhorns had multiplied during the war years. Cattle in Texas sold for about $5 each. A steer in New York would bring $50.

Texans loaded cattle on steamships or barges and sent them up the rivers. Cattle went down the rivers to New Orleans and then up the coast to New York. And cattle were rounded up into great herds and driven north to the railroads. The cattle barons discovered they could move cattle for only about a penny or so per mile per head with a trail drive. It enabled them to become very rich.

Life on the Trail

A real cowboy's life was far from romantic or glamourous. It was hard, dirty work. Each herd had a specific number of hands assigned to it. The leader, or trail boss rode ahead of the herd to scout for pasture and water. The chuck wagon, which carried food and medical supplies

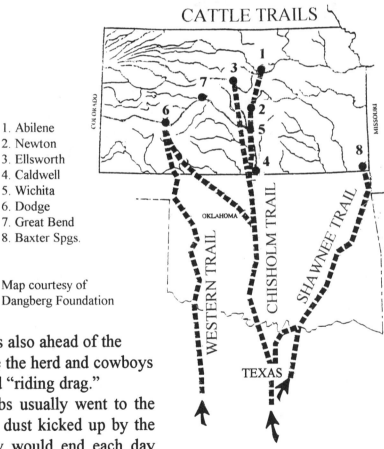

CATTLE TRAILS

1. Abilene
2. Newton
3. Ellsworth
4. Caldwell
5. Wichita
6. Dodge
7. Great Bend
8. Baxter Spgs.

Map courtesy of
Dangberg Foundation

was driven by the cook and was also ahead of the herd. Outriders rode alongside the herd and cowboys bringing up the rear were called "riding drag."

The rear of the herd jobs usually went to the youngest greenest hands. The dust kicked up by the herd would be awful and they would end each day coated in dirt.

Also on the drive were cowboys assigned to care for the horses. They were called "wranglers."

They also took care of the spare horses who were kept in a group called the "remuda."

Old Cowtown Museum, Wichita.
Courtesy of Old Cowtown Museum.
Photo by John Avery.

All day long, the cattle would be driven, then night they'd have to be watched. Cowboys would si to them to keep them quiet, often just making up t words as they went.

Thunderstorms were a big problem. Lightni and thunder would scare the cattle and make them st to run. To prevent a stampede, the cowboys would tu the lead cattle in a circle and get the entire he "milling"around rather than running.

Cowboys ate whatever the cook had in t chuckwagon and slept on a blanket under the stars. it rained, they got wet and had to dry out the next d as they rode.

For all this, they earned about $100 for three four months of work.

The Fear of Texas Fever

It was 1866 when a 16 year old named Jam Daughtery brought his first herd up from Texas. F planned to go to Baxter Springs. He ran into thieve Indians who wanted a tax to cross their land and m who claimed they were trying to protect Kansas her from a disease called Texas Fever. The longhorns d not get sick from Texas Fever. But they carried t ticks that caused the disease. Many states passed la saying Texas cattle would not be allowed there.

Kansas passed a law too, but it was not as str as those in Missouri, Colorado, Nebraska or Illino Kansas law did not allow Texas or Indian cattle come into the state between March and December. B it made an exception.

Most of the Kansas cattle ranches were in t northeast part of the state. So the legislature drew lin at the sixth meridian to the west and across the sta just north of where McPherson is today. They sa Texas cattle could be driven north into the state a shipped out as long as they stayed west and south of t two lines and paid a $10,000 bond to pay for a damages they caused.

Later, as settlements moved west, a new la would move the quarantine line west. It was chang six times during the cattle era, in 1867, 1872, 187

77, 1879, and 1883. As the Texas Fever line moved
st, so did the cowtowns.

The first law was written to favor the town of
lsworth, which wanted the cattle trade and expected
get a railhead on the Union Pacific Railroad. But
d weather and floods delayed the railroad and by the
mmer of 1867, the tracks had reached only as far as
 tiny settlement of Abilene.

he Chisholm Trail

Jesse Chisholm was a trader who operated at the
iction of the Little Arkansas and Arkansas Rivers.
 had a well defined trail for his freight wagons to the
my posts and Indian agencies in Indian Territory. He
o had a thriving side business in helping bring cattle
 from Texas. He sold them to the government as
d for the Indians. That route became known as
isholm's Trail and later "The Chisholm Trail."

When Texas cattlemen began looking for routes
drive cattle north to Kansas, they discovered the
isholm Trail.

Lots of little trails from Texas ranches fed into
 main Chisholm Trail. When it reached Kansas,
inches were formed to go to several cowtowns. Over
ie, it became common for cowmen to refer to the
ole length of the trail through Kansas to Abilene as
 Chisholm Trail.

Jesse Chisholm, an early trader respected by both Indians and early settlers. While on a camping trip into Oklahoma, he contracted food poisoning from eating rancid bear grease, causing his death in the spring of 1868.
Photo courtesy of The Kansas State Historical Society

bilene, the First Cowtown

Joseph McCoy was only 29 when he first came
Kansas. He was searching for places to drive cattle
 shipping to the east. He needed a town with good
iter and plenty of grass to fatten the cattle up after the
ig trail drive from Texas. He needed the railroad, he
ind it in Abilene.

There were maybe a dozen log huts with mud
d sod roofs and only one saloon in Abilene.

Joseph G. McCoy saw the chance for marketing Texas cattle at the Kansas railheads.
Photo courtesy of Wichita State University Special Collections

The town was east and north of the line where Tex cattle were allowed, but McCoy convinced th governor, Samuel Crawford, to allow the cattle to com into Kansas.

McCoy bought land for cattle yard and had railcars full lumber shipped in. Soon he ha holding pens for 3,000 cattle, barn, a bank, a livery stable, and big three-story hotel.

Abilene, 1875. Much of Abilene's growth came from the cattle trade.
Photo courtesy of The Kansas State Historical Society

On September 5, 1867, t first shipment of Texas longhor left Abilene in 20 railroad stockcars. By winter, mo than 35,000 Texas cattle had come into Abilene. T Texas drovers returned with the news that Abilene w a good, safe place to hold and ship cattle.

McCoy printed up circulars and took o advertisements in Texas newspapers, encouragi cattlemen to drive their cattle to Abilene. He also p ads in newspapers in Missouri and Illinois to attra buyers.

The next year there were 75,000 head of Tex cattle driven into Abilene. In 1869, the numb swelled to 160,000.

Soon the residents of Abilene had proble with the side effects of being a cowtown. One who street named Texas Street, was lined with saloo gambling houses and dance halls. Peace officers th were hired to clean up the town were either killed driven off. When townspeople started building a sto jail, the Texas cowboys tore it down.

In 1870, Abilene's marshall, Tom Smith post a law against carrying guns in town. For a time, Smi gained the respect of trail hands for using his fi: rather than guns to keep order. Months later, he w murdered as he tried to help the Dickinson Coun sheriff arrest two men wanted for murder.

Wild Bill Hickok, left, served as marshal of Abilene for a time. With him are fellow buffalo hunters, J. R. Obmonhundro, center, and William F. "Buffalo Bill" Cody, right.
Photo courtesy of The Kansas State Historical Society

His successor was James Butler "Wild Bi Hickok who became Abilene's marshal. According some people, during his term as marshal, he kill many men.

By 1869, the cattle business produced $3 million a year. Abilene was known all over the west and many visitors expected to find a much larger town. In fact, one Texan said:

"Well, I'll swar I never seed such a little town have such a mighty big name."

The year of 1871 was Abilene's biggest and its last. The permanent residents strongly opposed the activities on Texas Street and insisted that the gambling and dance halls be moved outside of town to an area called "The Devil's Addition." The saloons remained on Texas Street. That year 600,000 cattle came into Abilene. The men who drove them north to Abilene swarmed into the saloons and gambling halls to spend the cash they earned on the long drive. By the next spring, the Atchison, Topeka and Santa Fe Railroad had reached Newton. The fall of 1870, Joseph McCoy began building cattle pens in Newton.

ewton

Newton's only year as a cowtown was 1871, but it was enough time to make a reputation.

"Hide Park" was the designated area for gambling, drinking, and women -- the main entertainment of the cowboys at the end of the trail.

On August 12, 1871, Perry Tuttle's dance hall in Hide Park at Newton became the scene of the worst single night of violence in cowtown history.

Newton, 1872. The railroad tracks are a prominent part of the street scene.
Photo courtesy of The Kansas State Historical Society

This night became known as the "Newton's General Massacre."

The day before, Newton had held a bond election. The town policeman, Mike McCluskie and a Texas gambler named Bill Bailey had an argument that ended with McCluskie shooting and killing Bailey.

The next thing McCluskie was confronted by group of Texas cowboys and shot to death by cattleman named Hugh Anderson. McCluskie's frien Jim Riley, saw the shooting. He turned, locked t door and began shooting. The Texans shot back a when it was over, two men lay dead. Four others we wounded and three of them later died.

It was the end of wild times in Newton. A la and order committee gave every gambler, saloon gi and outlaw 12 hours to get out of town. O undesirable resident, sick in bed, was carried to t train on a cot.

For the cowboys, it meant a move to altern: locations Ellsworth or Wichita.

Cowboys whoop it up in town after a successful cattle drive and sale.
Photo courtesy of The Wichita-Sedgwick County Historical Museum

Ellsworth

It was the people of Ellsworth that had fi wanted to bring Texas cattle to Kansas. The Kans and Pacific provided a railhead at Ellsworth. T railroad even hired two men, Shanghai Pierce a Colonel W. E. Hunter, to build cattle pens at Ellswor Other men were hired to mark out a route from t Chisholm Trail to Ellsworth. Pierce was also sent Texas to encourage cattlemen to bring their herds to t new railhead.

Residents of the new soon-to-be cattle cen were well aware of the trouble in other cowtow They hired a police force and established a distr outside of town where gambling and drinking cot flourish. They called it Nauchville.

The police were given instructions to gi Ellsworth full protection and to ignore Nauchville.

Ellsworth's heyday was cut short by t financial panic of 1873. That fall, no buyers came the herds. The cattle had to be held for the winter a thousands died. By 1874, the herds had stopp coming to Ellsworth.

aldwell, the "Border Queen"

That same winter, 1874, the drovers of herds anded in Kansas found a new cowtown. The cellent grass and plentiful water around the town of ldwell made it a good spot to keep the cattle through e winter. Merchants supplied the goods the drovers eded and the town provided entertainment for the wboys.

Its location helped make Caldwell one of the ldest of all the cowtowns. It was right on the Kansas rder with Indian Territory (Oklahoma) which gave it e nickname "the border queen." It was the first town t of Indian Territory on the way up the Chisholm ail. And it was the last town where those returning wn the trail could enjoy the saloons and gambling lls before heading back through Indian Territory.

The average life span of a marshal in Caldwell 1874 was two weeks. Some quit the job before ing killed. Five were shot dead in less than four onths that year. There was common saying, *"In ildwell, you're lucky to be alive."*

Saloon and gambling hall owners had short lives well. Some died trying to break up fights in their sinesses. Others were shot by cowboys or card eats or outlaws.

ichita

In 1872, the Santa Fe Railroad ran a branch line, Wichita and Southwestern, to the town that had e been home to Jesse Chisholm's trading post. The t spring 400,000 Texas cattle came into Wichita. So many of Newton's gambling hall owners and lesirable citizens.

Joseph McCoy, as he had at every other cattle vn along the Chisholm Trail, came to build cattle ens at Wichita. By 1873, Wichita was the major tle market in Kansas. The town built a toll bridge oss the Arkansas River at Douglas Avenue. uglas was also the official route for driving cattle ugh town to the shipping pens.

John Henry Brown

Many of the lawmen of the old west were just one town away from being outlaws themselves.

So it was with Brown, the city marshal hired to "clean up" the wild cowtown of Caldwell in 1884. Brown had once been a companion of famed robber and killer "Billy the Kid" but had reformed.

He did such a good job that he was presented with a gold-mounted Winchester rifle by the grateful town. On the first day of May, his first weekend off, Brown, his deputy, and two Texas cowboys rode into Medicine Lodge, where they used the rifle to rob the bank.

The cashier, George George Geppert, was killed. The bank President Wylie Payne, was wounded.

A posse chased down the robbers and brought them back to the jail. Shortly after midnight, Payne died and a lynch mob formed outside the jail. Brown tried to escape and was shot and killed. His companions, according to the report of the coroner's jury, died "by hanging at the hands of a mob, composed of persons unknown."

Dixie Lee

In frontier life, there were few occupations that were open to single women. Jobs for clerks, secretaries or office help often fell to men. The average women turned to the few jobs she could secure - laundress, waitress, saloon girl, or dressmaker.

Lee was one of the last great saloon girls of Kansas. Her real name was Inez Oppenheimer. Drawn to money, jewels, men, and clothes. She drove up and down the streets of Wichita in her elegant carriage with a team of matching white horses.

At the time of her death in 1901, it was reported that she was known throughout parts of Kansas and she was worth about $150,000.

Wichita's Douglas Street was this cowtown's mainstreet.
Photo courtesy of The Wichita-Sedgwick County Historical Museum

Prairie Spirit

**Boot Hill Cemetery
(1872-1878)**

When Dodge City was a "wild cowtown," on a hill west of town, a cemetery was built and called Boot Hill.

Why Boot Hill? Because so many buried there died with their boots on.

Alice Chambers believed to be the only woman buried on Boot Hill died 5/5/1878. She is believed to be the last person buried there.

Like other cowtowns, Wichita attempted to control the unsavory aspects of the cattle business in a district called Delano. Most of the saloons and dance halls were confined to the area. Still, the intersections around Douglas and Main had plenty of saloons.

But there were other things that concerned the citizens of Wichita about that sinful place Delano.

Some of the people who had settled early in Wichita before it became a cowtown liked the money that the cattle business brought. But they began to question whether they wanted "everything" that a cowtown brought.

From 1872 to 187_ Wichita was the main trail town of Kansas. Cattle reached the peak of profits during these years and the Texas cattlemen grew wealthy. Wichita also prospered and grew rapidly. It became a center for the cattle trade and for trade with the Indian nations immediately south of the border as well.

Farms and fences around the town eventually cut off access to the trail drives and the cowboys moved further west. Another town had already established itself as a shipping center for buffalo hides. They discovered Dodge City.

Dodge City

Dodge City was then a rough and tumble place long before it became the "cowboy capital of the world." It opened as a cattle town in 1875. Dodge's heyday lasted more than a decade, in part because it also became a shipping point for cattle raised in Kansas.

Earlier, Dodge had not sought the cattle trade cause the buffalo-hide shipping business was making od money. Many of its residents were cattlemen, mblers, and gunslingers.

Dodge City had one saloon for every 50 idents and Front Street boasted a variety of sinesses, including the ng Branch Saloon.

Wyatt Earp and Bat asterson gained their ne as lawmen in Dodge ty's heyday.

The Santa Fe ilroad came to Dodge ty in 1872, and Texas tlemen began to use the orter route to Dodge led the Texas Trail.

Front Street in Dodge City, 1872, was main street. Note the railroad tracks in the foreground of the photo. Also notice the Long Branch Saloon in the row of businesses.
Photo courtesy of The Kansas State Historical Society

But as it did in all the cowtowns, the changing rld brought Dodge City's boom to an end. By 1884, Texas Fever line had been moved west of the nsas border.

Cattle grown in Kansas were still driven to dge City to be shipped, but the winter of 1886-1887 ught a terrible freeze. It was then that the end came Dodge City as a cowtown.

Place for African-Americans

Among the people who flocked to the new, raw wtowns were black men. They were freed during the vil War, but left to live in a society that did not accept m. So, they came west. More than 5,000 of them came cowboys and helped drive Texas cattle up the isholm Trail to Kansas.

Among those black men who made their mark early Kansas were:

"Tex," who was the first cowboy to die in a dge City gunfight. Tex was an innocent bystander, ught in the crossfire of two white cowboys who were oting it out.

There was Nat Love, better known "Deadwood Dick," who came to Dodge City in 186[ ] He found black cowboys were treated the same whites. At least that's what he said when he wrote book about his life. He earned his nickname [ ] winning roping and shooting contests in the town [ ] Deadwood in the Dakota Territory.

Ben Hodges was a fast-talker and a hustler [ ] cards. He died in the same year, 1929, as fam[ ] lawman Wyatt Earp and is buried in Maple Gro[ ] Cemetery in Dodge City.

The Dalton Gang

One of the more notorious of the outlaws th[ ] raided Kansas towns in the Wild West years was t[ ] Dalton Gang. On October 5, 1892, five members of t[ ] gang rode into Coffeyville to rob the town's bank[ ] Graf Dalton, Jack Moore, and William Powers enter[ ] the Condon Bank shortly before 9:30 a.m., Bob a[ ] Emmett Dalton went into the First National Ba[ ] across the street from the Condon Bank.

The bandits were recognized and an alar[ ] given. Two of the town's hardware stores opened the[ ] gun supplies and ammunition to the citizens who to[ ] up positions in the street and fired a burst of shots i[ ] the windows of the Condon Bank.

The robbers came running for their horses a[ ] fired back, killing the marshal, three townsmen a[ ] wounding a fourth.

The townsmen kept firing steadily. Emm[ ] Dalton, 16, was the only bandit who survived and [ ] was shot 23 times. He was sentenced to life in priso[ ] He was pardoned after serving 14 years. He lat[ ] moved to California and became a contractor and re[ ] estate dealer. He lived to the age of 66 and died in L[ ] Angeles in 1937.

The Dalton Gang.
Photo courtesy of The Kansas State Historical Society

Jack Ledford

A horse thief, murderer, and robber, Ledford and his Star-Bar-Half-Moon Gang ruled the Arkansas River Valley during Wichita's early cowtown days. Most local women and children feared him, except Alice Harris, step-daughter of one of the town's most prominent families.

He first met Harris in her stepfather's hotel, the Buckhorn Tavern. Alice and Jack fell in love. She was 16 and he was 27.

For nearly two years, he made a living robbing stagecoaches and stealing horses.

When Ledford was wounded in a stagecoach robbery and thought he was dying, he sent for Alice. As he healed, he asked her to marry him. She said she would if he gave up his outlaw ways. Ledford bought a hotel and named it the Harris House. He even ran for sheriff promising, *"If I am elected sheriff of this county there will be no more horses stolen around these parts."*

On December 22, 1870, the two applied for a marriage certificate. All was going well until an Sam Lee, an old boyfriend of Alice's showed up in town. Noticing there was a $2,000 reward out for Jack, Lee notified officers at Ft. Harker that Jack was in Wichita.

Jack was shot by the troops and died an hour later at the hotel.

All This in the Victorian Era

The Victorian era was a time of ornate decoration both in homes and in fashion. Houses had ornate woodwork trim. Baseboards were as a much as a foot wide even though wood was scarce. Such building indicated wealth and even the roughest cattle towns had an "upper crust" of social order. Merchants, bankers, railroad owners, and cattlemen spent lavishly and were at the top of the order.

Women's clothing was elaborate with ruffles, bustles, and fancy hats. Men wore vests, gold chains, and polished boots.

The benefits of the time had great influence on the way Kansas and the entire United States developed.

It made the town builders happy to believe that western towns would someday be just as cultured as the cities back east. It also made them happy to know that when that day came, they would be very rich.

Hays, 1880. This street scene gives an indication of the influence of Victorian style on the buildings of the day. Note the building to the left in the background.
Photo courtesy of The Kansas State Historical Society

Dodge City Cowboy Band. *This cowboy band played at President Benjamin Harrison's Presidential inaugurati*
in 1889.
Photo courtesy of The Kansas State Historical Society

Settling Down

By the 1890s, even Dodge City was seei
calmer times. Since the railroads had arrived in Tex:
and there was no longer any need to make the long tr
drives into Kansas.

The towns established by the Indian trade a
the cattle markets looked for new ways to grow a
thrive and new businesses were opened.

New residents began coming to Kansas to ma
it their new home.

Cowboy Capital of the World

DODGE CITY, KANSAS

Dr. O.H. Simpson, a pioneer dentist, created the cowboy sculpture which is located on Boot Hill. Completed in 1927 and dedicated in 1929, the base inscription reads, "On the Ashes of my Campfire This City is Built" written by Lane Dutton, a Dodge City attorney and judge.

Distributed by Avery Postcards, 6102 E. Morris, Wichita, KS 67218

POST CARD

We just saw Front Street in Dodge City. Did you know it was all built like a movie set in the 1950s? All of the buildings were made to look the same as the old ones. It's cool, though, pretending cowboys are having gunfights in the streets. And Dodge City is STILL a cow town. There are hundreds of cattle pens outside of town. I didn't see any trails, though. Just a lot of trucks.

© Photo by John Avery (DC-2)

Historical Events

1865 - Blizzard of New Year's Eve

1870 - Mennonites come to Kansas

1873 - The Timber Culture Act Passed

1874 - Grasshoppers eat Kansas

1877 - Nicodemus community started

1887 - Prairie fire near Nicodemus

1887 - Cyclone hits Prescott

1880-1890 - Drought in Kansas

Chapter 5

Civilizing Kansas

Chapter 5

Civilizing Kansas

The word was out! Great deals were to be had in Kansas. The state had prime untouched farmland just for the taking.

All it would take was hard work. Some investment in the local community was needed. There was another ability one must have. That was the ability to stand up to windstorms, blizzards, prairie fires, drought, blistering heat, insects, and floods.

If one could beat the odds, one could built societies, create economic empires, and reach one's dreams in Kansas.

This chapter is about the people who did just that. The Kansas you know today is very different from the one the pioneers first settled. But in many ways, it is still very much the Kansas they built.

The Timber Culture Act

America needed people to tame the West, the land west of the Missouri and Mississippi rivers. The government knew just what it would take to make people risk the move to the frontier land.

Congress added the Timber Culture Act of 1873 to the offer of the Homestead Act. A person who planted 40 acres of trees and maintained the timber for 10 years could get a grant for 160 acres of land.

Much of the unclaimed land was in the western two-thirds of the state. The fact that this was the same land promised to the Indian Territory tribes for permanent hunting grounds was ignored. There was also the problem of a long drought in the land that Stephen Long once called "The Great American Desert."

Railroad companies, especially the Kansas Pacific, wanted to sell the land they had bought from the Indians to the settlers. They built experimental farms in several areas. They hired promoters to write glowing advertisements about the new land. They talked about the beautiful blue skies. One Kansas Pacific handbook of 1870 stated: *"the weather and condition of roads enable you to do more work here than elsewhere."*

Early farmers soon saw that farming here would be different. It rained much less than in the east. They needed to grow crops that could survive without much water. Wheat proved to be a better crop than corn for that reason. Moreover, in other areas of the state, ranching was better than farming.

In 1873, T. C. Henry of Abilene became one of the first farmers in the state to do experimental farming.

A KANSAS LAND-OFFICE.

After the Civil War, as more and more people came to Kansas to settle, land offices often became the place to be. Deals were made, gossip could be heard and land often changed hands. This illustration showing a Kansas land office was originally published in the Harper's Weekly in July 1874. Photo courtesy of Wichita State University Special Collections

T. C. Henry.
Photo courtesy of The Kansas State Historical Society

Baker's horse driven elevator, Pawnee Rock in Barton County, 1890.
Photo courtesy of Wichita State University Special Collections

R. S. Elliott.
Photo courtesy of The Kansas State Historical Society

That year, he plowed 500 acres of Kansas Pacific land. By 1875, he had a 1,200 acre farm in wheat. He used new (hybrid) crop varieties and dry-land farming techniques.

R. S. Elliott was another experimental farmer. He published a pamphlet in 1870 called "Climate on the Plains." He worked with the Kansas Pacific Railroad. His job was to prove farming was possible in Kansas. He was one of several people who said that cultivating the ground and planting crops would cause more rain to fall. Another group of people suggested that planting trees would make it rain more.

For several years, there was rain. And it seemed to many settlers that the experimental farmers were right. Historians and climatologist today, however, believe that those rains were simply part of a cycle of wet and dry years. That cycle still occurs in 20 to 30 year intervals all across the Great Plains. There will be a period of wet years and a period of dry years.

When the rains didn't come, western Kansas farmers tried irrigation. Near Dodge City, Asa T. Soule planned a canal that was to run from Gray County into Edwards using water from the Arkansas River. The project was soon abandoned when some of the water upstream in Colorado was diverted before it reached western Kansas.

Other farmers used windmills and created ponds to help bring water to their parched land. In fact, the windmill would soon become one of the icon images of the prairie.

The Colonists

Once people were convinced that the wild prairies could be tamed, the next problem became the organization of settlements.

New settlers came and settled in colonies because there was safety in numbers and it was the most practical way to live and they were used to living near other people who had common interests or ways of living. Religious and racial groups, veteran's organizations, and Utopian societies all sought out similar groups.

The Emigrant Aid Company offered to help settlers in the new land. One promotional ad read:

"The inconveniences and dangers to health to which the pioneer is subject who goes out alone or with his family, only in meeting a new settlement are familiar to every American. The Emigrant Aid Company has been formed to PROTECT EMIGRANTS, as far as may be, from such inconveniences..."

Drawing by K. Fay for The Dangberg Foundation

That in a nutshell included most of the reasons why people wanted to settle in colonies. They were afraid of being cheated or robbed. They were afraid of being attacked or hurt. Many of them needed help in understanding a new language. Some wanted to practice their religion, political or personal beliefs without fear of persecution. But mostly they wanted to know that if trouble came, friends would be nearby. Settlements were often miles apart.

Creating Shelter

Prior to the Timber Culture Act of 1873, there were almost no trees on the plains. Families had to build two kinds of dwellings: sod houses or dugouts.

To build such a sod house, ground was broken by turning the sod over with a "breaking plow" pulled by a horse.

The plow had three curved rods, which turned the sod grass upside down. Pieces of sod were usually about three inches thick, a foot wide and two to three feet long. Settlers would lay the sod like bricks, so that the joints overlapped on successive layers.

They would use some wood to frame the windows and doorways, but the rest would be sod. The roof was a combination of wood supports and sod.

A dugout was made by digging a cave into a hillside to a depth of at least six feet. Stones were placed along the roof edges. Planks were then placed over the roof and covered by sod.

A Lonely Life on the Prairie

Providing a homestead claim was a lonely life. Settlers often came to Kansas with friends. But individual families had to settle their 160 acres alone. The desolation of the prairie caused one woman, Mrs. Gottfrid Magnuson, to exclaim when she came to the Smoky Valley in 1870: *"Why should I have come to a wilderness like this? Listen to the sighing of the wind as it sweeps over the rolling prairies. What a lonesome life. Thousands of miles from friends and civilization."*

In September of 1869, Lindsborg Paster Olaf Olsson wrote to a friend in Sweden: *"We have no planting yet around our house, since we are surrounded on all sides by what is called flat prairie, that is fields with long, luxuriant grass. If we live until next year, we intend to plant trees and grow flowers as much as possible."*

Civilizing Kansas   109

Early farmers used what materials they could find and improvised for the rest. The homestead of Henry Meyer in Barton County in 1876 featured a house made of logs with a sod roof.
Photo courtesy of Wichita State University Special Collections

Fine gravel or crushed rock was packed firml inside to make a solid floor. The walls were brace with rock or logs and some were plastered with mu and sand, then whitewashed with a heavy coat of lime

The sod houses and dugouts were usuall cool in the summer and warm in the winter. They als attracted some unwelcome critters. Early settler would often tell stories about how bugs or snakes fron the dirt roof would drop down, as the family would ea meals at the dinner table.

This illustration shows the interior of a temporary home of Russian Mennonites. Look at how crowded the building was, what kind of trunks people traveled with, and how clothes were hung to dry.
Photo courtesy of Wichita State University Special Collections

The Mennonites

The population of Kansa grew by more than a millio people between the Civil Wa (1860) and the census of 189(Many of the people who cam to live in Kansas during tha time were from Europe. Man of those people were fron German-Russian ancestry.

The Mennonites came t Kansas in the 1870s to escape religious persecutio They were mostly farmers whose religious beginning were formed in Switzerland and Holland during th 16th century. This was in a religious period known a the Reformation. They did not believe in war. Nor di they believe in being part of the military. In Europe th Mennonites were persecuted by various groups and, a times, by other religions.

Frank Leslie's Illustrated Newspaper,
March 20, 1875. Central Kansas - The
Russian Mennonite's Settlement.
Photo courtesy of Wichita State University
Special Collections

In 1871, Russia passed a law that required everybody to be part of the military. The Mennonites refused. They began looking for somewhere else to move where they could be free to live, as they believed.

At the time, the Santa Fe Railroad was advertising land for sale. The railroad appointed C. B. Schmict, a German resident of Lawrence, as its Commissioner of Immigration. It was largely through his efforts that the greatest number of Mennonites came to Kansas.

Something else appealed to the Mennonites. In 1874, Kansas passed a law that men did not have to serve in the army if it was against their religion. They had only to declare their faith at the local county clerk's office.

Jacob Wiebe led one of the first groups of Mennonites from Russia to settle in Kansas. They built long houses which also served as a storage shed and barn. Many of them settled near Hillsboro in Marion County. They called their community, Gnadenau, which in German meant "Meadow of Grace."

They bought land from the Santa Fe Railroad and grew wheat, watermelons, and sunflowers for seed. Soon other groups of Mennonites came to Kansas and settled in Marion, Harvey, Reno, McPherson, and Barton counties. (See the county map on page 302.)

Jewish Communities

Courthouse at Ravana. *Ravana was a Jewish community in Western Kansas.* Photo courtesy of The Kansas State Historical Society

In the late summer of 1882, twenty-four Russian Jewish families braved the frontier of western Kansas. They came to a place a few miles north of Cimarron and a few miles northeast of what is now Kalvesta. From the sod, they built a Synagogue and a cluster of tiny houses. They called their town Beersheba after an ancient city in Israel.

The colony stretched over several sections of land. Each family homesteaded 160 acres. Cowchips were used for fuel. Wells were dug and the native prairie was plowed and planted.

The families got help from the Emigrant Aid Committee of Cincinnati. The Committee provided the settlers with wagons, horses, harnesses, agricultural implements, some livestock, and poultry.

Soon, six other Jewish settlements followed in Finney, Ford, Pratt, and Comanche counties, and in Motefiore, Lasker, Leeser, Touro, Gilead, and Hebran.

The Jewish people who came to Kansas were part of the same European migration that brought the Mennonites and Volga Germans. By the time the Jewish people came, most of the prime farmland was already claimed.

They held to the land through blizzards, droughts, and grasshoppers. But farming proved too unprofitable for the Jewish people. Finally, they sold their equipment and livestock and took jobs with the railroad. They mortgaged their land and established businesses elsewhere.

By the 1890s, the Jewish farming colonies had all but disappeared.

Other Settlements

"In God we trusted, in Kansas we busted," was the slogan for many settlers in the late 19th century. They came with hope. They left shattered and broken.

In the beginning, Kansas was a land where Methodists, Baptists, Catholics and Mennonites all had strongholds in the communities.

In many ways, the Kansas frontier was an ideal place for diverse groups to live in harmony. It was often six miles by horse and buggy between communities. There were no phones, TVs, radios, or computers. They were isolated by distance and had little or no social contact with one another. German Russians settled in Ellis and Rush counties in the 1870s and 1880s. They named their new communities for their old communities in Europe: Catherine, Schoenchen, Herzog (Victoria) and Liebenthal. Every man in their congregation helped with the building of St. Fidelis Church in Victoria. This church became known as the "Cathedral of the Plains."

Bohemians settled in Kansas from the area of Croatia, Bosnia, Czech, and Slovakia. Many of these people were mechanics and merchants, but farming was more profitable in Kansas. They settled Ellsworth County and soon moved into Russell County as well. Like the Swedes, they have kept their cultural traditions. The annual Czech festival at Wilson is one example.

In 1869, with help from the First Swedish Agricultural Company, Swedish Lutherans came to the town of Lindsborg. They built New Scandinavia and encouraged fellow Swedes to come. Among their leaders was Dr. Carl Swensson, founder and president of Bethany College and Rev. Olof Olsson, who helped found Lindsborg. Some of the greatest singers in the world have come to Lindsborg during the Christmas season. They took part in the performances of Handel's Messiah, which have become a Kansas tradition at Bethany College. The Swedish Agricultural Company helped the Swede settlers buy guns to protect themselves against Indians. The company also helped build a store. The company also gave away lots to would be residents if they planted trees or built homes.

Land of Hope for Freed Slaves

More than a decade after the Civil War, southern black people were drawn to Kansas. It had become known as a free state.

The state also offered them a chance to make money and to live well.

By the late 1870s, many former slaves had settled in most parts of Kansas. A former Tennessee slave, Benjamin "Pap" Singleton became famous for his efforts. He was convinced that blacks could not prosper in their old slave states. He began urging them to come to Kansas during the 1870s. Singleton became known as the "father of Kansas black immigration."

Many came with the intent of establishing all black towns; others were drawn to existing cities such as Kansas City, Lawrence, Leavenworth, Topeka, and Wichita.

For blacks with little money, the cities often were their first stop. Many of those who had dreams of farming would abandon their dreams once they obtained jobs in the city. Others moved to the black towns or became farmers only to become victims of crop failures and harsh economic times. Some farmers were forced to go back to the cities to find jobs.

Freed slaves were drawn to Kansas.
Photo courtesy of The Kansas State Historical Society

Nicodemus.
Photo courtesy of The Kansas State Historical Society

Nicodemus was an all-black community settled in 1877 by a group of 300 Kentuckians. The town was promoted as the largest black colony in the United States. Most of its early residents lived in dugouts.

Other all-black settlements were formed in Kansas from a mass migration after the Civil War. Those who migrated, African-Americans were called "Exodusters." This name was drawn from Biblical reference to the chapter of Exodus when the Hebrew slaves were freed from Egypt.

Of several communities founded, only Nicodemus survives today. In 1996, it became national historic park site.

ther European Settlers

George Grant started the community of Victoria Ellis County in 1873. Grant was a Scottish silk erchant. He bought nearly 31,000 acres of Kansas cific Railroad land. He believed British farmers uld raise cattle and sheep in Kansas. He named his wn Victoria in honor of the English queen. Victoria ver grew to the size that Grant had dreamed. He did ove that sheep could survive Kansas winters. His ttle herds of Angus and Galloway helped upgrade estern stock.

In Harper County, there was Runnymede. An iglishman named F. J. S. Turnley offered to teach the ns of British men the secrets of good farming. He arged the wealthy families of Great Britain five ndred dollars per son. He promised he would teach em to be successful farmers and help them to build eir own farms on the American frontier.

Once the wealthy sons rived in Kansas, they found it sier to race horses and have rties. They didn't take to the ork of farming, thus, the tlement was never truly ccessful.

In Franklin County, a enchman by the name of nest Valeton deBoissiere gan Silkville. He envisioned Utopian community where all e residents would share work d money. They would thrive making silk. He planted ilberry trees and imported worms from France and oan. The community turned t 250 to 300 yards of award nning silk a day. However, eign countries could sell silk less money. Eventually, the nmunity failed.

George Grant.
Photo courtesy of The Kansas State Historical Society

A Silkville gathering.
Photo courtesy of The Kansas State Historical Society

What's in A Name

As settlements grew, there was a need for local government. However, Kansas was divided into counties. More than 30 counties were formed during the period known as "Bleeding Kansas." Almost all of them were in the eastern part of the state. Like everything else of this period, it was done with argument, fighting and sometimes violence and bloodshed.

It was not unusual for these early counties to have their names changed. Changes happened because residents fought over how their counties should be known.

Between 1861 and 1870, 18 counties were added, most in the central and far southeast part of the state.

In 1873, all of the remaining area of the state was divided into named counties by the Kansas legislature. However, some of the names were changed as the counties became organized.

Who'll Get the County Seat

As counties organized, local communities fought over which town would become the county seat. Most counties changed their county seats at least three times. Where the railroad ran was often the deciding factor for a new county seat. So, there were bribes and battles to get railroads to come.

In McPherson County, the battle was between McPherson and Lindsborg. A group of McPherson men went over to Lindsborg and asked the men guarding the county papers to step out and talk things over. While they were talking, a McPherson man put the papers into a spring wagon and drove off.

Iuka was Pratt County's first county seat winning over Saratoga and Anderson. When the railroad came, Pratt Center became the favorite. The fight turned violent. The courthouse was burned and people were wounded in shootings. The state's adjutant general was called to restore order. The county seat wound up in Pratt.

As many as seven small towns in Howard county actively sought the county seat. There were elections, court injunctions and stolen records. At one point, the county treasurer collected half the taxes for the year, kept the money, and left town. The residents, sick of the expense and fighting, came up with a unique solution: They divided the county up and formed two new counties: Elk and Chautauqua. Now there could be three county seats.

Some of the worst violence erupted between 1880 and 1890. On several occasions, the state militia had to be called to restore order. In three counties, people were killed in the effort to organize.

Eventually, the land was settled. Counties were typically divided up into six or seven hundred square miles. The idea was that every citizen should be able to ride by horseback from his home to the county seat and return in one day.

After all This, Beaten by Grasshoppers

Try to imagine what it was like to be a Kansas pioneer in 1874. The Civil War was over, but people were still angry and bitter. Neighbors still had strong feelings and even fights.

Imagine building a house and farm with few tools or materials. There were no trees for logs. There was limited lumber, if one had money. Most people had only a mule or a horse, a plow, and some seeds.

Picture living in a dark, damp little sod house where bugs and an occasional snake shared the space. Imagine the mud and the smell of wet dirt. There was no electricity, no sinks and no toilets. There was no radio and no TV. The most read book was the Bible. Food was what one planted and harvested. Meat was available if one killed, dressed, and cooked an animal. There was no refrigerator and ice only in the winter months.

The summers were windy and blistering hot. The winters were cold and windy, swirling the snow in drifts that buried the houses. In the spring, there were sometimes floods that destroyed the crops.

An editorial cartoon *is picturing the demise of Mr. G. Hopper of Kansas.* Photo courtesy of The Kansas State Historical Society

And if the floods didn't come, hailstorms might destro the crops. If the rains didn't come, the land becam dry. Prairie fires swept the land destroying everythin;

Life was hard. However, in July of 187 farmers had reason to hope. They had planted ne crops, which were green and growing.

Then, one day settlers awoke to a dark cloud o the horizon. They watched it come closer, fearing th wind, the lightning, the hail, perhaps a tornado. The they heard it: a buzzing, crackling, rasping sound. I there a fire they wondered?

Then, somethings fell to the ground -- thousand and thousands of long-winged grasshoppers. Th insects piled up on the ground, 2 or 3 inches dee[shining in the sun like silver dollars. Then they wer on the move, eating their way across the prairie.

The grasshoppers stripped the trees of the leaves. They ate all the garden vegetables, even onior growing beneath the ground. Clothes hanging outsid to dry were eaten.

For three days, the grasshoppers ate and at Then they flew on to another location, traveling ; much as 40 miles in a day.

It was so bad that the United States governmer had to help. President Ulysses S. Grant ordered the U Army to donate coats, blankets, and boots and shoes t Kansas families.

One good thing is, it will never happen agair At least, not with that species of hopper. Within thre years of the great grasshopper plague, the specie simply vanished.

Snow Plus Wind Equals Blizzard

There can be a lot of snow, but snow alone is n(a blizzard. On the other hand, a lot of wind with n snow is just a windy day. But when you put sno\ together with wind of more than 35 miles per hour, yo have a blizzard. Many history accounts still conside the blizzard that struck Kansas from New Year's Eve (1885 to January 7th of 1886, as the state's mo devastating winter storm.

This photo of a locomotive making its way through drifted snow Western Kansas shows what a challenge it was to "dig out" from a blizzard.
Photo courtesy of Wichita State University Special Collections

ozens of people died. Thousands of cattle and wild nimals were killed. It took almost a week to dig out f the snow and more than a month to survey all the amage.

Hardest hit were the people in western Kansas. Many of them lived in crudely built dugouts or sheds. They had little protection from the cold. The howling ind buried their homes in drifts. Many could not get ut of their homes and they ran out of fuel and food.

The great storm was actually two blizzards which were a week apart. The first hit on New Year's ve of 1885. The second on January 7, 1886. Some ewspaper accounts say snowdrifts reached as high as e tops of railroad cars. For nearly a month after the orms, newspapers were still writing of the damage.

In 1935, The Dodge City Journal published a ory on the anniversary of the storms, recounting the 886 losses:

> On Jan. 5, 14 people froze to death near Dodge City. Two brothers were found nine miles from the city. They had died clasped in each other's arms. An entire family - father, mother and three children was also found frozen near Dodge City.
> By Jan. 13, officials with Santa Fe Railway had hired 300 men to clear tracks near Spearville. They had to dig through towering snowdrifts.

ater, the paper reported, *"the railroad offered $2 a day and board for additional men to shovel through the drifts."*

Residents of western Kansas used whatever fuel ey could find to keep warm -- wood, corn or buffalo d cattle chips. In some cases, they fed their furniture the fires. Some homesteaders even survived by aying in bed after they had used all their resources.

Once temperatures stared to rise, a search was ade of all dugouts, shanties, and other prairie homes western Kansas to find the survivors.

rairie Fires

A most terrifying disaster for many settlers was airie fires.

Sometimes, pioneers would have enough time prepare for an approaching fire. They would load

This illustration published in Harper's Weekly, A Journal of Civilization, February 28, 1874, which was called, "Fighting The Fire." Photo courtesy of Wichita State University Special Collections

barrels of water, buckets and sacks onto wagons an prepare to fight the flames.

Lightning started fires. Sometimes spark flying from a railroad track or a steam engin smokestack started fires. Other times, people we: simply careless. Winds would quickly whip the fi through the dry prairie grass and, in no time, it wou be out of control.

Farmers tried to protect their farms from fire b plowing a furrow about 50 feet wide on either side of strip of land. They would mow the grass in the str while it was green.

One of the worst prairie fires broke out ne: Nicodemus on April 10, 1887. Nine people were kille in that fire. The fire, pushed by a 40 mile per ho wind, swept into Rooks and Phillips counties.

One of the reasons prairie fires are not the thre: today as they once were is because of conservatic efforts.

Pioneers kept records of what happened. Many Flint Hills ranchers today carefully burn their pastures each spring to destroy weeds and brush. The grass then grows green and lush and cattle keep it grazed short. The green grass is much less likely to catch fire from lightning or sparks. Today's ranchers also know about setting backfires and watching the forecast for the wind and rain conditions.

Tornadoes could be just as terrifying for early settlers as it is for today's present Kansans. Frank Leslie's Illustrated Newspaper, May 7, 1887. Terrible effects of the Cyclone of April 21st at Prescott -- two hundred buildings demolished, and thirty persons killed and injured.
Photo courtesy of Wichita State University Special Collections

Drought

Farmers need rain in order to produce go[od] crops. And when rains didn't come, families on t[he] frontier had to fight for their very survival. Stro[ng] winds whipped dirt into the air making a howli[ng] sound. Some settlers, it was said, almost lost th[eir] minds from the unrelenting sound of the wind.

One of the worst windstorms occurred duri[ng] droughts that came in a 10 year cycle from 1880 [to] 1890.

The Pioneer Legacy

You might sometimes hear people today t[alk] about the pioneer heritage. What the pioneer herita[ge] means is that Kansans have a long tradition of worki[ng] hard, surviving through tremendously difficult tim[es] and carrying the hope that tomorrow will always b[e a] better day.

It was such a tradition that gave rise to [the] state's motto, printed in Latin on the Kansas State Fl[ag] *Ad astra per aspera - "To the stars throu[gh] difficulties."*

The early settlers helped define and sha[pe] Kansas to what it is today. With the settlement of [the] state, the frontier disappeared. Between the Civil V[ar] and the beginning of the 20th century, the lifestyles [of] Kansans improved. Many ornate Victorian hou[ses] replaced sod houses. Cattle replaced buffalo. Wh[eat] replaced the prairie grasses.

There was much hope that wealth and grow[th] would continue through future generations.

The Great Seal of Kansas.
Photo courtesy of Wichita State University Special Collections

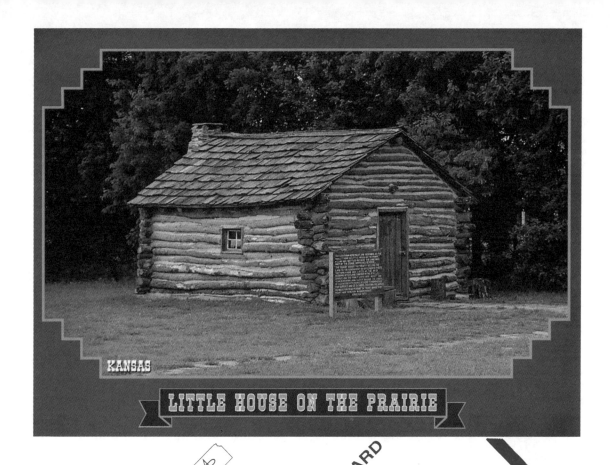

KANSAS

LITTLE HOUSE ON THE PRAIRIE

POST CARD

Avery Postcards, P.O. Box 20346, Wichita, KS 67208

SPACE BELOW RESERVED FOR U.S. POSTAL SERVICE

KANSAS HISTORY

This log cabin southwest of Independence resembles the Ingalls' home described in Laura Ingalls Wilder's "Little House on the Prairie." The family lived here for about a year, and in her book, Laura describes the building of the cabin, encounters with Indians, and going to Independence for supplies.

Little House on the Prairie is really little. I don't see how everybody could fit, especially with all the stuff they had to have to work in this. Independence sure is a lot bigger than when Laura lived there, though. I wonder what she would have thought of highways?

Historical Events

1853-1927 - Orphan Trains come to Kansas

1870s - Corruption in Kansas politics

1870-1890 - Kansas population grows rapidly

1871 - "My Western Home" is written, later to become "Home on the Range

1890 - Extreme western Kansas counties settled

1893 - Showdown between Poplists and Republican parties

1893 - Cherokee Strip Land Run

1899 - Samuel Crumbine begins Kansas health programs

1900 - Carry A. Nation wrecks saloons against alcohol

Chapter 6

Bad Times and Reform

Chapter 6

Bad Times and Reform

Without a doubt, changes were bound to come.

By the 1890s, farms were mortgaged to the hilt and there was drought in Kansas. Farmers, businessmen, and women all looked for a sign of hope. Even religious leaders agreed that changes were needed.

At first, there was hope in the "signs of progress." The railroads crossed the state. The Indians and the settlers had been separated. The buffalo were gone. Many believed the land was conquered. They looked for prosperity and good times.

But many of the newcomers to the state were not farmers. They knew nothing about the prairie. They hadn't counted on fires, floods, disease, drought, blizzards, and grasshoppers.

Long-range weather forecasts were in the distant future. No soil tests had ever been made. No one knew how much rain fell each year or which months were dry and which months were wet. Newcomers had no idea how hot the summers were or how cold the winters would get. They just assumed this land would be like the land they had left behind.

ude Awakenings

From 1870 to 1890, Kansas grew rapidly from st over .3 million people to 1.4 million.

Industries in the east were in need of western etals and other raw materials. Machinery allowed rms to grow bigger. Wells were drilled. Water imps were invented. Windmills were built.

Farmers tried growing everything. Corn, wheat, its, barley, sorghum, cotton, and tobacco were anted. Even grapes for making wine were grown.

State agricultural agencies told settlers not to orry about the dry, hot conditions. They pointed to assuring "facts" such as these:

* Everyone knows that iron attracts lightning id that lightning brings rain. Therefore, the railroads ill bring rain because the iron of the rails will attract ghtning.

* It always rains where there are large numbers ' people. Therefore, if more people come to the state, ore rain will come too.

During the 1880s, settlers poured in. At first, ey staked out homesteads along the railroads. Then e settlers moved out in all directions. By 1890, even e extreme western counties were settled. The State oard of Agriculture encouraged farmers in the west to ow wheat. Even without irrigation, wheat would ake 30 to 40 bushels to the acre.

But, with irrigation, the promise grew. So 'gation projects were going full-tilt in Finney, Gray, ord, and Hamilton counties.

Most of the new settlers worked hard to survive. it there were also swindlers among them. They ould homestead quarter sections of land and live on em for six months just so they could obtain loans ainst the land. They would take out a loan, take the oney and skip the state. Farmers who wanted to stay so took out mortgages on their land. By the 1890s, ore than 60 percent of all the acres in Kansas were ortgaged. Kansas had more mortgaged land than any her state in the nation.

In June 1897, Wichita ranked third in the nation the volume of real estate transactions.

Kansas State Song by Brewster Higley

A doctor and poet from Gaylord wrote the Kansas State Song.

B. Higley homesteaded in Smith County in 1871. In 1873, he wrote the poem, "My Western Home" in his home along Beaver Creek.

No original copies of the poem survive, however it was printed in the Smith County Pioneer that year and later reprinted by the Kirwin Chief in Phillips County.

The poem contains six versions and chorus about Higley's feeling of living on the Kansas prairie. His neighbor, Daniel Kelley, set the poem to music - together the song and poem was enjoyed by people throughout the area.

It was published 1910 by a Texas college professor.

Home on the Range was adopted as the state song in 1947. The lyrics are:

Oh, give me a home where the buffalo roam,
Where the deer and the antelope play,
Where seldom is heard a discouraging word and the skies are not cloudy all day.
Home, home on the range,
Where the deer and the antelope play,
Where seldom is heard a discouraging word and the skies are not cloudy all day.

New York City was first and Kansas City ranked second. Chicago, Philadelphia, and Brooklyn fell behind Wichita in terms of growth and land deals.

There was a booster spirit throughout the whole state. All things seemed possible. All dreams could come true, Kansans thought..

Six railroads now linked the state to the rest of the nation. Six colleges and universities were built and two more were proposed.

Scandals in Politics

The 1870s were a time filled with corruption in politics.

In 1872, the state auditor in Topeka, Alois Thoman was accused of stealing $4,500 by registering fake city bonds.

In 1873, Kansans were used to political fraud. But they were about to get an embarrasing lesson in how bad it could get. Senator Samuel "Pompous Pom" Pomeroy was seeking a third term.

During his first term; however, he was accused of mishandling relief funds and supplies intended for victims of drought. In 1873, a letter proposing a scheme to split profits from the sale of goods to the Pottawatomie tribe came to light. Pomeroy was accused of writing it, a charge he denied.

When fellow Senator John P. St. John asked for an investigation, Pomeroy tried bribery to quiet the matter. The issue seemed to be over when Pomeroy lost his bid for re-election. But it wasn't. The Senate held a caucus and Colonel Alexander M. York spoke before the joint session. His speech was this:

"I visited Mr. Pomeroy's room, in the dark and secret recesses of the Teft House on Monday night, (Jan. 27th), and at that interview my vote was bargained for, for a consideration of $8,000; two thousand dollars of which were paid to me that evening; five thousand dollars the next afternoon, and a promise of the additional one thousand when my vote had been cast in his favor."

Samuel Clark Pomeroy (1861-1891)
Photo courtesy of The Kansas State Historical Society

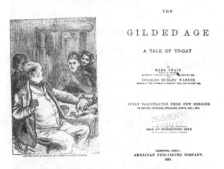

The Gilded Age, *written by Mark Twain featured a politician who was patterened after Senator Pomeroy.*
Photo courtesy of Wichita State University Special Collections

Pomeroy eventually moved to Whitinsville, Massachusetts where he died on August 27, 1891.

Pomeroy was replaced in the Senate by John J. Ingalls from Atchison, who is considered one of the greatest senators in Kansas history. Ingalls is credited with the state's seal and motto, *Ad astra per aspera*, meaning *"To the stars through difficulties."*

In 1874, State Treasurer Josian E. Hays, hastily resigned before he was impeached. He was charged with a crime. Samuel Lappin, the new State Treasurer, in 1876 was accused of forgery, counterfeiting, and embezzling school bonds from four counties.

So, Kansas went into the 1890s humbled and ready for changed in all areas of their lives.

John J. Ingalls, *helped write the state's constitution. He was considered one of the nation's greatest speaker in the 19th century.*
Photo courtesy of The Kansas State Historical Society

Mortgage Foreclosures

The sudden increase in numbers of people growing corn and wheat made the price of cereal grains drop. Droughts caused crop failures and blizzards killed livestock. Mortgages were foreclosed and sheriff's land sales became commonplace as farms failed.

City growth could not be maintained. People moved to the cities when their failed farms were lost, others also came. Businesses, too began to fail. Marshall Murdock, the editor and publisher of *Wichita Eagle*, wrote an editorial urging readers to "call a halt" to all the spending, wheeling and dealing of the time.

By 1889 businesses, schools, and farms were in trouble. The state's capitalists were losing thousands of dollars. Some people, in frustration, pulled up stakes and left their homes.

Disease also took a toll, especially in the country. Nothing was more frightening than being sick, because there were few doctors and virtually no cures for many diseases.

Widespread knowledge of germs was yet to be understood. People didn't know what caused epidemics of diphtheria, scarlet fever and smallpox, even though these diseases often swept entire communities. Home remedies were widely used.

Ads appeared offering farmers financial help.
Photo courtesy of Wichita State University Special Collections

Things like mustard plasters, onion syrup an poultices, sheep manure tea, tobacco poultice whiskey, castor oil, and patent medicines were standa "cures" for any ailment.

Poverty, hardship, and disease were too mud for some. They gave up the land they had claimed western Kansas. They moved to another place Kansas hoping to start over. Or, failing that, th caught a train back to the homes and families they l on the East Coast.

Land and More Land

Just as it had been when Kansas was Indi Territory, the answer for many farmers and oth people seemed to be in having more land. Now, th looked toward the new Indian territory to the south land that could be taken.

One by one, parts of the land given to t Indians were taken for white settlers. The governme staged "runs" to stake claims to land.

The first was on April 22, 1889. More th 50,000 people dashed into Oklahoma to stake out 9,0 homesteads.

On September 22, 1891, land that had be given to the Iowa, Sac and Fox, Shawnee, a Pottawatomie people was now open to whites. A y later, lands of the Cheyenne and Arapaho were tak for more white settlements.

That was not enough. Settlers wanted the pri grassland that ran 220 miles long by 58 miles wi covering 13,108 square miles south of the Kan border. That land, known as the "Cherokee Strip" the "Cherokee Outlet" had been set aside so Cherokees could travel to hunting grounds with having to cross other tribe's territories.

David Payne became known as the *"Father of Oklahoma" because of his efforts to settle Oklahoma long before it was legally opened for settlement.* Photo courtesy of The Kansas State Historical Society

Cattlemen had discovered the strip as they drove herds up the Chisholm Trail. It was rich in mixtures of bluestem, buffalo, switch and bunch grasses. They wanted to graze cattle there to fatten them up before moving them on to Kansas cowtowns. The Cherokees agreed, for a price. They asked $1 a head for grazing rights, then eventually lowered the price to 40 cents per head. Many cattlemen were glad to pay. Others were not. Trouble was coming.

The *Arkansas City Daily Traveler* reported on April 28, 1882:

> *"Advise from the Cherokee nation say that a company of United States soldiers have begun removing the stockmen on the Cherokee strip who have failed to pay the tax levied by the Cherokees on cattle grazing on the land. There is a good deal of excitement and some talk of resistance, but it is believed that owners of cattle who are not able to pay will remove their stock without making trouble."*

Soon there were reports of Indian retaliation against those who did not pay. On August 1, 1883, *The Traveler* reported:

> *"Reports come to us the effect that parties have been killing sheep and driving stock off the range...on Willow creek south of Arkansas City. Tuesday afternoon Mr. Fouts...received a telegram that a party of seven men had driven the stock off the range..."*

The answer for many seemed to be to just take the land.

Some objected. Marshall Murdock wrote against the idea, voicing fears that it would pull settlers away from southern Kansas.

Beginning in 1889, thousands of families from around the world were flocking to cities like Wichita and Arkansas City in hopes of moving quickly on into Oklahoma's Indian Territory.

The Cherokees did not willingly give up their territory.

Barbed Wire

Barbed wire, also known as The Devil's Rope came to the Plains in the 1860s and farmers discovered that the simple sharp strands would turn away even the stubborn Texas longhorn.

The Herd Laws of the 1870s and 1880s required cattlemen to fence their cattle.

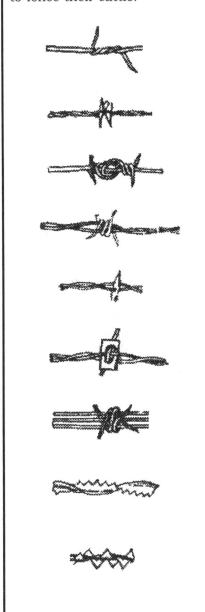

The Arkansas City newspaper reported on March 13, 1893:

> *"The Cherokees seem to have an aversion to selling the strip except upon a strictly cash basis. This will put us under the painful necessity of doing what we had to do before, many a time, send missionaries to reason with them on their depravity and take the land in payment for our services in trying to civilize them."*

On April 3, 1893, an agreement was ma(e between the Cherokees and the government. The str' would be lost to the Cherokees and to the Tex: cattlemen. The land would be opened to tl homesteaders and the date was set, September 1 1893.

The Biggest Land Run of All

Border towns beg: making big plans. Tl Arkansas City Travel(reported that one reside: wanted to take 10,000 copies (the newspaper's boom editio to the Kansas building at tl World's Fair in Chicago, 189 for distribution. After lengthy discussion, one leadin businessman stood and sa: 10,000 copies wasn't enough 100,000 copies of the pap should be taken.

Cherokee Strip Land Rush, September 16, 1893 *was one of the great land runs in Oklahoma. The scene was a blur as the run started.*
Photo courtesy of Wichita State University Special Collections

On September 11, 1893, nine registration boot] for land rush entrants were opened along the border.] Oklahoma there were booths at Stillwater and Orland north of Hennessey and south of Goodwin. In Kansa booths were in Kiowa, Cameron, Caldwell, Hunnewe] and Arkansas City.

To make a claim, people had to be 21 years ol(head of a family, or a widow, a single man or woma: and a United States citizen. They would receive on quarter section, 160 acres. Pre-survey marke:

signated each plot. Each entrant received survey
arkers to mark his claim. When land was claimed the
rvey marker was to be placed on the land.

Registrants poured in Kansans as well as
tsiders. Winds were hot and strong, clouds of dust
ocked out the sun. Still, more people came. Three
ys before the great race for land, almost 3,000
rtificates were written in Arkansas City registration
oths. Thousands more came each day. People
ayed all day and all night to hold their place in line.

Some didn't wait. "Sooners" people who
eaked across the border to gain early claims, were
rested and brought back if they were caught. Soldiers
ought 53 people into a camp and reported that more
re hiding along streams.

Two days before the race, The Arkansas
aveler reported that suffering in the lines was intense.
ree men died of dust and exhaustion at the Arkansas
ty booth.

he Gun Goes Off

As excitement goes, not
uch can beat High Noon on
ptember 16, 1893. Greed,
ssion, daredevilry, and
ffering were all rolled up
to the moment.

> "Arkansas City, Kan....Just
> before the hour, with a
> field glass the long line
> of horses and men densely
> packed for 200 feet back
> could be seen.
>
> At high noon the sharp
> crack of a revolver was distinctly heard and
> immediately following came the reports of the
> carbines. A hoarse yell went up, softened by the
> distance, and the line got in motion.
>
> Horses were seen to shoot out from the ruck
> and dash across the prairie. Then a dense cloud
> of dust obscured the line for a moment, but a
> brisk wind from the west cleared it away, and
> the men and wagons could be seen scattering as
> the slowest were left behind. Now and then a
> wagon would go over with a wheel knocked
> off." -The Burden (Kan.) Eagle, Sept. 23, 1893

Crowds wait on the Kansas/Oklahoma
border for the moment they could
claim land. Note the number of people
crowded onto the train.
Photo courtesy of The Kansas State Historical
Society

James Naismith
Photo courtesy of The Kansas State Historical Society

Prairie Spirit

It was **James Naismith** though of Lawrence who invented basketball in the late 1880s. He was the University of Kansas's first basketball coach in 1899. Naismith is also credited with inventing the football helmet — a bonnet using several layers of flannel and chamois.

Competitors used just about anything that woul get them across land. Some settlers simply walke across the border and staked a claim. Others used ol work horses, fast racers, carts, buggies, covere wagons, and bicycles. Trains from Winfield an Wichita were brought in to carry thousands of ticke holders to points in the territory.

Historians estimate that of those thousands c people who staked claims in the Cherokee Strip Lan Run, only about 20 to 30 percent were able to make living on their land. The hardships that had made lif so difficult in Kansas were also present in Oklahom; Some were able to hang on until the Dust Bowl yea and the Great Depression of the 1930s before givin up. Others succeeded by buying up the land as the neighbors gave up.

There were a few more small land runs befor the final shrinkage of Indian territory was over. Th Kickapoo lands were taken for white settlements i 1895 and parts of the Kiowa-Comanche and Wichit; Caddo reserves were declared "surplus" and opened b lottery in 1901. Five years later, all 480,000 acr; reserved for these four tribes were opened to whit settlement in a last run for land.

The Age of Reform

Across Kansas and the nation, struggles wer taking place to make real and lasting changes. Th period of history from 1890 to 1920 has been labele the "Age of Reform."

The Kansas farmer was perhaps the most read for change. The mortgages that made it so easy to g; a start in the new land were hard to pay as crops faile and livestock died. When loans slipped into defaul bankers took the land and sales continued.

The rise of the Populist Party was brought abo by the discontent of a large part of the Kans; population. Many of this discontented group we former Populists. During the 19th century, the philosophy was that the rich get richer and the poor g; poorer.

SHERIFF SALE!

You can purchase a vacant lot, residence or business property in Sa-
na at the Sheriff's Sale.

The County Commissioners of Saline County, Kansas, have fore-
losed tax liens and the properties have been ordered sold. U. S. McDonald,
heriff of Saline County, Kansas, will sell at the east front door of the Court
House, in Salina, Saline County, Kansas, approximately two hundred fifty
250) properties all of which are located in Salina, Kansas, to the highest
nd best bidder for cash in hand commencing

*farmers struggled to make ends meet, their mortgaged land was sometimes sold and posters like this one were
 t uncommon in the late 19th and early 20th century.*
to courtesy of Wichita State University Special Collections

The American farmer often fell victim to big
siness or, in this case, the railroads and the bankers.

The strength of the Populist Party was that it
lated to unhappy farmers and promised that by
orking together their problems could be worked out.
at struck a chord with Kansas farmers, even though
e leaders of the party were not farmers and were
pically businessmen, women, and some doctors.

The Republican Party, which had long been the
werhouse in Kansas, didn't fear the Populists until
e election of 1890 when the State House of
epresentatives fell to the control of the Populists.
nong those elected to Congress was Jerry "Sockless"
mpson from Medicine Lodge. He was known as
ockless Jerry" because of a speech he gave in which
said that his Republican opponent was a prince who
ore silk stockings while he, a rancher from Kansas,
d none.

A Legislative Showdown

After Populist Lorenzo Lewelling from Wichita was elected the state's 12th governor, there was a showdown between the Republicans and the Populists in the winter of 1893. Angry fists and words flew in the Kansas House of Representatives and gattling guns were brought in for control. The incident became known as, "The Lewelling War."

For the Populists, it was a chance to show they were a vital party in Kansas politics. For the Republicans it was simply a matter of party politics and survival.

The problem with The Lewelling War was that it went on for several days, it was emotionally charged and at times, dangerous.

The year before, Wichita had served as the meeting place for the state convention of the Populist Party. Lewelling, a small grocery store owner welcomed the convention goers with a speech so impassioned that he was selected as the party's nominee for governor. Later that year, as the Populist Party's momentum grew, the Democratic Party swung its support in favor of the Populists.

The party controlled a majority in the Kansas Senate and about half of the 125 member Kansas House of Representatives.

On January 10, 1893, the first day of the legislative session in Lewelling's term, the House of Representatives erupted into chaos. Both the Republican and Populist parties were determined to be the majority party, so each elected its own speaker and tried to bring the House to order. Neither party would budge or recognize the powers of the other.

Stubbornness set in and the politicians remained in their chairs for several days. Each side was afraid to adjourn and each side allowed tensions to build.

Finally, by February, tensions had risen to the point that Governor Lewelling called in the militia and a battery of gattling guns.

The Populist Party, traveling on a country road in Dickinson County.
Photo courtesy of The Kansas State Historical Society

On Valentine's Day, the Republicans tried to rest Ben Rich, the Populist Chief Clerk who, they aimed, had interrupted the house by loud and oisterous language, and unlawful noises.

Both sides began swearing in sergeants at arms.

Soon, the state grounds began to resemble a attleground, with sentries posted, soldiers camped and ums beating.

A war almost did result from this. Men were urrying arms to the site. There were fistfights. nally, the conflict was resolved by the Kansas State upreme Court.

In a compromise, the militia was released from ity, and the Republicans met in the House while the opulists met elsewhere.

While in office, the Kansas Populists passed a ilroad freight rate bill and enacted a law demanded the farmers, in which a debtor had 18 months to deem his land. After that period, it could be sold der mortgage. They also passed the Australian ballot hich is still used in Kansas today. This is a ballot inted at the public's expense and lists all candidates d is marked secretly by the voter.

Kansas soon became known as the heartland of e Populist's Party even though it was popular in veral states and, by 1892, was nominating esidential and vice-presidential candidates.

The Populists soon fell from favor though, when sagreements between the party's political leaders uldn't be overcome and the party literally could not gress. Populists could not agree on who should be eir leaders and what should be the issues.

But what the Populist Party did do was to bring the forefront the issues of the day. Some of the orking man's lot, helping the farmers get regulations stockyards, and on the handling of grain. These ues needed to be reformed. From there, other ders stepped forward and other issues were tackled.

The Populist Party was associated with reform d the Progressive movement. The Progressive ovement favored or advocated progress, change, and provement or reform. This was in opposition to eping things as they were.

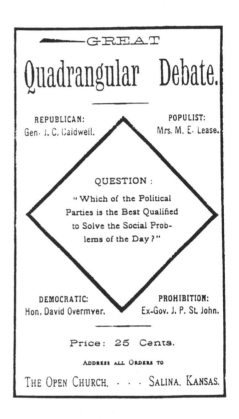

Debate Poster.
Poster courtesy of Wichita State University
Special Collections

Movement Against Alcohol

As people began looking for ways to make life better, an old opposition to alcohol gained new strength. Alcohol had long been a sore spot with many Kansans because of the trouble it caused. As early as March, 1856, John Brown, Jr., had called for strict laws concerning alcohol. In 1861, The Kansas State Temperance Society held its first meeting in Topeka. Shortly afterward, a group of women in Mound City broke up a newly opened saloon. In the 1870s, The Independent Order of Good Templars, a national temperance society, The Kansas Temperance Society and the Women's Christian Temperance Union all became active.

In 1878, John P. St. John was elected governor, in large part because he stood for prohibiting alcohol.

In November, 1880 St. John was again elected governor with a large majority. The legislature passed a prohibition amendment. Kansas then became the first state in the United States to outlaw alcohol. However, enforcing the law was difficult. Bootleggers and stills were constant reminders that the liquor issue wasn't really solved.

Fearless Women Taking Action

During the heights of the Populist movements, there was one women in particular who was a visible force in the party and that was Mary Elizabeth Lease.

In the late 1880s, Lease and her husband, who was a pharmacist, arrived in Wichita. Things were a bit strained in their relationship.

Mary Elizabeth set up a laundry in downtown Wichita. While she washed other people's clothes, she began reading law books, and eventually became a lawyer.

But while this was going on she decided that women of like-mind should come together. At that time, there were only two outlets that most women had in terms of social gatherings. They could form recipe clubs or sewing circles.

Mary Elizabeth Lease.
Photo courtesy of The Kansas State Historical Society

On January 21, 1886, Mrs. Lease changed that
th an ad in the *Wichita Eagle*. It read:

*"We would most earnestly invite the intelligent
women of Wichita, the artists, musicians, teachers,
actors, lecturers, and all women having the
advancement of their sex in view, to meet
Saturday, Jan. 23 at 3 o'clock at the residence of
Mrs. Harry Hill..."*

The ad caused much turmoil in the community.
 the day they were to meet, a huge blizzard came
ong. Nevertheless, nine women did band together to
rm a social club. They named themselves after
pathia, a fifth century Greek female philosopher and
ucator, known for her beauty. Their intent was to
omote the cultural and intellectual interests of
men.

The club is still in operation today and is one of
 state's oldest women's clubs.

Carry A. Nation was a woman
ose displeasure was definitely raised.
r hatred of alcohol was fuel because
r first husband, Charles Gloyd died
m alcoholism. The Medicine Lodge
man who opposed liquor and tobacco
d already raided Kansas saloons. But
 didn't make the national news wires
til December 27, 1900 when she
rched into the Wichita's Hotel Carey
d wrecked the bar. Using a billiard
ll and short pieces of iron attached to
ane, she broke the massive mirror
ind the bar and smashed glasses and
tles. Then she hurled two rocks at
 saloon's life-size painting of
leopatra at the Roman Bath."

Nation was arrested and placed
the old Sedgwick County Jail. A
chita Eagle newsman gave the story
the wire services and advised the
ion that a hatchet would be a more
orful weapon to use against the bars.

Carry A. Nation was a leading prohibitionist who made
national news by wrecking saloons throughout the midwest.
Her trademark became a hatchet.
Photo courtesy of The Kansas State Historical Society

Kiowa County's Mabel Chase became the
ion's first elected women sheriff in 1926.

Susanna Madora Salter, of Argonia who in 1887 became the first woman mayor in the United States.
Photo courtesy of The Kansas State Historical Society

Sister Frieda Kaufman, was instrumental in construction projects at Newton's hospital and Bethel Home for the Aged, 1932 to 1928.
Photo courtesy of The Mennonite Library and Archives Bethel College, N. Newton, Kansas

Amelia Earhart
(1898-1937)

Amelia Earhart was born in Atchison in 1898. In 1928, Earhart became the first woman passenger to fly across the Atlantic Ocean.

Then in 1932 she flew it alone, which she sat a new record time for the crossing: 13 hours, 30 minutes.

In 1935, she became the first woman to fly alone from Hawaii to California.

In June of 1937, she and her navigator, Frederick J. Noonan started a round the world flight. Their plane disappeared mysteriously on July 2, between New Guinea and Howland Island. Their actual fate has been questioned for years.

Photo courtesy of The Kansas State Historical Society

Changing the Way We Live

There were other Kansans who had lasting effects on the way we live. One such person was Samuel Crumbine who crusaded for health.

Crumbine was a doctor from the Spearville and Dodge City area who started getting recognition in the 1890s. He persuaded the local manager of a restaurant, owned by Fred Harvey, not to dip milk out of uncovered pails because of the germ factor. Harvey, owned a chain of restaurants in the Atchison, Topeka and Santa Fe Railroad depots across the nation. Taking Crumbine's advise Harvey soon began serving milk in sealed glass bottles.

In 1899, Governor William Stanley appointed Samuel Crumbine to the Kansas State Board of Health. He later became the board's executive secretary and moved his family to Topeka.

By doing this, Crumbine became the state's first full-time public health officer.

Some of the public health issues he crusaded for were the purification of public drinking water, the eradication of the disease carrying house fly and the general use of a common community drinking cup.

HIS DEATH OR YOURS!

Another contribution he made was to endorse the use of flyswatters and screens on windows because of a campaign he had against the common housefly. He warned the public through posters and newspaper articles about the diseases the flies could be carrying. He urged Kansans to cover food, haul away animal manure from their farms and cover their windows with screens.

The idea caught on and soon towns across Kansas were offering bounties for dead flies. In some towns, children could trade containers of dead flies for free movie tickets.

Crumbine also did away with the community drinking cups and towels.

THAN A CHILD IN SOME OF OUR CITIES?

Kansas thinks too much of her children and has better manners than to permit the use of the common drinking cup.

Crumbine Cartoons courtesy of The Kansas State Historical Society

Samuel Crumbine, August 31, 1908. Shown with his two assistan
Warren Crumbine and Bernice Vreeland. By today's standards his
office or laboratory in Topeka looks primitive.
Photo courtesy of The Kansas State Historical Society

People used the same drinking cup over and
over in businesses, trains, schools, anywhere peo
would gather. He showed how that could spr
disease. Soon, the common drinking cup was outlaw
and paper cups that could be used once and thro
away were introduced.

In public bathrooms, it was common to have
towel that everyone used. He advocated fresh towe

He also fought against tuberculosis
convinced Kansas brick companies to stamp "Do
Spit on Sidewalks" into thousands of bricks that w
then placed in public places.

Crumbine ordered the hotels to char
bedsheets each day and made regulations to h
prevent sexually transmitted diseases and prov
better infant child care.

In 1926, Samuel Crumbine resigned as Kans
first public health officer.

A circular was sent out from Valley Falls last week as follows:

WANTED! Homes for orphan children

A company of orphan children under the auspices of the Children's Aid Society of New York will arrive at Valley Falls, Thursday afternoon, December 8th.

These children are bright, intelligent and well disciplined, both boys and girls of various ages. They are placed on trial, and if not satisfactory will be removed. Parties taking them must be well recommended. A local committee of citizens of Valley Falls has been selected to assist the agents in placing the children. Applications must be made to and endorsed by the local committee. Bring your recommendations with you.

The following well known citizens have agreed to act as a local committee: J. T. B. Gephart, L. H. Burnett, Alex Kerr, A. D. Kendall, Dr. A. D. Lowry and Neil McLeod. Distribution will take place at the opera house, on Friday December 9 at 10 a.m. and 2 p.m.

Come and see the children and hear the address. B. W. Tice, Western Agent, 105 East Twenty-second Street, New York; Miss A. L. Hill, visiting and placing agent, 105 East Twenty-second Street, New York; W. W. Bugbee, state agent for Kansas, Eldorado, Kansas.

Orphan Trains

Perhaps one of the more unique experiments on the western frontier was that of the Orphan Trains.

From, 1853 to 1929, at least 200,000 children were part of a relocation program that attempted to find homes on the frontier for the urban poor. Traveling on that were known as Orphan Trains, the children and several thousand homeless adults were shipped from Boston and New York to small towns in the midwest and west.

Some sources estimate that the trains brought between two and five thousand orphans to Kansas alone between those years.

Anita Sprout was only 16 months old when an orphan train carried her halfway across the nation from New York to a new family in Wellington.

Now, more than eighty years later, Anita Sprout, who lives in Peck, Kansas, still holds tight to the only three possessions from her life before adoption: a suitcase, a little dress, and a nightie.

She spoke to a Wichita Eagle reporter in 1996 and this is what she had to say regarding her orphan train experience:

> *"On my adoption papers, it says my mother was a mere child and the father was unknown. That was World War I. I have no way of tracking back and trying to find anybody. I think people were ashamed of what they were doing. When you think of all those years and all those children."*

Sometimes, she says, even now after all these years, she looks at her children and grandchildren. She wonders what traits they carry that come from relatives she has never met. She wonders why so little information was ever recorded about the 75-year period when orphan trains were a common sight in small towns across the nation. Nearly every state in the United States would eventually be visited by the orphan trains.

She now frequently attends orphan train reunions, even so, she has yet to meet another passenger from her train.

Descendants including Betty Glidewell o Clearwater, the daughter of an orphan train rider, want more recognition of the orphan train experience as part of American history.

> *"We are at a point now where we are losing our original train riders, they are passing on from this earth...,"* said Betty Glidewell.

The trains were the brainchild of the Reverend Charles Loring Brace, founder of the Children's Ai Society in New York City. At his suggestion, the placement in foster homes out west was free, so more children could be adopted.

Reverend Brace believed the children should be sent to rural homes, where there was always room for one more pair of hands to help with the chores.

Prairie Spirit

During much of the 20th century, **Margaret Hill McCarter's** works were well-respected for her novels portraying Kansas. In 1920, she became the first woman to speak before the Republican National Convention.

At each rail station and sometimes at the local churches, schools or opera houses, the children were lined up to be chosen by families. Those not chosen were loaded back on the train to repeat the process at the next stop.

The orphan train concept became so popular that other east coast children's agencies began using it, including the New York Foundling Hospital, the New England Home for Little Wanderers in Boston and New York Juvenile Asylum. For a time, the Chicago Home Society and the Minnesota Home Society also placed children on orphan trains.

Many of the children who came west never wanted anyone to know they were from an orphanage. Some were told they weren't wanted or loved, but they were expected to work hard on the farms and small businesses of their new parents. Because of social taboos of the times, orphan train experiences and following adoptions often weren't discussed openly.

Today, less than a dozen of these riders remain living in Kansas.

By the 1920s, the orphan trains were becoming fewer and fewer because of child labor laws and a growing movement to keep families together.

Teresa "Jessie" Martin, an orphan train passenger said,

"Being an orphan train rider means you have learned a lot in life and are more understanding of other people's pain. You simply become grateful for the kind people along the way."

Prairie Spirit

Joseph "Buster" Keaton from Piqua is known as a silent film actor and filmmaker during the 1920s. He pantomimed stunts and deadpan stares and was known as "The Great Stone Face." His popularity faded with the arrival of talking movies.

John Coffey's Letter

When Betty Glidewell of Clearwater began researching her mother's family history she discovered her mother had been an orphan train rider. Her mother, Blanche Thomas was 7, along with her sister, Ruth age 4 boarded the orphan train in New York. She received the following letter from John Coffey.

The orphaned sisters traveled to Sulphur Springs, Texas, where Fannie Coffey, a 70 year old widow agreed to take them in on a trial basis.

But Coffey was both ill and too old to care for the girls and returned them to officials from the Children's Aid Society in New York. They were later adopted by different families. A family in Weatherford, Texas adopted Ruth and Blanche was adopted by a family in Tucson, Arizona.

September 13, 1995
Route 2 Box 400
Commerce Texas.
75428

Dear Betty Glidwell:

At the time of the 1917-1918 orphan train Mrs Fannie Coffey was a widow.

Her own three children had all died while very young. Her husband had been dead for many years.

Fannie Coffey belonged to the First Baptist Church in Sulphur Springs where Revern Wallace Russell was Pastor

Fannie Coffey took the two orphan girls from the train on trial. Fannie Coffey was seventy years old at the time and just could not handle it, so the orphan train people took the two girls back.

Fannie Coffey became ill a few years later and died of cancer in 1925. So you see she really could not have made it with the children.

And now for the rest of the story.

I was six and one half years old when Aunt Fannie took the girls off the train.

Goldie and I were strongly attracted to each other immediately, I think in part because I paid attention when she talked and answered her many and varied questions.

At six and a half years old, I was a pillar of strength and wisdom to the little four year old girl. She called me "my boy".

For my part I adored Goldie and thought she was the most wonderful person I had ever known.

When they took Goldie away, she and I cried and protested vigorously but hoplessly.

Parting with Goldie was probably the saddest point of my early childhood.

I have remembered her with an ache in my heart all these years, and had no hope of ever hearing from her again.

I think from the wording of your letter that the girls are no longer living.

If this is the case, I would like to know where they are buried?

I will visit the place and leave one perfect yellow rose on Goldies grave.

I think God and Goldie will understand

John L Coffey

*rphan Train. This never before published photo shows an orphan
ain child and her escorts.*

oto courtesy of Betty Glidewell

19th Century Draws to a Close

By the end of the 19th century, reform an progress had changed the way Kansans looked themselves. No longer was it a struggling frontier. had become a home for second, third and four generation families. Many Kansans had led the natic by their "first time ever" actions.

It was not just a place to make a living. Kans was a way of life. It was reflected throughout th nation. Other people in other states looked to Kans to see what the wave of the future would be.

ATCHISON, KANSAS

A

Amelia Earhart first brought fame to her hometown of Atchison by being the first woman to fly the Atlantic alone. Five years later, during a globe-circling flight, her plane disappeared somewhere over the Pacific.

I just saw the bedroom where Amelia Earhart was born. Her grandparents had lots of money and the house in Atchison is beautiful. It looks out over the river and it would've been fun to play where she did. She used to "fly" her sled down the banks. The jacket she wore in her airplane is here, too.

© Avery postcards, P.O. Box 20246, Wichita, KS 67208

© 1991 Photos by John Avery AT-3
L-5055-E Printed in Canada

Historical Events

1877 - George Washington Carver comes to Kansas

1885 - Turkey Red Winter Wheat brought to Kansas

1898 - The Spanish American War begins

1903 - Helium discovered in Dexter

1909 - Kansas Salt Mines rank 4th in the U. S.

1910 - Curtis Baldwin invents the Standing Grain Thresher

1911 - Clyde Cessna builds a plane

1915 - Woody Hockaday marks Kansas highways

1917 - United States declares war on Germany

1921 - Twenty-one plane manufacturers in Kansas

1924 - Baldwin invents the Gleaner-Baldwin combine

1927 - Wichita named "Air Capital of the World"

CRUZPAGAN 99

Chapter 7

Kansas in the 1900s

Chapter 7

Kansas in the 1900s

Kansans were quick to learn that fame and fortune could be had with just a little ingenuity.

When Kansas became a territory the few opportunities for industry and commerce that existed were mostly in trapping and hunting. As long as the beaver and buffalo flourished and beaver hats and buffalo coats and blankets were in fashion, the fur and hide businesses thrived. But when styles changed, then the ways and lifestyles of people making a living on those items changed too.

Enterprising people at first turned to the freight industry. Long wagon trains hauling freight became the major money maker. One of the most famous freighters was Russell, Majors and Waddell. At the height of their business, they had more than 6,200 wagons and used 75,000 head of oxen. Business owners who could bring food, dry goods, household supplies, farm implements and hardware into the territory could become extremely wealthy.

Once the land was settled though, more refined products were needed.

Sawmills carved out lumber for building. Grist mills ground out cornmeal and flour from corn and wheat. Money was quickly made.

People soon discovered more ways to make a successful living. At the beginning of the 1900s, there were many major industries in Kansas. Slaughtering and meat packing, milling flour and corn, building cars, general shop construction, building and repairing of railroads, producing dairy products, and printing and publishing were just some of the ways of becoming successful. Foundries, machine shops, making soap and candles, baking bread and other pastries, making brick and tile, mining salt, sawing lumber, and creating products from lime cement were some products of new industries.

With all this industry and commerce going on, people discovered there was black gold hidden deep within the ground. The state's rich mineral resources, oil, gas, zinc, and coal were where the real fortunes were quickly made, and sometimes they were just as quickly lost.

But first, there was milling.

lour is made

As early as 1839, wheat was being produced in ansas by the Shawnee Methodist Mission. But the pe of wheat grown was soft winter wheat. This heat did not always fare well in the Kansas climate.

The amount of wheat harvested, however, grew eadily. Records with the Kansas State Board of griculture indicate that there was a steady growth in e acreage growing wheat in Kansas from only 68,000 res harvested in 1866 to about 3 million harvested in)00.

In 1886, there were 300 mills producing flour, lued at $15 million. Whereas, today there are 19 illing plants producing flour worth $484 million llars every year. Kansas has ranked first in the tion for amount of flour milled for the last half of the)00s.

The milling industry has been one of the staples the state's economy for well over a century.

One of the early millers was Bernhard arkentin of Halstead and later of Newton.

Warkentin immigrated to the United States from uthern Russia, in the early 1870s. He built a grain ill at Halstead and helped more than 5,000 ennonites to settle in the area.

In 1885, he brought a railroad car loaded with irkey Red Winter Wheat seed to ansas to sell. It was a variety that imigrant farmers had already oved could be grown in Kansas. e became the first miller in Kansas edited with making that type of heat make money.

He then bought a mill in ewton and replaced its stone llers with metal ones. Before that, ansas mills were only able to ind the soft kinds of wheat. The irkey Red wheat was too hard for ose rollers and the grains wouldn't eak down properly.

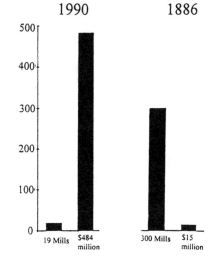

1990   1886

Bernhard Warkentin.
Photo courtesy of The Mennonite Library and Archives, Bethel College, Newton, Kansas

Unloading wheat by hand, Kreisel's Roller Mill, Olmitz, Barton County, 1906.
Photo courtesy of Wichita State University Special Collections Karen P. Neuforth Collection

Warkentin was able to grind the wheat into high-quality flour.

Other flour mills soon gained the ability t ground and the reputation for quality as well. Som still exist in business today.

Hudson Cream Flour

The next time you bite into the bun of you favorite cheeseburger, think Hudson Cream Flou Same goes for when you bite into tortillas, biscuit corn meal, cakes, cookies, and a lot of award-winnin recipes.

The Stafford County Flour Mills Compan which for nearly a century has ground their popula flour, is one of the smallest mills in Kansas but it ha developed a mighty reputation.

The gourmet magazine *Aveur* in recent years ha told readers they can order flour by mail. The flou they recommend? Hudson Cream Flour.

The magazine printed:

> *"Hudson Cream is not a blend of hard and soft wheat flour, as all-purpose flours are, but is made entirely from hard red winter wheat. The result: higher, lighter breads with a rich flavor, plus great pasta, pizza crust, dinner rolls and coffee cakes."*

Hudson is a small town in Stafford County. Th town has a population of 100 people. The flour m employs 35 people making the mill one of the county largest employers. More than 400 semi-truckloads flour are shipped from the Hudson mill each yea United Parcel Service trucks arrive twice a day just keep up with mail orders and each day the mill chur out 5,000 pounds of flour.

Although the mill is the state's smallest, it is on of the mightiest in terms of reputation.

Meat Packing

As Kansas approached the 1900s, one of th most important industries in the state was me packing. The cattle drives into Kansas encouraged t meat processors to locate near the early cowtowns.

Walter Anderson

One of the first chain hamburger restaurants in the nation opened in 1916 in Wichita.

Anderson borrowed $60 to buy equipment and supplies to open the little five seat restaurant but he didn't have enough money to buy ground beef. On the morning of his opening, he rushed to a local store and ordered 5 pounds of ground meat. As soon as it was wrapped, he promised the owner that he'd pay by noon. At noon, he returned with 50 cents in nickels and bought another 50 cents worth.

The concept of pressing meat into a patty, putting holes in it and then cooking it on a grill was genius. He'd place all the onions and pickles on top of the cooking patty to then absorb the juice of the hamburger.

So successful was his venture that within two years he opened another stand. He was joined by Edgar Waldo "Billy" Ingram and together they called their hamburger stands, "White Castle." The "White", they claimed, signified purity and cleanliness. The "Castle" was strength, permanence and stability.

Because White Castle burgers were cheap - a nickel apiece - they were almost always sold by the sack, to carry out. Within time, they were known and nicknamed "gut bombs," "Whiteys," "sliders," " "Castles," "Whitey one-bites," and "belly busters."

1867, Edward W. Pattison and William Epperson
tablished a packing house near Junction City. That
ar, he slaughtered more than 5,000 Texas cattle and
ld the meat and hides. A century later, Kansas is still
leader in meat packing. It ranks second behind
ebraska in the production of red meat. More than 5
lion pounds of meat are processed annually.

Every year, almost 7 million cattle are exported
om Kansas. The state also exports more hides and
ins than anywhere else in the world, about 290
llion dollars worth ($290,000,000.)

How Kansas became a leader in the agricultural
orld is part of the story of how Kansas grew as a state.

Pens of cattle await their next feeding
at Brookover Feed Yards on the
outskirts of Garden City, overshadowed
by a huge sign urging people to eat
beef and keep slim. The Brookover
operation was one of the first
commercial cattle feeding operations in
western Kansas.
Photo courtesy of The Wichita Eagle and Beacon
Publishing Company

ansans Show Ingenuity

As Kansas approached the 1900s, there was an
rease in inventions. These inventions aided the
nsas farmer in producing better crops. They also
led those who explored for minerals underneath the
mland.

Different varieties of seeds for both wheat and
rghum grains were introduced. Professors at Kansas
te Agricultural College known today as Kansas
te University, in Manhattan, came up with more
ormation to make the farmer's life easier and
rease his farm production.

Bales of Broomcorn.
Photo courtesy of The Wichita-Sedgwick County Museum

Kansas's only sugar refinery at Garden City and its only product -- 100 pound bags of sugar.
Photo courtesy of The Finney County Historical Society

Soil was tested and fertilizer experiments we conducted.

Other crops included apples in the northeaste Kansas counties and in Reno County. These orchar were among the nation's largest apple producers at t beginning of the century.

Sugar Beets in Kansas

The sugar beet industry in Garden City a became a prominent crop; however in later years few sugar beets were grown and the industry dwindled. I sugar beet production is cited in 1998, *Farm Facts f Kansas,* produced by The Kansas Department Agriculture and the U. S. Department of Agriculture

George Washington Carver

One of the foremost agricultural scientists of I day was George Washington Carver who lived Kansas during his youth. He was originally fro Missouri where his parents had been slaves.

His father died when he was a baby and I mother was sold. He came Kansas by himself when was only 13 years old.

He came to learn, and attend school at Fort Sco He supported himself doing other people's laundr

Carver graduated fro high school in Minneapo and in 1886 he homesteade claim near Beeler, N County. But before became a farmer, he was fi offered a scholarship Highland University northeastern Kansas.

George Washington Carver (1864-1943).
Photo courtesy of The Kansas State Historical Society

When he showed up to go to school, he was [tur]ned away from the white-only college because he [w]as an African-American.

In 1888, he left the farm to attend college at [Si]mpson College in Iowa. Later he attended the state [ag]ricultural college in Ames, Iowa.

He is best known for having joined the teaching [st]aff at Alabama's Tuskegee Institute in 1896 where he [be]gan work discovering how to make more than 300 [th]ings out of peanuts and sweet potatoes. Some of his [wo]rk over a half century at Tuskegee includes turning [so]ybeans into plastic and turning peanuts into milk, [pa]per, insulation, and wallboard.

[Ju]nius Groves

Junius G. Groves, another African-American, [ca]me to Kansas in 1879 with 90 cents in his pocket.

He got a job as a farmhand and started saving as [mu]ch as he could to buy his own land. He eventually [wa]s able to start his own potato farm near Edwardsville [in] northeast Kansas.

It turned out to be a great business.

About 1900, Groves was making enough money [on] his potatoes each year to build a railroad spur from [his] farm to the main line of the Union Pacific at [Ed]wardsville.

In 1907, *"The Negro in Business,"* a book [wr]itten by Booker T. Washington, wrote this about [Gr]oves:

"But why is Mr. Groves called "The Negro Potato King?" Let me answer. In one year alone he produced upon his farm 721,500 bushels of white potatoes, averaging 245 bushels to the acre. So far as reports show, this was 121,500 bushels more than any other individual grower in the world had, at that time, produced."

Groves was born a slave in 1859 in Green [Co]unty, Kentucky. He was part of the Exoduster [mo]vement, a wave of blacks who came to Kansas in [the] late 1870s.

Prairie Spirit

Lutie Lytle, graduated from Topeka High School. In 1892, she was the first female African-American in Kansas to become a licensed attorney.

The water wagon *was a welcome sight to farmers who put in hard hours cutting and shocking wheat. Note harness on the horse. The harness kept flies from biting the horse. The reaper cut the wheat, which was stacked into shocks to dry for the thresher.*

Photos courtesy of Wichita State University Special Collections

urtis Baldwin from Nickerson

As the 20th century began, the horse was still
portant in farming. It was about to be replaced by
ammoth tractors and threshing machines which soon
tted almost every field and county in Kansas.

In 1910, Curtis Baldwin, a farmer living 2 1/2
les south of Nickerson in Reno County, invented the
anding Grain Thresher. His thresher was pulled over
field by horses. It was a forerunner of modern
mbines.

In 1924, Baldwin invented the Gleaner-Baldwin
mbine. It is still one of the most popular combine
ands sold and used today.

Baldwin operated an assembly plant in
utchinson for many years, using Ford and
ntinental engines instead of horses to propel the
mbines.

The grain drill *could be adjusted for
both depth of planting and the amount
of seeds dropped into the ground.*
Photo courtesy of Wichita State University
Special Collections

hen Came Tractors

By the time settlements had begun in Kansas,
any farming implements such as the plow and chisel
d already been invented. But Kansas farmers, often
t of necessity, improved on farm equipment.

Between 1909 and 1920,
nsas farmers broke ground to
eate more land for wheat.
rest in world politics created a
g demand for wheat.

In 1914, a combination
rvester and thresher was
vented by a farmer near
earville. In 1926, Charles
gell of Plains developed and
arketed the one-way plow. His
ea was to set all the plow discs
the same vertical angle. His one-way plowed faster
d handled heavy stubble better than other plows.

The Baldwin Harvester-Thresher
Photo courtesy of The Reno County Museum

Windmills were an essential element of prairie life in the days before electricity. The power generated by the wind turned the blades of the mill which activated a pump in the well and water was pumped to the surface.

Several types of windmills were used by early Kansans.

This photo is from a sales display in 1890.

Photo courtesy of The Finney County Historical Society

Angell built about 500 plows on his Mead County farm before he sold the patent of the one-way plow to the Ohio Cultivator Co. Other farmer modified similar products, but his was the first to be mass-marketed.

Windmill Improvements

Another contribution in Kansas agriculture wa the windmill. At one time, Kansas had more than 5 windmill manufacturers. The most popular was the Currie Windmill. This windmill was popular from the late 1880s to late 1940s. The company was organize in the 1880s as the Currie Windmill and Pun Company. It was located in Manhattan.

The Currie Company was then moved to Topek in 1900. In the late 1940s, the Wyatt Manufacturing Company of Salina took over production of the Curri windmills and continued to use the name until the 1950s.

During the 1930s, the average price of a Curri windmill was $28. In 1950, you could still get a ne Currie for $39. Today this would be several hundre dollars.

Telephones, Electricity, Gypsum Plaster and Other Advancements

The telephone office at Dorrance, Kansas in 1909.

Photo courtesy of The Kansas State Historical Society

There were oth changes that played huge factor in shapin the way Kansans sa themselves in the 1900s. Most ci homes had telephon and electricity. Th made people feel le isolated and mo connected to the even happening globally.

In 1903, helium was discovered near Dexter in Cowley County

Discoveries in Kansas were in the area of mining. Zinc and coal mining and the making of glass, bricks and cement were leaders in the mining industry. By 1909, the Kanopolis, Lyons, and Hutchinson salt mines were ranked fourth in the nation in salt production.

Natural gas was mined. It flowed up in pipes from the oil and gas fields below.

Coal from Kansas was just as big an industry as salt was in the national market. In 1900, ten companies mined coal in southeastern Kansas.

A group of coal miners in Crawford County.
Photo courtesy of Pittsburg State University
Leonard H. Axe Library Special Collections

Lead was another important discovery having been found as early as 1835. It wasn't until forty years later that lead and zinc mining started gaining momentum near Galena.

Another industry was that of the manufacturing of gypsum plaster. It began by accident. In 1858, at a campfire near Blue Rapids, a settler accidentally melted a gypsum rock. Intrigued, he used it to close some cracks in his cabin's walls. So successful was his discovery that during the following year gypsum plaster was being used in the houses all over Blue Rapids. The first gypsum plaster factory west of the Mississippi River was at Blue Rapids.

But the best discovery, the closest thing to the riches of the gold mines in California and Colorado, was Kansas oil.

By no means did the discovery of oil happen overnight. American Indians had for generations used the oil oozing from Kansas soils for the treatment of their aches and pains. It was something almost magical and sacred to them.

Coal shaft in Osage City, 1920.
Photo courtesy of Wichita State University
Special Collections

The Indians soaked their blankets in oil and squeezed the liquid out before applying it to their bodies. Early settlers used the heavy oil as wagon grease and medicine.

The Aurora Oil Well brings in a gusher near Chanute.
Photo courtesy of The Kansas State Historical Society

Oil Boom towns had a special flavor. This 1917 house is shown here. Note the oil derrick in the back of the house. Also, along the side of the house, a huge board running down to a barrel. This was to catch the rain water to use for laundry and baths.
Photo courtesy of Wichita State University Special Collections

It wasn't until 1860 when oil was discovered. The exploration for more began near Paola. By the late 19th century, 1800s, there was drilling for oil at the Mid-Continent oil field near Neodesha. By 1895, the area drillers and producers were bought out by Standard Oil.

But the boom period didn't really begin until September 29, 1915 when Wichita Natural Gas began drilling the Stapleton No. 1 Well near El Dorado.

On December 9, the well reached 2,467 feet and the drilling stopped. It had hit all seven zones of oil found in the El Dorado field. The biggest oil boom in state history was on.

Drillers, mechanics, laborers, corporate executives, and speculators all raced to El Dorado from all over the nation, heading to what had suddenly become the largest oil field in the United States.

Among them were men like Wichitan Jack Vickers, a Kansas grain broker. He contracted to take crude oil from the fields and within a year had built a refinery at Potwin.

Vicker's company became the Vickers Petroleum Company.

Other companies to emerge from the field included Derby Oil, Skelly Oil and Cities Service.

Wooden derricks were laid out across treeless landscapes. Oil towns sprang up to house and offer services to the workers. One such town was Oil Hill, where 2,000 people once lived in company-owned "lease houses."

Each house had a front porch, two bedrooms and a kitchen. Indoor bathrooms came later. The town boasted its own golf course, swimming pool, and baseball team. The town, like the boom, is now gone.

Oil from the El Dorado Oil fields helped to keep the Allied forces fueled during World War I and ranked the state as one of the top producers in the nation.

DOROTHY'S HOUSE

Liberal, Kansas

Lyman Frank Baum

The evening of May 7, 1898, L. Frank Baum sat with his family in their Chicago ome. He was entertaining the children with his "made up" stories.

As Baum family lore tells, when the children ask where the made up characters lived, aum's eyes looked around the room, he saw a filing cabinet. The label on the top drawer as A-N and the label on the bottom drawer was labeled O-Z.

The rest of the story is history. Dorothy Gale, the cowardly Lion, the Heartless Tin oodsman, the bumbling Scarecrow and of course, the Wicked Witch all were in the Land of z!

In 1907, Baum put the "Wizard of Oz" story down on paper.

Dorothy's House in Liberal was built in 1907-1909 and was given to the Seward ounty Historical Society.

ostcard courtesy of Avery Postcards.

estern Kansans Try for Rain

Beginning as early as the 1890s when farmers re battling droughts in western Kansas, a few terprising folks came up with the idea of making n come from the clouds.

In the fall of 1891, folks in Goodland said they uld pay $500 to see it rain and they gathered around uilding on the county fairgrounds where mysterious ses were bellowing forth from a small hole in the of. Like the Wizard of Oz, "Melbourne the Rain zard" was creating his own magic.

The rainmaking efforts were short-lived thoug By the mid 1890s, most farmers were turning th hopes and attention to irrigation in order to water th crops.

It wasn't until the mid 1970s, that weste Kansas once again saw efforts to control the weath The Western Kansas Weather Modification Progra has operated since 1975. The main objective is reduce hail damage to crops using chemical cryst that reduce hail formation. The chemicals are dropp from a small airplane into the updraft of storm clou

Automobiles

Places like Topeka, Wichita, Hutchinson or ev Parsons could have been known as another Detr had it not been for World War I and Henry Ford.

The Great Smith, Topeka's automobile busine once thrived. Today, it can only be found in museur

The Cloughley Motor Vehicle Company Parsons, the Sellers Motor Car Company Hutchinson, and the Jones Motor Car Company Wichita were some of the leading car companies in state for only a decade from about 1910 to 1920.

In the fall of 1914, J. J. Jones started buildi his own car line. All told, he manufactured more th 3,000 cars before his company closed in 1921. T Jones Six Automobile was known for its bright col several coats of lacquer, soundness, and ability to go miles per hour.

However by the 1920s, aftermath of World War I and its effe on the economy destroyed the Kan auto companies. They couldn't comp with Ford.

Kansas Highways

While cars were being promot so were good roads. For years, it was each count responsibility to build and maintain roads.

Jones Motor Car Company.
Drawing courtesy of The Sedgwick County Historical Museum

As more cars were used
the roads by Kansans, the
ed became apparent for
tter roads.

In June of 1911, a
up of Kansans first met to
k about a dream they had to
nnect many of Kansas's
wns and cities with a
;hway.

It took nearly another
years before U. S. Highway

*Making a road in the early 20th
century was hard work. Early builders
used horsedrawn graders and their
own backs to build roads. Even then,
with no asphalt, roads were subject to
the whims of the weather. It was
easy to get stuck and stalled when a
rain or a heavy snowfall softened
the roads to mud.*
Photo courtesy of The Kansas State Historical
Society

was built. Eventually the highway would be billed
"The Main Street of America" and the "Meridian
ghway." Its purpose was to serve as a major
;hway stretching from Winnipeg, Canada to
apulco, Mexico.

It is hard to imagine the construction of a major
;hway in the summer of 1911. The builders had
at faith in the project. Until 1908, there wasn't a
le of paved concrete road in the nation.

So, for a group of people to gather in Salina to
k about a highway that would connect Canada to
xico, seemed a bit far-fetched.

Back then, getting from one place to another in
nsas was a gamble. Not only were the official
ections to places not accurate, but the roads on
ich motorists traveled left a lot to be desired.

Most drivers carried a copy of the "Blue Book,"
ich described how to follow the cow paths and dusty
ils from one town to the next.

The Wichita Eagle on July 28, 1938 cited such
ections as these taken from the book:

*"Straight ahead three miles to white school house
ı right; turn left two miles to stone fence at intersection;
ırn right four miles to end of road, taking the left hand
ad three miles to railroad track; follow railroad five
iles to four corners, taking right hand road two miles
Bingville."*

And if, by chance you did get to where you were
ng, bad weather could ruin the return trip. Why?
d roads.

"The term 'Kansas roads' will soon be synonymo[us] with bad roads," muttered Howard Wheeler to T[he] *Wichita Eagle* on December 9, 1926.

A close-up of a Jones 6 Automobile.
Photo courtesy of The Wichita-Sedgwick County Historical Museum

The paper explained: *"B[y] an absurd constitutional restricti[on] which was adopted in the infan[cy] of the state, Kansas must refrai[n] from indulging in internal improvements. The men who framed that provision in the Constitution probably had some motive for it, but it is very difficu[lt] to understand what that motive might be."*

On October 9, 1929, t[he] dream of connecting many of the nation's cities wit[h a] major highway crept closer to reality. Kans[as] celebrated in Belleville, Salina and Wichita as the ro[ad] was built south through their towns.

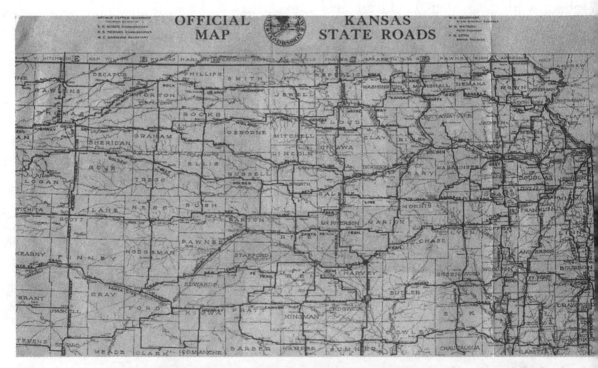

1918 Road Map. There are no highway numbers and travel must have been difficult. One ha[d] to travel from community to community by town signs, rather than knowing where the highwa[y] would go. Many of the major routes were given names at this time.
Map courtesy of Wichita State University Special Collections

The heyday of U.S. 81, which eventually extended south to the Dallas/Fort Worth, Texas area, came to a close on October 25, 1956. The Kansas Turnpike opened and most traffic moved by the turnpike. Today, the road, the old U. S. 81, is still heavily traveled but it is a far cry from the days when it was known as "The Main Stream of America."

U. S. 40 runs from the Atlantic to the Pacific. It known as the National Highway. U. S. 40, now Interstate 70, linked many of the old trails that connected the country before there were highways. In Kansas it closely follows the Smoky Hill Trail and is said to be one of the richest, historically, of any of the transcontinental roads.

Route 66, although only crossing the southeastern tip of Kansas, is an important icon of American life. It also came to symbolize the vastness and the promise of the West.

But by the 1930s and the Dust Bowl years, it also came to symbolize the homelessness of the West as well. It became the main route for thousands of mid-westerners traveling to California to start new lives.

U. S. 54 highway was originally called the Cannonball Stageline Highway, named after a stagecoach company. It was founded in the 1880s by Donald Robertson "Cannonball" Green. The original reason Green laid out the road was that he claimed his coaches were *so fast that even Father Time couldn't keep up* with him.

Another major roadway that aided Kansans was 70 which runs the length of the state. When it was completed in the 1960s, it became the first interstate in the nation. Another major artery is I-35, it runs north and south across the state.

Kansas Mapmaker

In many ways, we can thank F. W. "Woody" Hockaday for the maps we use today.

Hockaday, a pioneer mapmaker, put Wichita, Kansas City, Washington D. C. and San Francisco on maps and connected them with miles of highways. In

Woody Hockaday was an early Kansas mapmaker. He marked an "H" in red on posts and telephone poles to identify the highways. Today KS highway 96 still uses the Hockaday number.
Photo courtesy of The Wichita-Sedgwick County Historical Museum

1915, Hockaday hired a road crew to mark 60,0 miles of highways across the nation. Then, he hand out free Hockaday Road Maps at his tire store Wichita.

The maps gained national recognition. Some the highways that he helped mark are still we traveled, including U.S. 54, K-96, and U.S. Highways.

The Airplane Comes to Kansas

As cars were winding their way acro highways, so were airplanes beginning to cross Kans skies.

Few states have been so profoundly affected an industry as Kansas has with aviation. Wichita s holds the title as the "Air Capital of the World." Since the 1920s, more than a quarter of a million plar have been manufactured in Wichita. Thousands mc are expected to be rolled out in the years ahead.

The production of planes in Kansas started 1900 when Carl Dryden Brone began a factory Freedom, Kansas. He built a model but was never a to perfect the plane. He closed his factory in 1902.

In 1911, Clyde Cessna built a plane near Ra He put on a public fligh the Salt Plains near En Oklahoma. By 1916, had built a business out manufacturing planes a moved the business fr his farm in Kingm County to north Wichit The A. K. Long Airplane Company v formed in Topeka in 19 Three mechanics, Willi Janicke, and A. K. and

Clyde Cessna's early airplane, "The Comet" named by Cessna for its speed of 107.5 miles per hour.
Photo courtesy of Wichita State University Special Collections

J. Longren built a plane, and flew it 15 miles at 1,C feet. A. K. became the first man to successfully bu and fly a plane in Kansas. So encouraged were three that A. K. Longren became a stunt flyer at st and county fairs around the Midwest.

Then, in 1919, a man ...m the El Dorado oil boom ...ys, J. M. Moellendick ...vested in the Wichita ...rcraft Company. He ...rsuaded several men to ...n the company staff. ...me of these men later ...came powerhouses in the ...iation industry. They ...re Walter Beech, Clyde ...ssna, and Lloyd ...arman.

By 1921, the Kansas ...te census showed there ...re 21 plane manufacturers in the state. By 1927, ...chita had become the "Air Capital of the United ...tes."

Wichita's First Air Show, May 4, 1911
Photo courtesy of Kansas Aviation Museum
Bob Picket Collection

...er and Olive Beech
... courtesy of Wichita State University Special Collections

...anish-American War - A Kansas Hero ...m Iola

When the Spanish-American War began in ...8, many Kansans were ready. Kansas sent four ...unteer regiments: the 20th, 21st, 22nd and 23rd.

Spanish-American troops from Company K, 2nd Regiment, Garden City.
Photo courtesy of The Finney County Historical Society

None of those soldiers saw heavy comb[?] but the troops were exposed to malaria a[?] typhoid fever.

When the war with Spain threaten[?] Frank was one of the first to enlist [?] Montgomery County. He was placed [?] Company G of Col. Frederick Funsto[?] Fighting 20th.

While stationed 18 months in Cu[?] Funston was wounded three times and lost [?] horses, some of which were shot out fr[?] under him. He was captured by the Spanish a[?] sentenced to death but escaped before the execution. [?] wasn't until he became sick with malaria that he w[?] forced to return home.

After he recovered, he was then sent to [?] Philippine Islands where he captured a rebel lead[?] His actions helped end the years of fighting in [?] Philippines. He received the Congressional Medal [?] Honor and the rank of Brigadier General for his her[?] acts. At 34, he was the youngest general in the U.[?] Army and his name was common in households acr[?] the nation.

In 1906, when San Francisco suffered [?] disastrous earthquake, Funston was in charge of [?] Army's efforts to provide relief and supplies to [?] victims, once again making him a hero.

He died suddenly in 1917 from a heart atta[?] during a celebration held in his honor in San Anton[?] He was buried on a hill overlooking San Francisco a[?] the Army named an important World War I train[?] camp after him at Fort Riley.

Brigadier-General Frederick Funston U. S. V., 1899.
Photo courtesy of The Kansas State Historical Society

How Kansas Became Linked to The Pledge of Allegiance

Frank E. Bellamy was born September 16, 18[?] and at the age of 15, in Cherryvale, he entered a cont[?] sponsored by *The Youth's Companion*, a popular yo[?] magazine of the day. The contest was for the Natio[?] Columbus Public School Celebration of the 40[?] Anniversary of the Landing of Columbus.

The magazine published an offical program for all schools in the country to use on Columbus Day. In the program was "Salute to the Flag" and it featured Bellamy's pledge minus the "to" before "the Republic." Also included was instructions on saluting the Flag. The "Salute to the Flag" did not include the author's name. He did receive $25 prize money, a badge dated October 21, 1892 with the words: "National Public School Celebration, Columbus Day, October 21, 1492-1892," and a statement saying that "all writings submitted in contest shall remain the property of Youth Companion."

In 1915 Bellamy died with the authorship unresolved. Two years later, James Upham of Boston, editor of the *Youth's Companion,* and Francis Bellamy past editor of the magazine claimed authorship. The New York Bellamy claimed two versions of how he penned the allegiance.

In one account he was having dinner with Upham at a restaurant when they started talking about the pledge. After discussing a number of ideas, they returned to the magazine office where he finished writing it. In the other, he was locked in his office writing the pledge, while Upham paced outside.

The words "the flag of the United States of America" was changed from "my flag" in 1923. The phrase, "under God" was added and signed into law in 1954 by President Dwight D. Eisenhower, who was a native of Kansas.

As World War One Nears

Kansas changed dramatically from the 1890s to 1918 the year World War I, ended. The United States had entered the war in 1917. After the war, Kansans no longer looked at themselves necessarily as Kansas Pioneers but more as informed United States citizens. Things like the telephone and the fact that more Kansans were educated and could read newspapers, connected them to events happening around the world.

Prairie Spirit

Tom Henry of Arkansas City made the "O'Henry" candy bar out of his small candy factory in 1919. He sold the recipe to a larger company where the O'Henry became a popular favorite throughout the nation. His son Pat Henry opened a candy factory in Dexter in 1957 and it is still run by the Henry family. Each year, they make nearly 70,000 pounds of candy.

Wichitan **A.A. Hyde** is best known for inventing and manufacturing Mentholatum in the late 1890s and early part of the 20th century. He first sold it door-to-door but soon its popularity allowed him to hire salesmen and it was sold all over the nation. The company headquarters is now in Buffalo, N.Y. Hyde was also known for his charitable works for more than 60 organizations. He helped build the YMCA camp in Estes Park, Colo. He believed in giving away nine-tenths of his salary to charitable organizations. And even though he died in 1935 at the age of 85, his money is still helping fund organizations today.

The dial telephone was invented by Al Strowger of El Dorado.

Kansans were patriotic. They were passio about ideas. However, Kansans were not ready fo that a world war would bring them.

The home of Mentholatum in the 1890s.
Photo courtesy of The Wichita-Sedgwick County Historical Museum

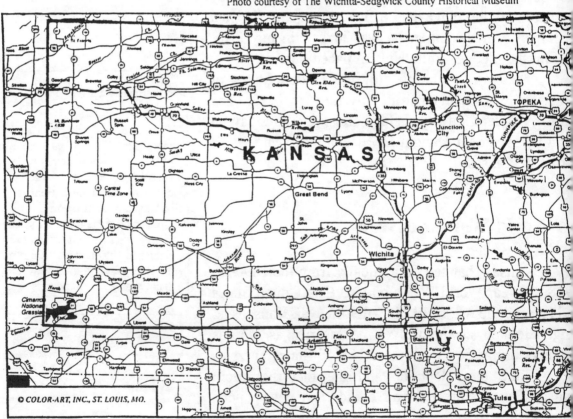

1999 Kansas Road Map, showing the Kansas Turnpike and the other major highways and roads.
Map courtesy of Color Art, Inc., St. Louis, Mo.

Greensburg, Kansas

THE BIG WELL

POST CARD

We saw the hand dug Well today. This Well was built for the railroad in 1887.

It's a big wishing Well — with 105 steps to the water.

Historical Events

1905 - Idea for 4-H comes to Kansas

1915-1916 - Most Kansans favored Allies over Germany

1917 - German submarine attacks shipping

1918 - 77,000 Kansans served, 2,500 died in the war

1918 - Armistice signed

1918 - Kansas flu epidemic

1920 - Charles Curtis becomes United States Vice-President

1920 - Capper Fund established

1934 - Capper Foundation founded

Chapter 8

Going To War

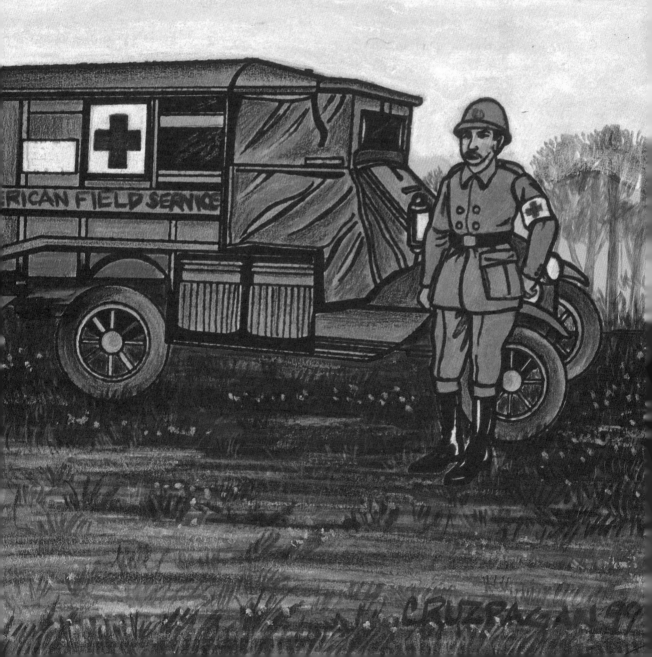

Chapter 8

Going To War

> In 1914 when a world war began in Europe, many Kansans were surprised and concerned that some of their relatives would be involved in the fighting. Like much of the rest of the nation, Kansans were not ready to be involved as a unified force.
>
> Some Kansans did get involved, though.
>
> For instance, when Belgium was crushed in 1914 by the German army, Kansas farmers quickly donated wheat and Kansas millers turned into flour for free shipment to that country.
>
> By 1915, under the direction of Governor Arthur Capper, most Kansas counties had some residents working in the war relief. The majority of people, however, supported neutrality.
>
> People were involved with their families, with their farms and businesses. The war was something far away. Kansans cared, but they were also very much involved in the events of their own lives.

eking Neutrality

In 1915 and 1916, most Kansans supported eping a neutral position between the Allied countries d the Germans, slightly favoring the Allied side over e Germans.

World War I began as a local European war tween Austria-Hungary and Serbia on July 28, 1914. ; the war escalated, it progressed into global war volving 32 nations. Twenty-eight of those nations re known as the Allies. They included Great itain, France, Russia, Italy, and towards the end of e war, the United States. The allied forces opposed e coalition of Central Powers, which included rmany, Austria-Hungary, Turkey, and Bulgaria.

The flashpoint for the war started over the sassination of Archduke Francis Ferdinand of ustria by Gavrilo Princip, a Serb Nationalist. But the derlying factors that caused the war were the litical and economic rivalry between nations having uge build-up of arms.

From 1914 on, as it looked more likely that the lited States would eventually become involved in the ir, some Kansans tried to oppose any military volvement. Groups such as The Peace and Equity ague, The Woman's Kansas Day Club, and The nsas State Grange opposed the state preparing for y military strife.

On the other hand, residents in Finney County pped out more than 100 horses from the county to gland for the Allied army use.

The United States declared war on Germany on ril 6, 1917.

ench Warfare in World War One

When the fighting broke out, both sides hoped a quick victory. But with huge armies involved, it n became obvious that the war would not end with ew short skirmishes. This was one of the first wars ere technology could kill with horrifying results, ere machine guns and heavy artillery could easily p huge marching columns of men, where mustard

Trench warfare during World War I.
Photo courtesy of National Archives

gas could be used to atta
unsuspecting troops and whe
airplanes flew overhead. So, f
protection each side began to d
down into the ground. The seri
of ditches they dug were call
trenches.

Any movement in
opposing army's trench drew t
enemy's fire. There was a sayi
on the Western Front that *"If y
could see it, you could kill it."* T
trenches helped soldiers hide.
the late fall of 1914, bo
Germans and the Allies h
created a series of zigzagging trenches dividing t
armies from the English Channel to Switzerland.

The average depth of a trench was between fi
and eight foot deep. They were covered with roofs a
interconnecting tunnels, making almost a who
underground city where troops lived for long periods

time. The bottoms of the trench
were cold and wet. Soldiers oft
placed wooden boards in t
bottom to keep from standing
the cold, wet mud.

In one of the more unus
incidents of the war, German a
Allied soldiers came out of th
trenches in a moment of truce
Christmas Day 1914, a
celebrated, giving each gifts
drinks and food. In one pla

*The men of the 130th Field Artillery
Company, part of the 35th Infantry
Division, are shown during their rifle
practice at the Topeka Fairgrounds.*
Photo courtesy of The Kansas State Historical
Society

soldiers from the two armies played soccer gam
against each other. But by the next day, both sides h
climbed back into their trenches and resumed the wa

Later on in the war, barbed wire was placed
front of the trenches by soldiers to slow down attacki
troops.

Soldiers would often stay in the trenches
months at a time. Sometimes the trenches of opposi
armies were separated by only a few hundred yards
open ground called "no man's land." These trench
were dirty and stank hideously.

soldiers would often joke that you could smell the front line miles before you could see it.

While in the trenches, soldiers lives were plagued by rats, mice, and insects. The lice they referred to jokingly as "cooties."

How Kansans Became Involved

In 1917, Germany began submarine attacks on the shipping industry and that prompted the United States to cut all diplomatic relations with Germany. Some Kansans, like residents in other parts of the United States, feared that there were German spies in their midst. People feared that railroads, bridges, and major industries might be blown up. Guards were placed at many of those possible locations.

To aid the war effort, the governor of Kansas, Arthur Capper, proposed that every back yard and every vacant lot have a garden to help the war effort. Kansans responded by planting vegetable gardens.

There was a need for officer training camps. Fort Riley became one of the Reserve Officers' Camps for new men. In the summer of 1917, 2,500 candidates received training at the fort. At Fort Leavenworth 5000 men received engineering and aviation training in the new Army Air Corps.

Camp Funston at Fort Riley, named in honor of the Kansas general from Iola, became a training ground for thousands of the soldiers.

Also, at Fort Riley there was Army City, which from July 1917 to late 1922, served as a home for a unique community that housed tens of thousands of American soldiers and their families.

Army City had its own utilities company that provided water, sewer, and electrical lines to the new community.

Soldiers at Fort Leavenworth practice their skills on an obstacle course.
Photo courtesy of The Kansas State Historical Society

The city itself was a large area of the Fo[rt] between Camp Funston and the town of Ogden. It ha[d] its own bank, post office, theaters, lumber yard, hote[l] pool halls, restaurants, photo studios, dry good store[s] drug stores, laundry, and ...the world's largest barbe[r] shop.

After World War One, because there were n[o] permanent industries located at Army City, there wa[s] nothing that could keep the city going so it died awa[y].

But in its heyday, by most standards, Army Cit[y] was huge. In the spring of 1918 there were 8,00[0] soldiers and civilians crowded around Army City's ba[ll] field to watch the 89th Division All Stars split [a] double-header with the St. Louis Cardinals. On Apr[il] 12, the same year, seven thousand fans showed up [to] watch the World Champion White Sox defeat th[e] soldiers by 12 to 1.

Army City was visited by vaudeville troop[es], talent shows, sports competitions, and Wild We[st] shows that entertained soldiers who trained at Cam[p] Funston.

A Glimpse of the Soldiers

The Kansans who fought in World War I cam[e] from all different walks of life. Private Lyman Tapse[?] from Horton who fought in the 137th Infantry die[d] from gas poisoning in Commercy, France on Februar[y] 2, 1919. He never made it home and is buried [in] Commercy.

What is known about him is that his India[n] name was Op-tuck-tap-see. He was born on th[e] Pottawatomie reservation near Mayetta in 1900 an[d] was only 19 when he died.

There was also Private Charlie Spear who wa[s] one of eight Kickapoo Indians from the reservatio[n] west of Horton. He volunteered shortly after th[e] outbreak of the war and enlisted in Company B of th[e] 137th Infantry. He died of wounds near Montrebe[au] Woods, France in the Argonne on October 6, 1918.

He was born on the Kickapoo reservation an[d] his Indian name was Pip-ko-kuk.

Donald Thompson

World War I photographer Donald Thompson had his roots in Kansas.

He grew up in Topeka and some of his first news photos published were of the Topeka flood of 1903.

When the war broke out, Thompson traveled to it - and even slipped behind enemy lines. His graphic footage of movie reels and photographs helped Americans back home understand how horrifying the war really was.

After the war, during the 1920s and 1930s, he produced travel films in Hollywood.

Another Kansas soldier was Erwin Bleckley who was raised in Wichita and was one of the first men the area to volunteer for World War I.

During one of the more famous battles of the war, the U. S. 77th division, which became known as the "Lost Battalion," was surrounded by Germans in the Argonne Forest in France.

Bleckley, a member of the 50th Observation Squadron, repeatedly flew his plane over the battle site to drop supplies to the Americans.

The *Wichita Eagle* reported that as Bleckley leaned over to survey the ground, every German rifle and machine gun within range turned loose on him.

"For a moment the enemy forgot all else," the paper reported. "This lone plane over them signified what they hated and wanted to overcome, and at it they hurled thousands of bullets with all the skill they had."

The plane skidded and made turns, climbed and dived.

For some of the soldiers below, the plane seemed charmed as it continually flew and was rocked only occasionally by the big shells that passed within inches of it.

All throughout the day, Bleckley tossed food and supplies to the men below and would fire his guns into a German machine gun nest. Finally, the plane was hit and crashed to the ground, killing Bleckley.

All that remains of the Bleckley name in Wichita is a memorial to him at the Veterans Administration Hospital.

Earl Browder

Some Kansans were concerned about life in a different way. In his day, Earl Browder was a political force, and a two-time Communist Party presidential candidate.

Earl Browder was born in 1891. He began studying the writings of Karl Marx at the age of 16. He sold a large popular Socialist newspaper, on local Kansas streets.

During World War I, Erwin Bleckley of Kansas was awarded the medal of honor.
Photo courtesy of The Wichita-Sedgwick County Historical Museum

Prairie Spirit

Oscar Micheaux of Great Bend is honored in Hollywood with a star along the city's most famous sidewalk, the Walk of Fame. Micheaux was an author and movie producer who produced more than 45 movies and several novels. In 1918, he became the first African-American to produce a full-length motion picture with an all black cast, *The Homesteader*.

In 1911, Browder moved to the Kansas C
area. He became active in both the labor and Social
movements. He went to jail rather than serve in t
armed forces during World War I.

He helped organize the Communist Party in t
United States in 1919, just after the Bolshev
Revolution in Russia, 1917.

In the United States, Browder was secretary
the Communist Party from the early 1930s until 194
Twice he was the Communist Party candidate
President. In 1936, he got 80,000 votes. And in 194
he only got 47,000. But he was so out of sync with
fellow Kansans that not a single vote came from
hometown.

Henry J. Allen Becomes Governor

In 1918, Henry J. Allen won the election
governor and he hadn't bothered even to campaign.

Allen, who was editor and publisher of
Wichita Beacon, was far away from Kansas when
1918 election was held. He was on the battlefields
France giving aid to soldiers.

He was nominated after the governor, Artl
Capper, ran for the Senate leaving the seat open. Al
was a prominent Republican whom the majority
Kansans preferred.

Allen's position in journalism had alm
always kept him in the public's eye. In 1917, wl
state political leaders gathered to decide
Republican candidate for governor, Allen was a logi
choice.

However, Allen had left Kansas for France
become Organizer and Superintendent of the Ho:
Communication Service of the American Red Cross

When the election rolled around, he was still
France.

His absence for both the nomination and
election is the only such instance in the state's histo

At the Continental Hotel in Paris on Novem
10, 1918, Allen was handed a Paris edition of
American newspaper that told him of his landsl
election on November 5.

Once in office, he helped bring women the right vote in Kansas. He also set up laws providing for the gistration and licensing of vehicles.

he 1918 Flu Epidemic

More than eight decades ago, the world's adliest outbreak of influenza began in Kansas.

To this day, scientists search for answers, ping to avoid similar epidemics in the future.

It was 1918 and the nation was at war.

Fort Riley teemed with soldiers from all over Midwest, training for Army duty in France. It also med with horses and mules. Each month, animals ated 9 thousand tons of manure, and piles of it were med daily.

Some say the burning played a part in what ppened on March 9, when a blinding dust storm uck. The storm mixed the ashes of burned manure h flying dust. Coughing and sneezing, men huddled makeshift buildings at Camp Funston, a subdivision the base.

Less than 48 hours later, a company cook came wn with a bad cough, fever, a severe sore throat, a idache, and muscular pain.

By the end of the week, 500 cases of influenza re recorded and 46 resulted in death.

The epidemic of the ages had begun. The flu ead quickly throughout the military and into the eral population.

Before it ended, it claimed at least 20 million iths worldwide. Some reports say 40 million.

Many people say that the epidemic probably ted at Fort Riley. The first recorded cases came m there.

The flu spread when many of the men, some still overing from the first wave, completed their ning at Fort Riley and were shipped to France. With m went the influenza.

The flu was most commonly called the Spanish uenza. Some called it the Spanish lady. Old-timers ed it the grippe. German soldiers called it Flanders er.

Prairie Spirit

Chanute's **Martin and Osa Johnson** have some of the most exciting wildlife photographs ever taken in the world. The couple from Chanute In 1918, Martin joined the Explorers' Club of New York and Osa was given an honorary membership. For more than 20 years the couple traveled to exotic locations around the world.

People were advised to avoid public gathering wear masks in public, keep their feet dry, and try not get chilled.

In early October, Dr. Samuel Crumbin Secretary of The State Board of Health, issued statewide shutdown order to stop the spread of the disease. Visitors were barred from all state institution places of amusement were closed and local authoriti were told to discontinue public meetings.

One in every four Americans caught the flu a 12,000 Kansans died of it or its complications.

German-Americans and Others To Blame

With all the hardships and the horrible ne stories reported back home, Kansans wanted someo to blame. With fears of spies in their midst, sor Kansans sought revenge with the only people th knew who spoke German. In these cases, it w usually devout German Catholics or Germ Mennonites who had by then lived in Kansas for nea a half a century.

Part of the Mennonites hopes and dreams f coming to America in the first place was to worship they chose, discrimination and persecution were supposed to happen.

People who weren't of German ancest mistrusted these "new" Germans. Some of them s spoke the language of their mother land. Some of the refused, out of religious convictions, to carry guns, a go off to war.

It was not uncommon to see signs in stores t said, *"Speak American in this Place."* Same su signs were above public telephones. The Kans Germans did, as much as they could. Speaki German was also forbidden in some schools acro Kansas. Speaking German was also forbidden in ma church services.

Most persecuted were the men of "war ag who refused to serve in the military. Also persecut were the families who refused to buy war bonds.

ome were tarred and feathered by other Kansans.
ome were sent off to military camps where they were
orced to put on the military uniform, salute officers,
ngage in drills and fire guns.

Governor Capper
quired that in each of the
05 Kansas counties, the
eriff, county clerk, and
ounty physician would
onstitute a board to
upervise the draft
gistration of men for the
ilitary.

Young women were
so called on to show their
atriotism. Canning clubs
ere organized and young
eople were asked to help out on the farms. These
omen, 16 years and older, were asked to register with
e Women's Council of Defense and sign "food
edge cards."

*Women volunteered through the Red
Cross to do their part of the war effort.
This group of women is rolling
bandages to be used in hospitals.*
Photo courtesy of The Kansas State Historical
Society

usiness was Regulated

Business owners were also subject to the
gulations of government during the war. Prompted
a shortage of coal, the Federal Fuel Administrator
r Kansas, ordered the following: When they closed
night, business owners should turn out all electric
gns, display lights and all lights in the buildings,
cept those that were necessary for safety. Street
hts were also to be dimmed. Business hours were to
from 9 a.m. to 5 p.m., with some exceptions.
ocery stores, drug stores, department stores, news
nds and hardware stores, for example, could stay
en until 6 p.m. except on Saturdays, when they could
se at 9 p.m. All this was done to save electricity.

Kansans were encouraged to buy "Liberty
ans" and "Victory Loans" as saving bonds.

Kansans made bandages for hospitals, gather
clothing for the people of France and Belgium, a
provided gifts for the servicemen.

Kansans were also told that Kansas flour mi
were milling grains for the troops and selling direc
to the United States Food Administration.

*"The Mills already have produced enough flour
to last us until harvest if every person does the right
thing,"* Walter P. Innes, Kansas State Fo
Administrator said to Kansans:

*"The right thing is to live on a maximum of one
and a half pounds of flour per person per week.
Families where bakers' bread is used should limit
themselves to one-half of a pound of flour per person
a week. A household with two members should not
have more than 12 pounds of flour on hand at any
time. Twelve pounds is a month's supply for a family
of two, and to have more than a month's supply is
hoarding."*

Grocers were ordered not to sell more than
month's requirement of flour to families.

If people were found guilty of hoarding flo
they were fined up to $10,000 and/or four years
prison. Store owners who sold people more than th
allotted share of flour were also subject to the sa
penalties.

Like the rest of America, Kansans participat
in "Wheatless Wednesdays" and "Meatless Tuesday
all in an effort to conserve food.

Night Riders, a persecution group, circulat
warnings against families with German backgroun
Houses and stores were sometimes painted yellow
families did not appear enthusiastic about the v
cause.

Kansans were also instructed as to how to w
their loved ones serving in the war. They were told
thank them for the service they were giving and
them know how much America and their hometo
counted on them.

The key word of the day was patriotis
Kansans wanted to believe they were helping win
war. Sometimes whole groups or organizations of n
enlisted together, such as town bands or colle
classes.

Thousands of the Kansas men served in the war. Many Kansans served in the Meuse-Argonne Battle, one of the largest battles in all of military history.

National Guardsmen from Kansas served and also participated in the Argonne offensive.

During the war, there were approximately 7,000 Kansans in service, of that number 2,500 died.

More than 00 Kansans received the distinguished service Cross.

When the war was about to end, and it became apparent that the Allies would win and Germany would be defeated, people all over the nation discussed among themselves how that end should come.

Kansas troops returning home from World War I, marching under a giant *"Victory Arch," in downtown Wichita.* Photo courtesy of The Wichita-Sedgwick Historical Museum

Governor Capper sent a telegram to President Wilson saying Kansans wanted "a complete military victory that would put an end to militarism forever."

The Armistice was signed on November 11, 1918. After that, Kansas was awash in victory parades.

Hoping there would never again be a war like this one, most Kansans supported President Wilson's Ideas for a League of Nations.

Vice-President of the United States is a Kansan

In the fall of 1928, Charles Curtis became the first Kansan to serve as Vice-President of the United States. He was also the nation's first Native American to fill such a high position.

Curtis of Topeka was born in January 25, 1860. He was one-eighth Indian and a full member of the Kaw tribe. He had spent much of his boyhood years on

the Kaw reservation near Council Grove

During his teenage years, he was a jockey at horse races in eastern Kansas. Curtis operated a horse-drawn cab that carried passengers between Topeka's depots and hotels.

In 1881, at the age of 21, he became a lawyer. By the mid-1880s he had entered politics and was elected Shawnee County attorney. The first month he was in office he closed 88 saloons in Shawnee County. He enforced the prohibition law against selling liquor.

In 1892, he ran for the U. S. House of Representatives, and won. He served there until 1907.

That year, Kansans nicknamed him "Our Charley," and when a U. S. Senate seat from Kansas became vacant, he was appointed a U. S. state senator. During his time, he was considered a powerful Republican leader because of his ability to help others make compromises.

In 1928, when Herbert Hoover became the Republican nominee for President, Hoover selected Curtis as his vice-presidential candidate to help him win votes from the midwestern farmers.

When the news came that Hoover and Curtis had won, drums on the Kanza reservation sounded in celebration.

Charles Curtis (1860-1936) is shown with Herbert Hoover.
Photo courtesy of The Kansas State Historical Society

Prairie Spirit

Billy Mills was a Sioux Indian from the Pine Ridge reservation in South Dakota when he was sent to Lawrence in the 1950s to attend the Haskell Institute. He won two state championships in the mile and three state titles in the two-mile cross-country run. He then attended the University of Kansas on a full scholarship where he became a Big Eight cross country champion and led the Jayhawks in the NCAA championships. In the 1964 Olympics he ran in the 10,000-meter run. During the last 300 meters of the race he was accidentally pushed by one of the other runners. He caught up with the rest of the runners and won a gold medal.

Haskell Indian Nations University

This university educates American Indian and native Alaskan students that are federally recognized tribal members.

It is one of the oldest federally supported educational institutions in the United States.

Located in Lawrence, the University draws upon the Sacred Circle as the foundation for American Indian/Alaska Native philosophy.

Haskell's vision is to become a national center for Indian education, research, and cultural programs that increase knowledge and support the educational needs of American Indians/Alaska Natives.

Henry Roe Cloud

Henry Roe Cloud was a graduate of Yale, listed in Who's Who of America. He became one of the nation's leading reformers for the rights of American Indians.

One of his first efforts at reform started in Wichita in 1915 with the founding of the Roe Institute.

Henry Roe Cloud and his family, 1918.
Photo courtesy of Wichita State University Special Collections

It was later named the American Indian Institute. At that time, it was one of three all-Indian high schools in the nation.

The all-male school was one of the first American Indian high schools in the nation. The majority of its students came from Oklahoma. It encouraged American Indians to become part of mainstream society.

Kansas Ties to 4-H

Beginning as early as 1905, an idea was brought to Kansas that eventually evolved into what we know today as 4-H.

4-H itself originated out of Clarinda, Iowa. But its roots in Kansas started out first as corn and canning clubs, then spread to tomato clubs, and poultry contests. Finally, in 1926 it was referred to for the first time as the Boys' and Girls' 4-H Club Work. The 4-H

33 RD. ANNUAL 4H ROUND-UP
MANHATTAN, KANSAS. MAY 28-JUNE I, 1957.

4-H Round-Up, 1957.
Photo courtesy of Kansas State University
Department of Special Collections

Organization helped bring culture and knowledg
well as social skills to rural people.

4-H began as a way to teach children ho
develop farm and household skills but it ende
teaching much more. Early organizers believed
were not just teaching children how to succeed in
but they were teaching their parents, as well.

The "H"'s in 4-H stand for Head, Heart, H
and Health.

"Few recognized what they saw as the beginnι
of a new movement, that was destined to spread
across the entire state and to enter farm homes
and influence the lives of thousands of rural boys
and girls, and their parents as well," said the Ka
Extension Service Department.

It wasn't unusual for individual counties and the [s]tate fair board to offer contests with sizeable rewards [fo]r the winners of the 4-H clubs. Winners were [so]metimes given trips, money and even livestock or [ap]pliances.

Even the governor of Kansas became involved. [Fo]r years, Arthur Capper, governor and successful [ph]ilanthropist from Topeka, generously rewarded [w]inners of various club projects. He and his wife never [ha]d any children, which may have been one of the [re]asons why he was so involved.

When he was governor, he received a letter from [a] Kansas farm boy asking Capper to help him buy a [pi]g. The governor loaned the boy the money and then [re]peated the act for others. Soon up to 10 children [fr]om each county could sign up for an animal project [an]d buy livestock with money borrowed from Capper. [Af]ter their animals were sold, members repaid the [lo]ans and kept any profits.

It was not unusual for club members to have [$1]50 in profits. By the 1920s, Capper had loaned more [th]an $100,000 to 4-H members across Kansas, only [$2]00 was not returned. The program was discontinued [in] the late 1920s when an agricultural depression hit [K]ansas.

But even so, the popularity of 4-H continued. [D]uring the Depression, 4-H fairs were a source of [en]tertainment as well as education. 4-H is still a [po]pular organization for Kansas families today. 4-H [cl]ubs now offer dozens of projects for urban as well as [ru]ral young people.

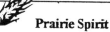

Prairie Spirit

Pete Felden, Jr. is a sculptor from Hays who was selected in 1978 to sculpt four famous Kansas to be placed in the rotunda of the capitol building — Amelia Earhart, Arthur Capper, Dwight D. Eisenhower and William Allen White.

[T]he Capper Foundation

With a concern for children with physical [di]sabilities, Senator Arthur Capper established the [Ca]pper Fund on Christmas Day in 1920. During the [ye]ars, the costs of hospitalization and surgery from any [ch]ildren were paid from the Senator's personal [fin]ances.

Arthur Capper made his fortune through his [pu]blishing business. He worked his way up the ranks [an]d eventually owned several newspapers and

periodicals. He served the State of Kansas as it
twentieth governor and then as United States Senato
from 1919 to 1949.

An employee at Capper Publications had
daughter with polio. He encouraged Senator Capper t
"do more for the children." On September 26, 1934
The Capper Foundation for Crippled Children, a non
profit corporation became a reality.

Today, The Capper Foundation serves thousand
of children and adults yearly. With a mission "t
enhance the independence of people with physica
disabilities, primarily children."

How the War Changed Kansans

After World War I, Kansans grew weary o
progressive social reform, and Populist type partie
They had, as a whole, turned inward toward themselve
and their state. They had also become mor
conservative.

The war had been horrifying for most Kansan
and there was a tendency for intolerance. Intoleranc
for others grew and organizations like the Ku Klu
Klan quickly gained momentum in Kansas. Labo
disputes also were common.

The war took away Kansas's innocence. Neve
again would Kansas be the same.

ABILENE, KANSAS

EISENHOWER HOME 1898-1946

POST CARD

We visited Eisenhower's home today.
He graduated from high school in 1909. He worked for Belle Spp Creamery for 2 years, then he entered West Point, June 3, 1911. He was commissioned a 2nd Lt., Sept. 1915.
We learned alot about him and the house was beautiful.

Historical Events

1916-1919 - Labor strikes

1920 - Electricity arrives to Kansas farms

1921 - William Allen White takes on the Klan

1929 - The Great Depression

1931 - Topeka High School built

1932 - Franklin D. Roosevelt elected President

1932 - New Deal program in Kansas

1935 - Palm Sunday dust storm

1935 - Alfred Landon re-elected Kansas Governor

1936 - Landon wins Republican nomination for President

1938 - Revived minimum wage law helps Kansans

Chapter 9

Roaring Twenties, Dirty Thirties

Chapter 9

Roaring Twenties, Dirty Thirties

The War to End All Wars was won.

Now it was time to build a future.

These were times of exploding wealth and grinding poverty. They were times of rapid growth in some places and dying towns in others.

Kansas, like the nation, recoiled from war and began to relax. They danced a swinging, free-moving dance called the Charleston. Women wore straight dresses, cut above the knee, with long fringe. Coats made from the fur of raccoons were in style.

Prohibition was federal law, as it had been in Kansas for half a century. However, "speakeasys" or private clubs where alcohol was served, flourished. It was a wild and crazy kind of atmosphere that earned the decade the name "the roaring twenties." In spite of an almost party atmosphere, there were serious questions that needed answers. Kansas, like the nation, was searching for answers.

What should be the role of labor and what should be the role of management in an industrial age?

How can the water be conserved and the soil saved from erosion?

How can a free nation with free speech fight the rise of bigotry and hatred in new organizations of hate?

How can the nation endure a Great Depression and emerge even stronger than before?

This was a time of great challenge and great defeats. But also a time of great spirit and great triumph. It was a time when the fighting pioneer spirit came through. It was a time when people were determined not just to survive but to create a future. And, that's just what Kansans did.

Economy Based on Agriculture

Farming was the foundation upon which the developing state economy relied.

During the war, the demand for grain had soared and Kansas farmers answered the call as they turned over thousands of acres of prairie sod. They planted Turkey Red Winter Wheat. "Win the War with Wheat," was the Kansas slogan.

After the war, Kansans were urged to grow more crops as the demand grew for grains to export. Tractors and trucks had taken the place of horses and steam engines. Now the farmers could cultivate more land. While the acres in wheat grew, the number of flour mills decreased. There were 300 mills in 1866. Today there are only 19 mills.

People were just beginning to see that natural resources, especially the land and water, would not last forever without help. Between 1900 and 1917 there were four droughts and 55 floods. The fertile prairie topsoil washed away into the rivers. Once the root system of the native grasses was plowed up, the soil blew easily in the wind. Sometimes it drifted, like snow. People could see this was a problem. But nobody knew then how big the problem would become.

As early as the 1920s, farmers in western Kansas began to use the one-way plow, a new kind of plow. It left some reside of the previous year's stubble in the ground to help prevent soil erosion.

In 1927, the Division of Water Resources warned state officials that a statewide irrigation and flood control plan was needed. But nobody could agree on how to design and build such a thing, let alone pay for it. Water and wind continued to take their toll in Kansas farmland. Irrigation lowered groundwater levels. As much as 80 percent of the population was in danger of losing its water source.

Most experts agreed it would be a good idea to harness rainfall by terracing the land and by building reservoirs and ponds. In 1929, the legislature voted to give a tax break to any farmer who built a pasture pond.

This display of farm machinery shows the equipment that was considered necessary to run a farm in 1905.
Photo courtesy of Kansas State University Special Collections

An example of contour plowing in Western Kansas. But it wasn't enough to prevent disaster when prolonged drought struck.
Photo courtesy of Kansas State University Special Collections

Irrigation Pump and Ditch, Garden City, 1925.
Photo courtesy of Kansas State University Special Collections

Electricity had arrived on Kansas farms by the 1920s, with it came a variety of labor-saving devices like these in a special display in 1925.
Photo courtesy of Kansas State University Special Collections

Engineers said the state needed five bi reservoirs in every county and 50,00 farm ponds to solve the problem. Som were built. But it was not nearly enougl

Farmers planted more and mor land in wheat, corn, soybeans, and grai sorghum. Disaster was just ahead.

The Automobile, Movies Vacumn Cleaners, and Mor

Industry and technology boomed an Americans reaped the rewards.

The automobile was not new. But after the wa it rapidly gained popularity. When Henry Ford bega making cars that sold for $295, more people coul afford to buy one.

Cars increased the demand for gasoline and tl Kansas oil fields boomed. Travel also increased tl demand for good roads and 335 miles of highwa were built in 1924 alone. Two years later, however,

survey ranked Kans; behind 46 other stat in the building roads. The state aske for federal money help build and pav more roads.

Electricity came Kansas. This brougl convenience to dai living. The ice b was replaced with tl refrigerator, vacuu cleaners replaced tl brooms, the wring washing machines were replaced by electric washer and electric milking machines saved on human labc The radio became a source of information ar entertainment. Movies were popular. Big beautif theaters were built.

This publicity photograph for Cessna Aircraft, taken in 1927, was designed to show the wing strength of the airplane.
Photo courtesy of The Kansas Aviation Museum
Bob Picket Collection

But there was no fascination greater than the idea of traveling through the air.

In 1925, flights from Wichita to Kansas City were offered. It took three hours to fly one way and a ticket cost $30.

Wichita businessmen jumped ahead of all other places in building flying machines. Laird, Mollendick, Stearman, Cessna, and Beech took the lead. Investors from all over poured money into Wichita. They built one-fourth of all the commercial planes built in the entire nation. The following year, the industry built 2,500 planes in Kansas.

Like the social life in the clubs and dance halls, industry was "roaring" in the 1920s.

1929, Beech Travel Air 6000, the interior of the 6-seater plane.
Photo courtesy of Wichita State University Special Collections

Labor Strife

The economy grew and industrial giants sought greater profits; however, some segments of the work force did not get to share in the overall success.

One such group was the miners in southeast Kansas. Health problems were related to working underground and constantly breathing dust. Many died of lung-related illnesses.

The workers wanted better pay, better working conditions, and shorter hours. Labor strikes were commonplace in Kansas. From 1916 to 1919 there were 364 different strikes.

Charles Lindberg lived in Bird City during the summer of 1922. He moved there to star in a local airshow. He is shown with Walter Beech, he approached Wichita's Travel Air Company asking them to build his plane for his Atlantic crossing. When they turned him down he went to St. Louis, there a St. Louis company built his Spirit of St. Louis plane.
Photo courtesy of Wichita State University Special Collections

Alexander Howatt, wa
president of the Kansas district c
the United Mine Workers o
America. He organized the min
workers in southeast Kansas.

In the fall of 1919, Howa
called for a strike in the Kansa
mines. The Kansas supply of co
was almost exhausted.

Governor Henry J. Alle
was afraid another strike woul
leave people without heat an
factories without power. H
decided that this just would not b
allowed. He put the mines unde
state control, saying coal was
vital necessity. While the mine
strike was on, college student
members of the American Legio

Alma, Kansas Farmers Cooperative,
1920. Times were good for farmers in
the years immediately following World
War I.
Photo courtesy of Kansas State University
Special Collections

and other volunteers took over the labor of minin
coal. Governor Allen called out the National Guard
protect them from angry miners.

The Court of Industrial Relations·

Governor Allen wanted to mak
sure future problems with labor d
not stop the state's industries.
created the "Court of Industri
Relations." The court wa
intended to protect the public k
keeping production going. It wa
supposed to give labor a way
appeal against low wages, lor
hours, and discrimination. Indust
was expected to benefit because th
would be no picketing, r
boycotting, and no strikes.

This Cherokee County demonstration
in support of farm labor took place
during the Great Depression.
Photo courtesy of National Archives

Samuel Gompers, Union head of the Americ
Federation of Labor, was very angry about the Kans
court.

He wrote:

> "Kansas cannot legislate men into serfdom. Kansas cannot put upon her statute books a law that will compel men to submit to involuntary servitude."

Gompers and Governor Allen agreed to debate the topic at Carnegie Hall in New York City. Never had any other state tried such a thing as the Court of Industrial Relations. The whole country was watching to see how it turned out for Kansas.

In some cases, the court worked well. However, it soon created arguments over the question of the workers right to strike and other people's right to support them with signs and picketing.

In 1923 the United States Supreme Court declared the Court of Industrial Relations to be unconstitutional and it was abolished.

Change, Challenge and Bigotry

The rapid growth of Kansas industry and the arrival of thousands of new immigrants to compete for jobs also helped create another kind of strife.

People who lost their jobs to the newcomers, especially when they were employed as strike-breakers, found it easy to blame their own problems on other races or ethnic groups. In the early 1920s, the Ku Klux Klan was growing across the nation. Many people were becoming very concerned.

Burning a cross against the night sky was a common activity for members of the Ku Klux Klan in the 1920s. The Klan, was ousted from Kansas after Emporia newspaper William Allen White ran for governor, calling attention to the need to rid the state of the organization.
Photo courtesy of The Kansas State Historical Society

This was not the same Klan that formed in the South following the Civil War.

The father of this Klan was William Simmons, a extremely conservative Georgia minister. The Klan was against everything it did not consider "American." This included Jews, Catholics, Negroes, and anyone who opposed the Klan.

In Kansas, the Klan's organizers took advant
of labor unrest. In 1922, it found new members am
the striking railroad workers who had lost their job
black people who would work as strike breakers.

Some working men liked the Klan sim
because they didn't like Governor Allen.

Allen spoke out strongly against the Klan.
for some people, being in favor of the Klan was a v
to be against Governor Allen. But organized la
never solidly backed the Klan.

William Allen White Takes on The Kla

William Allen White had won two Puli
Prizes in his lifetime, the highest honor in newspa
writing. He won the first in 1922 for an edito
defending freedom of speech.

He wrote this editorial against the Klan in 19
It said:

> "It is an organization of cowards. Not a man
> in it has the courage of his convictions... The Kh
> Klux Klan in this community is a menace to pea
> and decent neighborly living, and if we find out
> who is the Imperial Wizard in Emporia we shall
> guy (hound or ridicule) the life out of him. He is
> joke, you may be sure. But a poor joke at that."

By 1923, the Klan had 60,000 members
Kansas. Governor Allen tried bringing a suit aga
the Klan. Attorney General Charles Griffith attemp
a crusade against it. But the courts had trouble keep
witnesses.

The Klan was known to burn crosses on la
and lynch people. It was hard to find people willin
testify publicly against it.

White thought someone should run for gove
on a platform against the Klan just to make Kans
aware of how bad it was. In 1924, White decided t
it himself.

He told his friends that he didn't really war
run because he didn't want to be elected. He w
Governor Henry J. Allen, who was not a candidate
year:

*A 1924 cartoon featuring William
Allen White against the KKK.*
Photo courtesy of The Kansas State Historical
Society

What's the Matter With Kansas

One of White's Pulitzer
Prize editorials was written in
1898.

White was a staunch
Republican and he thought
the Populist movement was
bad for Kansas. His editorial
said in part:

*"We don't need population,
we don't need wealth, we
don't need cities on the fertile
prairies, you bet we don't!
What we are after is money
power. Because we have
become poorer and ornerier
and meaner than a spavined
mule..."*

White later apologized for
much of what he said and
became a supporter of some
of the Populist ideas.

White did not set up a campaign organization, but he was strongly supported by Allen, who owned the *Wichita Beacon*, and by Victor Murdock, who owned the *Wichita Eagle*. Frank Doster, a former Populist state supreme court judge, also opposed the Klan and supported White.

White did not win the election. The "regular" Republican, Ben Paulen, a conservative Fredonia banker, was elected governor. But White did do what he set out to do. He brought the Klan problem out into the open.

In 1925, the Kansas Supreme Court ruled that the Klan could not do business in Kansas without a charter. The Secretary of State refused to issue a charter to the Klan.

The Kansas City Star described White's effort as "one of those successful failures through which civilization edges forward."

Soon, however, all of Kansas and the nation were to be plunged into a test, not of their ability to edge forward, but of their very ability to survive.

April 30, 1914, William Allen White working at his desk, notice the old typewriter. White won his second Pulitzer Prize in 1947 for his autobiography.
Photo courtesy of The Kansas State Historical Society

The Great Depression and Dust

Kansas farmers had bumper wheat crops in 1929 and 1930. In 1929, however, the rest of the country was plunged into a great depression. The stock market failed. Private fortunes and businesses were lost. People who had wealth and money held on to it.

People didn't trust the banks and wanted their savings. There wasn't enough money in the banks to pay the demand. Many banks closed their doors. Kansas held on because of its earlier prosperity. Prices were dropping steadily, however. So farmers planted more acres so they'd have more grain to sell.

March, 1936. Wind blown dust piled up in large drifts near Liberal.
Photo courtesy of National Archives

Drifting sand almost covered up this schoolhouse near Cimarron in 1939.
Photo courtesy of Kansas State University Special Collections

In 1931, farmers raised a recor 240 million bushels of wheat. B the price fell to 30 cents a bush and farmers fed wheat to cattl and hogs hoping to sell th livestock for better prices.

The decade of the 193(brought double misery to Kansa The depression closed businesse and cost city dwellers their job Of the 16 Wichita aircra factories turning out flyin machines in 1929, only four wei left by the time the depressic ended.

A prolonged drought brought even great disaster to farmers.

By 1933, there was no longer enough moistu in the ground for crops to gro Some seeds didn't even g enough water for plants to con up. Other crops withered short after they emerged.

There was no grain to fee the livestock. Finally, mo farmers had to give up trying raise cattle and hogs.

With the moisture go and the plants stripped off th bare ground, dust began to blo The drought, and the du affected the entire Great Plain Texas, Oklahoma, Kansas, Colorado, and Ne Mexico. These states were called the "Dust Bowl."

Survivors of more than 40 dust storms th struck in the Great Plains during 1935 alone rec: blackouts of dust that lasted for days. Dust filled t air so that it was impossible to see the distance acro a city street.

The Tumbleweed

Tumbleweeds are famous from western movies and songs, they are not native to the American west.

The tumbleweed is a plant called the Russian Thistle and its seed came to Kansas mixed in with the seed of Hard Red Winter Wheat.

Tumbleweeds have shallow roots, that easily comes out of the ground. They have a lot of small branches and a round shape which makes them roll easily in the wind.

During the Depression, farmers attempted to keep their cattle alive by feeding them tumbleweeds, but the thistles provided to have little food value.

Some farmers on the Great Plains would use the plants as Christmas trees. Their shape and their abundance of stout branches decorate nicely.

Photo courtesy of National Archives

Howard Zook was 82 when he talked to the *Wichita Eagle* in 1995 about his memories of one of the worst storms of them all, on Palm Sunday, 1935. He lived in western Kansas near the town of Kendall.

"It just looked like a big solid bank rolling in When it hit, the sun disappeared and we beat it into the house...we stood there leaning against the wall. The only way you knew where people were was by feel. You couldn't see them a foot away from you. The dirt was just that thick."

People had to use shovels to scoop the dirt out of their attics after the storms or the weight of the dirt would make the ceiling of their homes cave in.

Ray Kraus was only five years old in 1935. He lived on a farm in Ness County. This is what he remembers:

1935 Palm Sunday storm. Dust storms of boiling, rolling clouds of dust blacked out the sun day after day.
Photo courtesy of The Kansas State Historical Society

"I remember going to the water pump to get water for the house. We'd put a cloth over the spigot and pump the water through it to filter it. Then we'd put a wet cloth over the bucket to keep the dirt out while we carried it to the house."

As the top layer of soil was stripped away, a fi[n] volcanic ash was exposed. Volcanic ash is under mu[ch] of the topsoil of western Kansas, eastern Colorado a[nd] extends into Oklahoma and the Texas panhandle.

The ash blew and drifted, finer-than-sand dus[t] it found its way through cracks and windows and und[er] doors. People became sick from inhaling the dust a[nd] developed pneumonia. Some, especially old peop[le] and babies, died.

Good Times, too

Oddly enough, many people who lived throu[gh] that time remember that there was also fun in spite [of] the weather. They remember ball games and ba[nd] concerts and listening to the radio.

The most prosperous of farm homes in the 1920s had running water at the sink in the kitchen.
Photo courtesy of Kansas State University Special Collections

One housewife in western Kansas wrote:

"Strange as it may seem we had fun. I can remember days when the wind and dirt would blow all day until along about sunset when the wind would go down and the air would clear. One of the neighbors would drive into the yard....and say 'come over for supper.'

We would hurriedly fix a dish of something to take and the whole family would go; after supper we would play cards and really have a good time. We also had party dances in our homes; there would be two or three men available who played a violin and a guitar; we would move enough furniture out of the front room so we would have enough room to dance...Most of us managed to buy a radio, which was something new, and we spent many a night listening to the programs and music."

Getting water *for washing clothes, cooking, bathing, and drinking meant a trip to the well for farm families in 1937.*
Photo courtesy of Kansas State University Special Collections

Western Kansas farming in 1920s.
Photos courtesy of Wichita State University Special Collections

A New Deal

In 1932, Franklin D. Roosevelt was elected President of the United States and promised a "new deal" that would pull the country out of the Depression and do something to help the farmers.

Kansas Governor Alf Landon and the state legislature were also in favor of help for farmers. During hard times, mortgage payments on farms and homes couldn't be made. A law was passed that stopped foreclosures of mortgages and liens for six months after March, 1933.

Roosevelt's new deal also involved other programs. Governor Landon supported most of them. Some that had a big effect on Kansas were the Works Progress Administration (WPA), the Agricultural Adjustment Act (AAA) and the Civilian Conservation Corps (CCC).

The AAA allotment checks kept many Kansa families alive.

The WPA was the object jokes and talk workers "leaning on shovels" for a living. Howeve the projects brought jobs to thousands who were ne otherwise able to earn a living.

The CCC taught men and women of Americ how to live independently and help the natura resources. This increased their self esteem.

Cecil Gomez, a retired chef, at the age of 79 f published a cookbook in 1997. It included a autobiographical sketch. His story tells what th chance for a job with the CCC meant, in those times.

Gomez was 12 in 1929 when his father die He said his mother tried to cope alone as the Dust Bo and the Depression grew worse. But she couldn't mal a living. In 1931, the sheriff came and took his fi younger brothers away on the train to the Orphan Home in Atchison. Gomez writes:

A WPA construction project, the Library on the Wichita State University campus, 1938.
Photo courtesy of Wichita State University
Special Collections

> *"The day they left, Ed Herschler, the school principal, felt so bad and tried to comfort me. He told me I didn't have to go back to school. I remember that I crawled into an empty boxcar and cried all afternoon."*

When he turned 18, Gomez got a chance to jo the CCC. It was a job that paid $30 dollars a mont The CCC sent $25 back home to help his family and I got the rest.

e learned to cook, and in a few months got a raise and
another $6 a month in his pocket. If it wasn't for the
CCC, his family, like others would have suffered more
than they did.

'Pay as you go'

Many western farmers were "land poor." This
meant they had a lot of land but were not making
enough money from their land. Governor Landon
believed they should receive lower property taxes. But
he also believed the state government should stay out
of debt and keep its budget balanced.

He pushed for a budget and a law that required
the state to have enough money in the treasury at all
times to pay all its bills. He also wanted each agency
of the government to have its own budget. His "pay as
you go" policy kept the state government running in
spite of how bad the times were.

Alfred "Alf" Mossman Landon.
Photo courtesy of The Kansas State Historical
Society

Landon also
supported a new
idea that came
from a group of
state government
workers.

That idea
established the
Legislative
Council, an
organization that did research for legislators and
provided them with the answers to their questions.
The Legislative Council was the first of its kind in the
United States.

A Landon campaign poster.
Photo courtesy of The Kansas State Historical
Society

Landon was a popular governor and was re-
elected to a second term in 1935.

Another Term and A Run for President

During his second term, Landon worked hard
for water and soil conservation, fair taxes and the
protection of the Kansas oil market. He also supported
most of Franklin Roosevelt's New Deal programs.

Alf Landon buying war stamps.
Photo courtesy of The Kansas State Historical Society

Alf Landon campaign button.
Photo courtesy of The Kansas State Historical Society

Kansas ratified (approved) two amendments t
the U. S. Constitution: one approved of feder
unemployment insurance and other approved th
Social Security Amendment.

People liked Landon and there was a tal
during his second term, suggesting he should run f
President.

He did and won the Republican nomination fo
president in 1936. Thousands of Kansans turned out
to cheer that announcement.

Landon, however, lost that election to Frankli
Roosevelt, a Democrat, who was so popular th
probably no Republican could have defeated hin
Landon did not run for office again, but he remained
powerful force in Kansas politics.

Unpopular "Huxies"

In 1936, for only the fifth time in its history, Kansas elected a Democrat, Walter Huxman, to the governor's seat. He had a Republican legislature and he was criticized as a puppet of the Roosevelt administration by those who did not like the New Deal.

The state badly needed money for social programs to take care of old people, the disabled and dependent children. The legislature, over Huxman's protest, passed a 2 percent sales tax to raise the money.

Small, metal tokens, each worth one-tenth of a penny, were used to pay the tax. People who didn't like Huxman began calling the tokens "Huxies." The tax program overall was badly managed and unpopular. Much of the money went toward cutting property taxes instead of relief efforts for the old, disabled and dependent children.

The legislature also wrote and passed a bill that legalized the sale of beer for the first time since Kansas passed prohibition in the 1880s. Opponents of alcohol blamed Huxman because he signed the bill into law.

In 1938, Huxman was defeated. But he went on to become a federal judge. He served many years and became well-known and widely respected as a judge.

Labor makes Gains

Labor unrest tapered off later in the 1930s after several legislative measures helped the workers.

The State Board of Health adopted a hygiene section for industry in 1936. It began checking companies to see what kind of dangerous substances workers might be exposed to. It also studied ways to eliminate dangerous risks to workers.

Federal Social Security, child labor, and unemployment compensation acts were ratified in Kansas. In 1938, the legislature revived the minimum wage law which helped the Kansas labor force.

Photo courtesy of The Kansas State Historical Society

Prairie Spirit

When doctor's told Elkhart's **Glenn Cunningham** that he might lose his legs following a horrible fire accident when he seven years old, Cunningham recovered by forcing himself to walk behind a mule, hanging on to its tail. He endured unbelievable pain and taught himself how to walk again — and then run. In 1936 he won a silver medal in the 1,500-meter race of the Olympics.

Building For the Public

Topeka
High School

Topeka High School, *built in 1931 at a cost of more than one million dollars. The flag pole was from the battleship "Old Ironsides."*

Photo courtesy of Avery Postcards

Prairie Spirit

Author and poet, **Langston Hughes** often faced racial discrimination as he was growing up in Topeka and Lawrence. Nevertheless, he rose to become one of the leading poets of the nation. During the 1930s, he was a motion picture writer in Moscow, then a news correspondent in Madrid. He wrote more than 20 books, most of them poetry, and several short stories, essays, plays, songs and an autobiography.

One lasting legacy of th prosperity of the 1920s and th public works projects of th Depression years was man public buildings.

In the 1920s, town competed to see who could buil the biggest, most elabora schools.

Topeka Central Hig School was a three-story bric building, trimmed in stone with tall Gothic tower. Wyandot High School in Kansas City wa built as a giant letter 'H.'

A unique building sty attempting to copy nature's colo and lines was characterized by th designs of Frank Lloyd Wrigh famous architect of the time ar followed by architects of th "prairie school."

Examples of the prair school are still seen in the hig school at Russell, at Wichita North High School, at the Capitol Loan Associatic Building in Topeka, and at the home that Frank Lloy Wright designed for Governor Henry J. Allen Wichita.

Across the countryside, there were also uniqt examples of the lifestyle of the Plains. Huge bar: were often two or more times the size of the house Kansas farms and tall grain elevators became known "prairie skyscrapers."

Developments in Art

There were Kansans who depicted pioneer li in drawings and paintings from the days of the territo forward. As the battles for statehood and the effort populate the state advanced, so did Kansas art.

As early as 1883, the State Art Association worked to build a permanent art collection in Topeka.

George M. Stone was a portrait painter and was commissioned to do a series of Kansas landscape paintings. His works also included murals and paintings on historic topics.

Frederic Remington became known for paintings and sculptures that illustrated the days of the Wild West. He lived for a time on a ranch in Butler County and used what he saw and learned there in many of his works.

Birger Sandzen, a Swedish artist and teacher, came to Bethany College at Lindsborg in the 1890s and helped to make it a unique art center.

He did etchings, lithographs, printings, and water colors using the southwest as his theme. The Sandzen Gallery in Lindsborg today provides a fine display of his work and offers space for exhibits of contemporary artists.

Hattie McDaniel and Clark Gable from a scene in Gone With The Wind.
Photo courtesy of The Kansas State Historical Society

 Prairie Spirit

Hattie McDaniel of Wichita became the first African-American to receive the Academy Award for her portrayal of "Mammy" in *Gone With The Wind.* When she received the award in 1939, she was severely criticized by the NAACP because of the role she played of a servant. McDaniel replied that she would rather receive $700 a week for playing a maid than work as one for only $7 a week.

Curry and the Murals

John Steuart Curry *in a self-portrait.*
Photo courtesy of The Kansas State Historical
Society

John Steuart Curry was born in Kansas a[nd]
trained at the Chicago Art Institute. He wanted [to]
portray reality in his work. He traveled with a circ[us]
for a time. He painted realistic scenes of Midwest li[fe]
and of circus life. In 1933, he painted two murals [for]
the Justice Building in Washington, D.C.

Many Kansans however, didn't like how harsh [and]
real his paintings were and he wasn't well liked in h[is]
home state.

A notable exception was William Allen Whi[te.]
When Curry left to become "artist in residence" [at]
Wisconsin University in 1934, White scolded Kansa[ns.]

*"It takes something more than factories,
something more than crowded cities and towns,
something more than per capita wealth to make a
civilization and Kansas would be able to hold her
head a little higher if she could have taken John
Curry under her wing."*

That kicked off a newspaper campaign th[at]
resulted in Curry winning a commission to pa[int]
murals in the state capitol building in Topeka. H[is]
paintings were of the historic struggle of man agai[nst]
nature. Perhaps most famous of all his murals is that [of]
John Brown, Bible in one hand, rifle in the oth[er.]
Many people said his paintings were too extrem[e.]
Curry was also criticized by some who said his anim[als]
were not the right size compared to his people and [to]
each other. One critic even complained that the tail [of]
the pig curled the wrong way.

Curry never quite finished all the paintings. T[he]
dispute that had arisen began to slowly disappear. [By]
the time the artist died in 1946, it was seldo[m]
mentioned.

> **Prairie Spirit**
>
> **Charlie "Bird" Parker** of Kansas
> City was a jazz saxophonist and
> composer during the 1930s and
> 1940s. He developed a new form
> of jazz called bob, or bebop.

Changes on the Farm

The 1930s had burned a lesson on the ent[ire]
American landscape. Soil and water had to [be]
preserved.

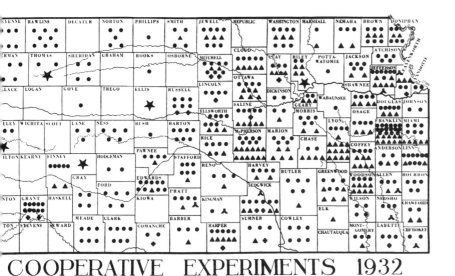

COOPERATIVE EXPERIMENTS 1932

- • VARIETY TESTS (372)
- ▲ SOIL TREATMENT TESTS (170)
- ★ EXPERIMENT STATIONS
- ▲ EXPERIMENTAL FIELDS
- ◆ OTHER TESTS (18)
  (86 COUNTIES)

Cooperative Experiment Stations, 1932.
Photo courtesy of Kansas State University Special Collections

In Kansas, as in other states, the role of research ll to the universities. These universities were those hich had been given grants of land to develop chnical and agriculture education.

With the help of the U. S. Department of griculture, Kansas State College of Agriculture and pplied Science at Manhattan, w Kansas State University, tablished extension services.

Extension agents, who orked in each of the state's 105 unties, provided help with ricultural methods to farmers. gents helped farm women in me economics and boys and rls through the 4-H clubs.

Researchers worked to me up with drought-resistant rieties of corn and wheat. ientists studied the best way to rm each of the crops.

Finally, everyone gave up on the idea that nply farming the land would change the climate of nsas and agreed that nature had to be respected.

Eleanor Roosevelt viewing a shelterbelt planted by Prairie States Forestry Project in Hutchison, 1938.
Photo courtesy of The Reno County Museum

Thousands of acres of land were planted bac[k]
grass. A government program called the S[oil]
Conservation Act paid farmers to stop erosion
simply letting their acreage remain in grass.

New Faces, Radical Political Ideas

There was a new face in Kansas politics in 19[ ]
Another independent candidate stepped forth.

He was Gerald Winrod, a minister with a ra[dio]
show. He organized a group of followers that he cal[led]
"Defenders of the Christian Faith." He used the mo[ney]
he raised with his church activities to run for U[.S.]
Senate.

Winrod made a trip to Germany in the
1930s and was impressed with the ideas he heard f[rom]
their leader named Adolf Hitler. He came back[to]
Kansas and campaigned on a platform that was a[nti-]
Jewish, anti-Communist, and anti-Catholic.

Much of what he said sounded very much [like]
Hitler. His attempt at being elected failed as not m[any]
Kansans were convinced to vote for him.

Caught up in their own problems, drought [and]
depression, not many Kansans were ready to deal [with]
political changes and the conflicts in Europe. W[orld]
War Two (WWII) was about to began.

Many, like Alf Landon, were opposed to [any]
involvement by America. Others, like William A[llen]
White, thought America should aid the Allies but [not]
join in the war. There was sympathy for Great Bri[tain]
in her stand against Germany. But there were [many]
arguments against getting involved in what many [felt]
were Europe's problems.

Soon, certain events would settle all argume[nts.]

EMPORIA, KANSAS

POST

AP

Today we went to Emporia and saw the house where William Allen White used to lived. He owned the newspaper and wrote a lot of stuff that made people think about changing the way we live. He even ran for governor because he thought the Ku Klux Klan was bad.

Historical Events

1940 - Hilter rolls into Poland

1941 - Attack on Pearl Harbor and war is Declared

1943 - B-29 Bomber Built

1943 - Coleman Company fills war orders

1943 - German POW camps in Kansas

1944 - D-Day

1945 - Victory in Europe and Japan

1950 - The Korean War

1950 - Brown vs. Topeka Board of Education

1952 - Ike nominated and wins Presidency

1952-1956 - Drought hits Kansas

1955 - Udall Tornado

CRUZ PAGAN 99

Chapter 10

Another Great War and its Aftermath

Chapter 10

Another Great War and its Aftermath

Kansans had enough to worry about with depression and dust. They didn't want to have to worry about the problems in Europe or going to war again.

World War I had been a bitter and unnerving experience for America. In recent years, they had also suffered huge losses at the hands of nature and they needed time to recover.

Conflicts Kansans had already seen, made government grow bigger. Kansans feared a federal government with enormous power over their lives. The growth of government in the Depression years had be accepted to prevent starvation. But now, many Kansans thought it was the time to back off, not speed up.

Kansans, however, would not get the time they so desperately needed. The rains came again in Kansas in 1938 and 1939 and the crops grew. But the winds of war that were sweeping Europe were forces so strong they could not be denied.

Re-Arming and The Draft

By 1940, Adolph Hitler's German "blitzkrieg," a lightening fast attack by land and air, had rolled over Poland and crushed Belgium, Holland and France. England stood alone against the German war machine and the United States watched with growing tension from the sidelines.

President Roosevelt pushed a rearmament program through Congress. It was designed to help England by supplying her with weapons. It was also intended to slowly beef up American defenses. Congress also passed a military draft.

Kansas was more divided than it had been since the slavery question of territorial days.

The congressional delegation, led by Senator Arthur Capper, was determined to keep the U. S. out of Europe's war. Capper called a draft in peacetime a "step toward dictatorship." He said America must mind her business, not the world's, if freedom was to be preserved.

Others in the state, liked and respected Emporia newspaper editor William Allen White, who took a different view.

White became head of the Committee to Defend America by Aiding the Allies. By sending weapons to Britain, American leaders could help stop Hitler without actually becoming involved.

Then, in December of 1941 came a blow that hurled America full force into war.

Kansas men registering for the draft in Wichita, 1942.
Photo courtesy of Wichita State University Special Collections

The Attack on Pearl Harbor

Most Kansans were at church on Sunday morning, December 7, 1941. They came home to hear radio reports of the Japanese bombing of Pearl Harbor, Hawaii. At 3:12 p.m., Kansas time, America was officially at war against Japan. The entire Kansas delegation, even Arthur Capper, voted in favor of the declaration.

In a matter of days, war was also declar[ed] against Germany and Italy. The Wichita Beac[on] pointed out that the Germans were behind the Japane[se] attack in an article on December 9, 1941:

"It was Hitler striking at Hawaii. It was Hitler flying over the West Coast. The elimination of the Japanese will not end the matter. We must go on and finish the job finally and completely...Until Hitler is finished there will be no security for any man or wom[an] on this earth."

Germany had negotiated a pact with Japan t[hat] bound the two nations together in their aggressions.

Kansas vowed to keep up a "ceaseless flow [of] defense materials from this area to America's arm[ed] forces."

Building the Machines for World War

The Kansas aircraft industry went into f[ull] swing. Wichita factories began to work day and ni[ght] producing airplanes for America's armed forces. [By] 1943, the men went off to fight and 31,000 wom[en] filled the factories. Every day, another four airplar[es] rolled off Wichita assembly lines. In Kansas City, [B-] 25s came off the production lines in the Fairf[ax] Industrial District.

Pre-fabricated housing was bolted together [to] provide shelter for the workers who flocked in fr[om] across the nation. Workers for the Army Corps [of] Engineers literally built a city in 15 months near t[he] aircraft plants in Wichita. They called it "Planevie[w]" because it offered a view of the planes being built [for] war. Planeview, with 4,400 dwellings and 20,0[00] residents, was the seventh largest city in Kans[as.] Planeview had the first shopping center in the Wich[ita] area, its own schools, police and fire departments, a[nd] the Fourth National Bank's first branch bank.

By percentage of population, Wichita had t[he] highest war-contract volume of any American city.

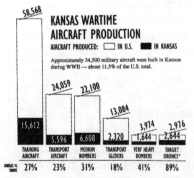

Kansas Wartime Aircraft Production
Chart courtesy of U. S. Army Air Force Office of Statistical Control

Kansas Aircraft Production

Beech Aircraft built and supplied some 5,257 Model 18 twin engine planes for training and use as light bombers for the United States and its Allies.

Cessna Aircraft also supplied several models of aircraft to the military during the war years. During 1941 the USAAF (U. S. Army Air Force) received 3 AT-8s with 295 horsepower Lycoming radial engines. These were used to train future pilots of multi-engine aircraft.

The Cessna Bobcat Series, was produced for the military in different formats for different jobs. Production continued until 1944 when a total of some ,504 Bobcats had been delivered.

The Boeing B-17 Flying Fortress, which entered into service in 1940, became the power punch against Germany. In daring daylight raids, the United States B-17 pounded German war factories cutting supplies to their military. These were strategic attacks meant to weaken Germany's ability to continue the war.

Assembly lines at Boeing *ran night and day to manufacture the B-29 for the war effort.*
Photo courtesy of Wichita-Sedgwick County Historical Museum

A Super-Bomber by Boeing

The first B-29 Superfortress heavy bomber was built in 1943. Almost half of the B-29s that flew in World War II were built in Wichita. In March of 1945, a formation of 325 B-29s created a firestorm over Tokyo. It was a B-29, the *Enola Gay,* that dropped the first atomic bomb on the city of Hiroshima.

The Boeing newsletter, *"Plane Talk"* often told the stories of workers. One family was that of Walter Moore and his daughters. Aril Elizabeth and Fern Maxine worked in the sheet metal assembly section of the aircraft company, commuting daily from their home in Kingman, Kansas.

They began working in December of 1942 and January of 1943. They were notified in November of 1943, that Walter Moore's son, Sgt. Boyd Eugene Moore had been killed in North Africa.

Walter Moore *and his daughters, Fern Maxine and Aril Elizabeth, are shown at work on the Boeing assembly line in 1943.*
Photo courtesy of Boeing, Wichita

Another Great War and its Aftermath   223

Other War Effort Towns

It was not just Wichita and Kansas City tha benefited from the boom in war business. Small towns also had their share of the effort.

Baxter Springs had a munitions factory.

Hugoton had plants producing carbon black fc ammunition.

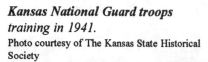

Kansas National Guard troops training in 1941.
Photo courtesy of The Kansas State Historical Society

Parsons and DeSoto had ammunition factories Atchison produced alcohol.

Otis produced helium fc balloons.

All told, Kansas had major role in building, trainin and equipping for the war. B November of 1943, it was amo the top 10 states in the Unite States in per capita share of wa contracts.

The Cavalry Becomes "Mechanized"

At Fort Riley, the war also brought rapid ar explosive change. The historic, somewhat romanti cavalry post that had been home to George Armstror Custer gave way to powerful new machinery.

(left) **Air Force Base in Garden City, 1944.** *One of 11 air bases during WWII.*
(right) **Garden City Air Force Training Base Cadets** *learning Morse Code, 1944.*
Photos courtesy of Finney County Historical Society

It was jeeps, tanks, trucks, and motorcycles that took the army to the front to fight. Horses were relegated to history.

It was also at Fort Riley, that black cavalry regiments were mustered, the descendants of the famed "Buffalo Soldiers." Heavyweight boxer Joe Louis was stationed there, training like other black Americans for a key role in the war. It was their experience that helped raise questions of America's own racial prejudice. If Hitler's racial superiority ideas were evil, how could America condone its own policies of racial segregation?

Like women, blacks found that the war opened new doors to them. The National Association for the Advancement of Colored People could challenge a system that called on black Americans to fight and die but denied them equal privileges at home. It was the beginning of a wave of questioning that would spread ever wider over the next three decades.

Other Military Bases

Fort Leavenworth also found itself in a new role as the war effort picked up speed. It became a major draftee induction center and a training post for ground troops.

Camp Phillips, near Salina, was another major infantry training center and Camp Funston was reactivated at Fort Riley for training infantry troops.

Around the state, other bases expanded, too. The Hutchinson Naval Air Station was built in 1942 on land purchased from Amish farmers. Another Naval air station was built at Olathe. Army air fields were established at Topeka, Coffeyville, Independence, Arkansas City, Winfield, and Garden City.

At Great Bend, Pratt, Walker, and at Smoky Hill Air Force Base near Salina, crews were trained to fly the B-29s. Smoky Hill became the biggest base in Kansas and the third largest in America. The first B-29s to fight in the Pacific took off from there.

There was another, unique training school at Smoky Hill. The military cooks were trained there in the only school of its kind in the nation.

This cartoon which appeared in a January of 1943 newspaper, addresses the women going off to work for the war effort.
Cartoon courtesy of The Wichita Eagle and Beacon Publishing Company

---

Typical B-29 flight meals

On long missions, flight meals were prepared for the crews:

Tomato soup
Swiss steak
Potato cakes
Buttered peas
Apple cobbler
Hot rolls
Coffee or cocoa

Today, the Smoky Hill base bombing range st
belongs to the Kansas Air National Guard. Fighter a
bomber aircraft from all over the United States still f
to Kansas to practice bombing skills.

*Coleman lamp employees are in front
of the company's downtown Wichita
factory in 1938.*
Photo courtesy of Wichita State University
Special Collections

Lanterns and Stoves

The Coleman Company had been in busine
since 1900. William Coffin Coleman, a man with pc
eyesight but a keen business vision, discovered
bright-burning lantern in a store window. He beg
working on ways to improve lighting. His stoves a
heaters warmed hundreds of homes during the Gr
Depression. Outdoorsmen found his portable stov
and easy-lighting lanterns to be useful campi
equipment.

But it was the U. S. Army's order for lanterns
1943, that brought the Coleman Company into the v
effort. Coleman's lantern soon quickly became
essential piece of equipment for soldiers at the front

Just months after Pearl Harbor, the U.
military asked Coleman for something more. Th
needed a stove that would burn almost any fuel
almost any condition. All the parts needed to
attached in order to prevent them from being lost
wartime conditions.

Working around the clock, Coleman employ
came up with the "GI Pocket Stove" in just 60 days

*Ad for Coleman's G.I. "Pocket
Stove."*
Photo courtesy of Wichita State University
Special Collections

"Gives the boy in the foxhole, tank or bomber a combination kitchen range, hot-water system, and heating plant that is easy to carry...The case makes a quart-sized stew pan. The top makes a smaller one. The stove lights instantly, burns with a blue flame that is practically invisible even at night. Temperature and altitude makes no difference, it works equally well in the humid jungle, in the Aleutians or high in a bomber."
Reader's Digest, August 1945.

In 1944, war columnist Ernie Pyle touted the stove and Bill Mauldin, famous war cartoonist, repeatedly included the "G.I. Stove" in his cartoons, thus securing the stove's reputation as one of the most popular non-shooting pieces of equipment to come out of World War II.

After WWII, the military's pocket stove was modified and manufactured on occasion. It was pressed into service during the Vietnam War. Until the early 1950s, Coleman manufactured a civilian model of the stove. The company redesigned a smaller stove that would burn unleaded fuel. The civilian single-burner stove is still manufactured in Kansas.

Doing Without to Win the War

As all of the nation's resources poured into making machines for war, food, clothing, and equipment for the armed forces, Kansans, like the rest of the country, went without.

Ration coupons allowed the purchase of small amounts of sugar, coffee, and meat. City dwellers planted "victory gardens" in their yards to provide food for their families. Farmers planted fence row to fence row in order to supply the Army.

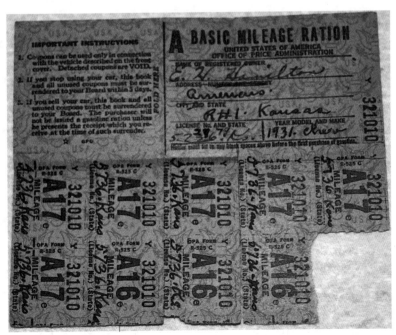

"A" Basic Mileage Ration Coupons.
Coupons courtesy of The Edmund H. Hamilton Family

MAKE THIS PLEDGE:
I pay no more than top legal prices
I accept no rationed goods
without giving up ration stamps

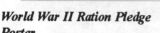

World War II Ration Pledge Poster.
Poster courtesy of Wichita State University Special Collections

Gasoline, too, was rationed. Passenger cars were limited to four gallons a week. Highway speed limits were reduced to 35 miles per hour to save gasoline. Rubber for tires became scarce. Flat tires became frequent.

People took "pledges" to do their share by not using up more rationed goods than they were entitled to ceive. Even the wealthy had to carry their ration coupons to the store.

When officials of the federal government made a statement about "sacrifice and suffering at home" a Kansas newspaper editor said there really was no suffering at home. He said it was all being done in Europe and the Pacific.

Farmers Answer the Call

War brought a need for the foods produced on Kansas farms and the state answered with an effort unsurpassed anywhere.

The slogan *"Wheat Will Win The War,"* popular in the first World War, came back. The "breadbasket of America" was now called the "granary (storehouse) of democracy."

Soybeans were called by some a "miracle crop." They would provide vegetable oil as well as protein foods and livestock food.

A combine in a Kansas wheat field.
Photo courtesy of Richard M. Berry for The Dangberg Foundation

They were added to the Kansas crop list. In 1942, Kansas farmers were asked to plant 125,000 acres. They responded with 300,000 acres.

Farmers could get all the gasoline they needed to raise crops, but finding labor to plant, cultivate, and harvest was not so easy. Thousands of farmers had left the land to go to war or to go to work in the aircraft factories, the munitions plants, and in the oil fields.

Again it was women who came to the rescue. Across America, women joined the "Women's Land Army of America." They marched into the fields as their fathers, husbands, and sons marched into battle. The old, the disabled, and the children joined the women. By 1945, the value of crops raised in Kansas had soared to $300 million, compared with $87 million in 1940.

Kansans who did not go to war worked in the fields to produce this great gain of crops. Many of them were women and children.

German Prison Camps

In 1943, the Army turne to Kansas for a place to hous German prisoners of war. Man of these German prisoner worked in the fields to hel increase the crop production.

A POW camp built nea Concordia housed about 4,00 prisoners. The 157-acre cam included 280 barracks and 2 auxiliary buildings, all wit electricity, and hot and col running water. The camp had it own hospital, library, fir

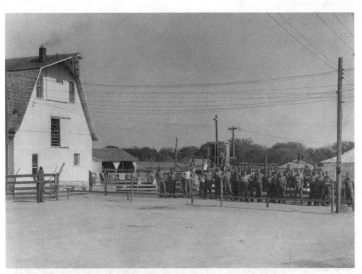

German prisoners of war were put to work doing crop research at Fort Hays Agricultural Experiment Station during World War II.
Photo courtesy of The Kansas State Historical Society

department, newspaper, gym, and athletic field. Whe the program proved popular, more camps were built a Hays and Peabody.

Unlike the resentment and prejudice that spran up during WWI, the Kansans of German descent wh were farmers in the area, had been U. S. citizens fc more than a generation.

They drew little attention. The prisoners foun little bitterness against them. They were well-treate had enough to eat and even were able to send foo home to their families.

Ben Neushafer was a boy in his teen when the German prisoners of war came t his family's farm near Enterprise to work

"They were real good help," said a 67-year-old Neushafer in 1995 in a newspaper interview. *"I never talked German, but my parents did. That was one reason they got along so well. They'd talk about the usual things -- about work, families."*

A barbed wire fence surrounds the German prisoner of war camp near Concordia in Cloud County.
Photo courtesy of The Kansas State Historical Society

The relationship that existed betwee Kansans and German POWs of World War II did muc to help heal the wounds of war.

Robert Linder, history professor at Kansas Stat University in Manhattan, said his father supervise prisoners at Camp Phillips near Salina.

inder says:

"It took the edge off the hatred that was being generated during the war. I can remember as a little kid singing patriotic songs and being taught to hate Germans and Japanese," he said. *"The experience, where German prisoners had contact with Kansans, helped Kansans see the human face of Germans and vice versa. It contributed to the healing after the war. And it contributed to the memory of lots of Germans who ended up in the Soviet zone and longed to have something better than they had, something similar to what they once had in Kansas."*

Some of the German prisoners had relatives ving in Kansas. It was not uncommon for one brother r sister to have immigrated to the United States and nother to have remained behind in Germany. Nieces nd nephews of some Kansas farmers wound up first in e German army and then in a Kansas prisoner of war amp.

These prisoners were visited regularly by members of their family who lived in Kansas. They ould bake cookies and bring the prisoners food and ther personal items.

Without a doubt, the impact of the Kansas-erman prisoner connection was extremely powerful nd enduring.

angerous Prisoners Turned ver to the Army

German prisoners who were considered escape sks were put to work doing hard labor at Fort Riley here they were under guard.

"The idea was to keep them so tired that they wouldn't have the energy to do anything," said Scott rice, a historian at Fort Riley. There was no escape.

The Army at Fort Riley gave the German risoners the task of building a tall stone wall that runs e full length of the Main Post, allowing them only owbars for tools. The wall still stands today, looking omewhat crude and ragged compared to the fine mestone masonry of the post's historic buildings.

Prairie Spirit

During World War II, **Joe Bossi** was a pilot from Arkansas City whose plane went down in the Bermuda Triangle — on the night of Dec. 5, 1945. His Avenger torpedo bomber and four other planes made up Flight 19, who were practicing a bombing run out of Fort Lauderdale Naval Air Base. The planes and their crews mysteriously disappeared and were never seen again. Their disappearance helped fuel the myth about the Bermuda Triangle.

Dwight David Eisenhower, 1909. His Abilene high school graduation portrait.

Photo courtesy of The Dwight D. Eisenhower Library

Ironically, it was primarily immigrant German stone masons, masters at their craft and having the correct tools, who had built most of those better looking buildings. They did it in the 50 years before the prisoners of war came and toiled on the wall.

A Kansan Leads Them All

There was no Kansan better known during World War II than Dwight David Eisenhower, who was Supreme Commander of the Allied Forces. He was born in Texas but moved to Kansas at a young age.

Eisenhower graduated from Abilene High School in 1909 and worked for two years at the Belle Spring Creamery before winning an appointment to West Point Military Academy.

Eisenhower was proud of his Kansas roots and the value system he learned by hard work in Abilene. He was known to the troops as a "regular guy" who talked and joked easily with the men under his command. As Supreme Allied Commander, he had the job of planning the most difficult campaign of the war, the invasion and liberation of Europe.

In the hours before the invasion started, Eisenhower visited the troops in the field. He was going to be asking a lot of them to give up their lives, he said, and he wanted to look them in the face.

Among those who remember Eisenhower's visit is Sherman Oyler, a retired Topeka school teacher, who grew up in Wellington.

Oyler said that he recalls the general had wanted to speak with *"anybody from Kansas."*

Oyler later parachuted behind the German lines at Omaha Beach with the 502nd Parachute Infantry Regiment of the

Unnamed American infantrymen line up for rations in this early 1945 winter photo.

Photo courtesy of National Archives

101st Airborne. He now calls the meeting with Eisenhower: *"one of the defining moments of my life."*

The General, fearful of the weather which delayed the landing for a day, drafted a news release. It read:

"The troops, the air and Navy, did all that bravery and devotion to duty could do. If any blame or fault attaches to the attempt, it is mine alone."

The Tide Turns

On June 6, 1944, "D-Day," the Allies landed at Normandy and the great, final push to free Europe from German control was begun.

Marshall Carlson's home is in the northeast Kansas community of Clay Center near where he grew up. He says he doesn't remember what he and the other men on board the landing ships were talking about in the hours before dawn of June 6th.

He does remember, he says, that a lot of the men were seasick and throwing up. The ship was dark and cold and smelled awful. He remembers the shell that hit before they landed, killing 20 of the men on board. He remembers men drowning because the water was too deep and their gear was too heavy for them to swim.

John Franklin Branson, born 1917 in Peabody, related to Jacob Branson of the Wakarusa War of 1855, became a Kansas oil well worker, built Liberty ships in Long Beach, California, and then prepared for the war in 1945.
Photo courtesy of The John Branson Family

A Kansan at the front

Merritt Worley grew up in Allen and was a cattle truck driver when the call to war came. He was 21 years old when he landed on Omaha Beach and with the 5th Armored, 85th Cavalry Reconnaissance he fought his way through Europe.

The above photo shows Worley (right) and a fellow soldier in front of an armored vehicle in France.
Photos courtesy of The Merritt Worley Family

KEEPER OF THE PLAINS

Photo courtesy of Avery Postcards

Prairie Spirit

Blackbear Bosin was a Kiowa-Comanche who came to Kansas from Oklahoma in the 1940s to work as an illustrator for Boeing Aircraft. One of his best known works is the *Keeper of the Plains*, a 44-foot steel statue of an Indian placed in 1974 at the confluence of the Arkansas and Little Arkansas rivers.

In World War II, 215,000 Kansas soldie served with other soldiers from across t United States, Great Britain and Canada.

On April 12, 1945, they got sad nev from home. Their commander in chie President Franklin D. Roosevelt, had died. T Vice-President Harry S. Truman of Missou was sworn into the office of President.

On May 8, 1945, Germany surrendere The war in Europe was over. Now, only Japa was left to conquer.

End of The War

President Truman had made a tough decisio He would use the most powerful weapon in America arsenal -- the nuclear bomb-- to bring a quick end to t war with Japan. It would save thousands of lives allied servicemen.

The pilot chosen to fly the mission was Bri General Paul Tibbets and the plane chosen to carry was a B-29 named the *Enola Gay*. On August 6, 194 the bomb was dropped on Hiroshima, Japan. Two da later, another nuclear bomb was dropped on Nagasal A week later, Japan surrendered.

A Kansan Brings the Flag

In Tokyo Bay, Admiral William Frederi "Bull" Halsey Jr., one of the leading U. S. nav officers, was in command of the Third Fleet, of whi the USS Missouri was the flagship. It was on the US Missouri that Japan was to officially sign documents surrender.

Halsey sent a dispatch to the U. S. Nav Academy requesting that a historic United States fla be rushed by officer courier on the next availab transportation to Tokyo.

The flag had only 31 stars. It was the on American flag ever to fly over the Japanese Empire.

Lt. John Bremyer, a McPherson native, was stationed Washington D. C. He did his art in World War II to make sure e top secret documents in the fficer Messenger Mail Center ent through as they should. He as the officer in charge.

Bremyer volunteered to ansport the flag. He gathered a ovie camera and a still photo amera to take with him. His urney involved 10 planes and ore than 100 hours of travel me.

The Navy's original tention had been to fly the flag uring the surrender ceremony, ut because it was so old, istorians feared that the banner ould be destroyed in the apping wind. Instead, the flag as displayed behind glass during e ceremony. Bremyer stood by e display, and returned with the ag after the surrender ceremony.

Today, the flag is in the possession of the U.S. aval Academy Museum in Annapolis, Maryland.

USS Missouri on September 2, 1945, the special flag, on the right, in the photo was on display.
Photo courtesy of Wichita State University Special Collections

he Soldiers Come Home

Abilene's favorite son, Dwight Eisenhower ame home for a visit in June of 1945. His reception as bigger than anything Kansas had ever seen before.

The Abilene Reflector-Chronicle wrote about it n June 22:

"General Dwight D. Eisenhower, back home at last among the people he grew up with, today expressed great emotion as he accepted their acclaim, then very seriously called for solid support by the American people of President Truman in his efforts to solve the war problems and unite the nation."

Eisenhower also paid tribute to his hometow
that reception. The Reflector-Chronicle quoted him

*"Every boy dreams of the day when he comes
back home after making good. I too so dreamed but
my dream of 45 or more years ago has been
exceeded beyond the wildest stretch of the
imagination. The proudest thing that I can say today
is that I'm from Abilene."*

When the news of the final surrender of Ja
came in August, Kansas, like the rest of America, w
wild. Church bells rang. People in cars formed li
for parades, honking their horns as they drove up
down the streets. Flags were waved and people wav

In Salina, the celebration was not planned, bu
happened all the same. The Salina Journal wrote th

*"There had been no celebration planned in
Salina. It was not necessary. The news, so long
awaited...was spark enough to touch off all the
exuberance needed. There was only the church
service, city-wide in scope, which began in
Memorial Hall at 8, where people of all
denominations, color and creed were asked to
gather and give thanks that the mighty conflict
had ended."*

In Kansas cities, towns and on farmsteads, th
were many who did not come home. More than 3,
Kansas men had died.

Thousands more were severely wounded.

One of them, Bob Dole of Russell, was hit by
exploding shell on April 14, 1945, less than a mo
before the war in Europe was over.

He was 22 and a college student who wanted
be a doctor. The shell ripped through his ri
shoulder, tearing his arm from his body. The fingers
his left hand were numb. His right arm was surgica
tethered to his body with muscle taken from his thi
When his wounds healed, his right arm was more th
two inches shorter than his left. And it was numb fr
shoulder to fingertips.

*1976, Gerald Ford kept his promise to
launch his campaign for President in
Russell if Bob Dole agreed to be his
Vice-Presidential running mate.*
Photo courtesy of Russell County Historical
Society

The young man who had wanted to be a doctor had to find another career. He became a lawyer, a politician and was then elected to the United States Senate.

Robert Dole in Russell, Kansas on the campaign trail for President.
Photo courtesy of The Wichita Eagle and Beacon Publishing Company

He became one of the most powerful senators Kansas has ever had. Eventually, he was a candidate for President of the United States.

Bob Dole in 1941 graduation from Russell High School.
Photo courtesy of Russell County Historical Society

Post-War Boom: Buildings and Babies

Americans had won the war and saved the world. Now was the time to get on with the job of building a nation worthy of its heroes.

In Kansas, Governor Alf Landon said:

"We have a reconstruction and rehabilitation job ahead that will tax the tremendous capabilities of our country to the limit. We must meet it."

Women could now leave their factory jobs and get back to making homes and raising children. Between 1946 and 1952, it seemed that every woman in America became pregnant. The post-war births created a population growth that has been labeled the *"baby boom"* and its members, the *"baby boomers."*

The drive to achieve "normal" created a decade that has become what everyone wanted, the ideal family life of the 1950s.

The Dymaxion House

A futuristic housing idea was the Dymaxion House. Designed by an architect Buckminster Fuller and built by Beech Aircraft after World War II.

Fuller actually conceived the idea for the house in 1927. The term "Dymaxion" was coined in 1929 by a copy-writer who combined three of Fuller's favorite words: dynamic, ion, and maximum.

When Fuller designed the house, he used sheet aluminu originally intended for Beech airplanes. The theory was that the house would be light, weighing only 3 tons, compared t a normal 150 ton house. The house could be packed in a case and shipped by air to any place in the world.

Beech became involved in the project after WWII in order to employ aircraft factory workers and solve the severe housing shortage.

Fuller was not completely satisfied with the house and the project fell through.

By the 1950s, interest in marketing the house wained.

In 1992, the one and only Dymaxion House ever assembled was moved from Butler County to the Henry Ford Museum & Greenfield Village in Dearborn, Michigan.

Lustron Houses

One of the government's short-lived answer to the national housing shortage was the Lustron home.

Carl Strandlund had the idea for houses, which were enameled metal exteriors, interiors, and roofs. The federal government loaned Strandlund $37.4 million.

They featured radiant heat, air conditioning, combination automatic dishwasher, large picture windows, built-in cabinets, and closets galore. Their strongest selling point: no maintenance. Homeowners could use magnets instead of nails to hang their pictures. Paint chips or dents could be repaired by taking the panel to the auto body shop.

Potential buyers could choose among 1, 2, or 3 bedroom homes ranging from $8,500. to $11,500. They could be shipped. It took only 7 days to assemble.

Almost 80 houses remain in Kansas and if built in today's market the cost would be $30,000 to $40,000.

At the time the "normal" life in Kansas was le than the ideal life elsewhere. There were not enou houses. There was a shortage of everything. Befo comfort could be created, things had to manufactured and houses had to be built. In Kans the housing that had been built for factory workers w needed to house the returning GIs. Structures intend as "temporary" became permanent.

Every family wanted a house of its own and backyard for a swingset. Government, mindful of t threat of communism, saw home ownership as a way define the American capitalist ideal and "eve homeowner a capitalist" became a slogan.

The "G. I. Bill" flew through Congress a returning veterans found themselves eligible f college eduction and living expenses. For no mon down, they could get guaranteed home loans.

The burst of technology that had built machin of war turned full force on manufacturing for domes life. Television was illuminated with shows li *"Ozzie and Harriet," "Leave it to Beaver,"* a *"Father Knows Best."*

Factories that had built planes for war began build planes for travel, mail and, other freight items

Factories that built tanks and army trucks beg

making cars, refrigerators, freezers and washing machines for the "goods-starved" consumers.

Medical "miracles" from the battlefield saved lives and limbs at home. Mental health care improved too. Changes in the law defined mental illness as a treatable disease and Topeka State Hospital was accredited as a psychiatric hospital.

Winter Hospital located in Topeka became a psychiatric hospital, administered by the Veterans Administration.

Private business helped. The Menninger Clinic expanded in December of 1946; and the close cooperation between the state and the veterans institutions made Topeka a world-wide center for mental health care. Drs. Karl and Will Menninger were involved in the clinic for the advancement of mental health care. Dr. Will Menninger helped the Veterans Administration to see the need for psychiatric care.

Dr. C. F. Menninger in his office.
Photo courtesy of The Kansas State Historical Society

The Issue of Alcohol Returns

Kansans could see much that needed to be done. More than 100,000 Kansas farms were still without running water and electricity. Better highways were needed. Returning GIs who wanted to start businesses needed loans. Thousands of the boys who had gone off to war were young men now who wanted to go to college.

In Kansas, there was another issue that could not be ignored. For 60 years, the state had outlawed the sale and manufacturing of liquor.

National prohibition had come and gone without changing anything in Kansas.

In the 1946 governor's election, the question of legalizing alcohol seemed to be the big one.

Prohibition in Kansas was all about the prevention of scenes like this one in the early 20th century.
Photo courtesy of Wichita State University Special Collections

Democrat Harry Woodring led the "wet" movemen
He argued that liquor was already being sold.

Republican Frank Carlson who had served s
terms in Congress opposed Woodring. Carlson didn
say much on the issue except that he would put it to
vote of the people. Carlson won the election. F
formed a program of social, economic, agricultura
and industrial reform. In 1948, the promised vote o
liquor came. Kansas, "dry" for 60 years, went "wet.

Getting Down to Work

Kansas got on with business in 1949. A twen
year highway plan was passed. Social welfare a
mental hospital programs were reorganized. T
medical school at the University of Kansas w
expanded and its dean, Dr. Franklin Murphy, made a
effort to get doctors to practice in rural communities

The state took a hard look at the problems wi
rivers and floods and decided that water conservatio
and flood control programs were a high priority.

Handling the Floods

Water comes through the dam and
enters the new river stream bed
following the construction of Cheney
Dam, a water reservior project.
Photo courtesy of Wichita State University
Special Collections

Kansas had a long way
go to build the flood contr
and irrigation systems that ha
been urged by the Division
Water Resources as early
1927. But in 1949, with th
help of federal money, the fir
two big reservoirs in Kans
were built The U. S. Arm
Corps of Engineers built dan
on the Smoky Hill and Fa
Rivers to create Kanopolis an
Fall River Reservoirs.

Not everyone, and especially not the farme
whose land was about to be flooded to make lake
agreed on where dams and lakes should be located.

The proposal to dam the Blue River and build Tuttle Lake made people especially angry because of the prime bottomland that would go under water. (See rainfall chart on page 284.)

In July of 1951, Kansas received a reminder of why the dams and reservoirs were needed. One of the greatest Missouri River basin floods in history occurred. Land from Central Kansas to Eastern Missouri went under water.

In Kansas, thousands of people lost their homes, several people died and billions of dollars in damage was done. Railroad bridges were swept away in Topeka. Industrial districts of Kansas City, built in the low lying areas along the Kansas and Missouri Rivers, were destroyed.

It didn't completely end the argument, but Tuttle Creek Dam was built.

The next year, 1952, a drought began that lasted until 1956. A possible return of the dust storms was a reminder for Kansans that soil conservation could not be ignored.

In 1958, the state became involved in the federal Water Supply Act. The act allowed water storage in federal reservoirs to be used for drinking water and for irrigation in times of drought.

Construction of the lakes often fell under the direction of several other agencies. Besides the Army Corps of Engineers, there was the Bureau of Reclamation and the Kansas Park and Resources Authority.

The state park system was spurred by the development of lakes; and the resulting reservoirs offered a recreation source for Kansans. Boats became commonplace in a land where they were once oddities.

Operations by the fishery division of The Fish and Game Commission were enlarged. New species of fish were introduced in Kansas water: white bass, followed by walleyes, northern pike, and the striped bass.

The large public land areas around the lakes provided hours of enjoyment for people from all walks of life. Camping and picnicking, once confined to the city parks, blossomed into a way of life for many families.

Prairie Spirit

The **Docking family** of Lawrence and Arkansas City has been one of the more prominent in Kansas politics. George Docking and his son, Robert, were the first father and son to become governor. George was elected in 1956 and 1958. Robert served as governor in 1967. He was the first governor to be elected four times to the office — and while he as in office the Kansas Constitution was changed from a two year term to four year terms. The law was also changed so that a person can serve only two terms in a row. Tom Docking, Roberts son and George's grandson, ran for governor in 1986 and lost to Mike Hayden. Tom Docking served at lieutenant governor in the 1980s.

After the 1955 tornado, National Guardsmen and volunteers search through the rubble that was once the town of Udall.

Photo courtesy of The Wichita Eagle and
Beacon Publishing Company

The twisted remains of an automobile found after the Udall tornado on May 25, 1955.

Photo courtesy of The Wichita Eagle and
Beacon Publishing Company

The Worst Weather Disaster

The night of May 25, 1955 brought the deadlie[st] tornado in the history of Kansas when Udall, a tin[y] farming community in Cowley County, was qui[te] literally blown off the away.

Seventy-seven people died that night and mor[e] than 400 were injured when the twister struck just aft[er] 10:30 p.m. It was just minutes after the televisio[n] weatherman had reported that the "danger of sever[e] weather is over."

Every home and building in Udall was eith[er] destroyed or damaged that night. This all happene[d] within a few seconds when the tornado struck.

In a little town, known for the elm trees whos[e] branches formed a canopy of shade over the street[s,] there were no trees left.

As late as the mid-1990s, residents still kept th[e] trees tightly trimmed, remembering all too well th[e] branches that crashed through windows and roofs th[at] night.

Looking back on the night 40 years later, residents talked of the miracles of people being alive among the rubble.

Rapid Industrial Growth

Kansas businesses solved the problem of what to do with the thousands of people who had flocked to the cities and to the war production centers during the war: Put them to work building all the things Americans wanted.

Aircraft plants began building commercial planes and business planes for rapidly growing companies.

The four big companies that had prospered during the war continued to build aircraft for peace. Beech, Boeing, Cessna, and now Learjet all found that the demand for airplanes kept their factories busy.

Not only building planes for peacetime business, Boeing continued building military aircraft such as the B-52 introduced in 1954 because of the Cold War.

The Kansas oil fields produced the gasoline..

Kansans wanted a house built with the new sheets of "plasterboard" or "drywall." These were produced in factories in Kansas's "Gypsum Hills" around Medicine Lodge.

Boeing assembly lines *ran day and night to manufacture passenger planes.*
Photo courtesy of Wichita-Sedgwick County Historical Museum

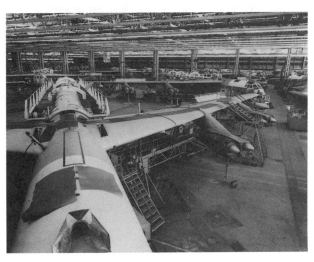

B-52s being built *during the arms race with the Soviet Union.*
Photo courtesy of Wichita-Sedgwick County Historical Museum

A 'Cold War' with The Soviet Union Emerges

The Soviet Socialist Republic, America's ally in WWII, was forcing more and more of Europe under communist domination. The Soviet Union was, on paper, a confederation of states.

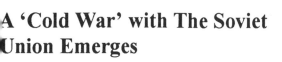

Another Great War and its Aftermath   243

In reality, it was a group of countries ruled from Moscow, the capital of the Soviet Union.

The Communist Army of Mao Tse-tung fough and pushed the Nationalist Chinese Army forcing the leader Chiang Kai shek and the movement f democracy to flee to the island of Taiwan. There the asked for help from the United States to remai independent and free.

The term 'Cold War' was coined to describe th struggle to maintain the balance of power (weapon between the free world and the growing Communi world.

A Hot War in Korea

American infantryman comforts a fellow soldier during the Korean conflict.
Photo courtesy of National Archives

In 1950, North Kore soldiers crossed the lir separating Communist Nor Korea from Democratic Sou Korea. The United Natior had guaranteed South Korea security since World War with the help of the Unite States and other soldier stationed in South Kore. North Korean guerrill fighters, aided by Communi China and the Soviet Unic began attacking the south an the United Nations troops. Their goal was to brin Korea under Northern communist rule.

Kansas and all of America was war weary. B as the conflict grew so did U. S. involvement with th United Nations against the North Koreans war was n declared. It was called a "conflict," or a "polic action," a "war."

However, in this "police action" for the Unite Nations, 53,000 Americans were killed in two years some of the bloodiest fighting in American histor. Other U. N. member countries also lost troops in th conflict. For the first time, the conflict involved a active battle for minds as well as an assault of bodies

As it had in conflicts before, Kansas responded with both troops for battle and training at home. Fort Riley trained a new group of soldiers and Fort Leavenworth's Command and Staff College educated a new group of officers. World War II veterans found themselves recalled to duty in a different kind of war and young soldiers were trained to join them in combat.

It was a new kind of conflict, one that involved American soldiers not just in a campaign to win battles. It was two differing governments, each wanting to win with its own political strategies.

The United Nation's strategy was to maintain a balance of power between the forces of Democracy, led by America and its allies and the forces for Communism led by the Soviet Union and Communist China.

Marshall Army Airfield at Fort Riley.
Photo courtesy of The Kansas State Historical Society

Brown vs. The Topeka Board of Education

In Topeka, in 1950, Oliver Brown wanted his six-year-old daughter, Linda to attend their neighborhood school, Sumner Elementary. It was only a few blocks from the Brown's home. However, it was an all-white school.

When Brown took the issue to the Topeka Board of Education, the board told him she would have to attend at Monroe Elementary, an all black school. Monroe Elementary was across town, which meant that Linda would have to walk to school and cross several railroad tracks to get there each day.

The Browns and several parents in their neighborhood petitioned to school board members to change their minds. The board didn't.

The Browns took the case to court. In 1951 panel of three Kansas judges ruled against the paren

The Browns and other parents appealed, whi sent the case to the United States Supreme Court Washington, D. C. Although there were three oth cases that were similar to the Brown's and ready to heard, theirs was the first case.

In 1954, the Supreme Court ruled that "separ but equal" schools for different races was illegal.

The vote had repercussions all across Ameri especially in the south where governors vowed th schools would not be integrated.

On October 26, 1992, Congress passed pub law 102-525 which established the Monroe Schoo National Historical Park Site. It is in the process being restored so that people can visit it and learn me about the importance of this site sometime soon.

A Kansan for President

President Eisenhower and his wife, Mamie, wave to well-wishers during *Ike's 1956 re-election campaign.*
Photo courtesy of The Dwight D. Eisenhower Library

In 1952, Kansas's greatest hero, Dwight Eisenhower, was nominated as the Republic candidate for President of the United States. November, he won in a landslide over Senator Ad Stevenson of Illinois, who was the Democra candidate. The Korean War ended in 1953 and pe was at hand. Eisenhower was easily re-elected t second term in 1956. In 1957, President Eisenhov sent 1,000 federal troops to Little Rock, Arkansas enforce the integration of a Little Rock High Sch resulting from the court decision of Brown vs. Topeka Board of Education.

In the remainder of his term, Eisenhov presided over a time of prosperity, hope, and optimi in America. The national feeling of quiet and w being was so great that his administration was of criticized for "doing nothing."

The record shows, however, that times were so quiet as the memories might portray them to be. fact, a great many things were happening, some which would become far more noticed in the deca that followed.

More Questions Raised

Women were also beginning to question why their roles must be in the background, why women should stay home and men should have careers.

Their efforts during the war had shown many women that they were just as capable as men of making decisions, having a job and deciding how to spend money, and how to vote.

In Washington, Senator Joseph McCarthy was questioning the loyalty of everyone from other congressmen to movie stars, business leaders and ordinary citizens. This was a time when fear of Communism, and what it might do to America, ran wild. McCarthy's hearings on "Un-American Activities" accused a widely divergent number of people of having communist leanings. McCarthy's claims were not sustained. He was condemned by the Senate, and he resigned in disgrace.

Eisenhower was seeking answers on how to keep America safe and how to stop the spread of communism both at home and abroad.

He negotiated a peace in Korea, but it was a pact that involved long-term commitment to maintaining order with international troops. As late as the millennium year 2,000, American troops are still on duty in Korea, patrolling the border that divides the north from the south. Fears of North Korean aggression, including the possibility that nuclear weapons might be built in Korea linger today, in the 21st century.

Eisenhower pledged to send U. S. troops to any Middle Eastern country requesting help to fight communist aggression, a policy that became known as the "Eisenhower Doctrine."

President Dwight David Eisenhower in the Oval Office of The White House, February 29, 1956.
Photo courtesy of The Dwight D. Eisenhower Library

With his Secretary of State, John Foster Dull[es] he created the Southeast Asia Treaty Organizatio[n] pledging American resources to stop the spread [of] communism in that part of the world.

He proposed an international agency to sha[re] information on atomic energy.

During his presidency on October 4, 1957 t[he] Soviets launched the first man-made satellite, Sputn[ik] One. In response, on July 29, 1958, Preside[nt] Eisenhower signed the National Aeronautics and Spa[ce] Act. The next day he then requested $125 million [to] fund the project of the National Aeronautics and Spa[ce] Administration.

Eisenhower invited Soviet President Nik[ita] Khrushchev to visit the United States and w[as] scheduled to make a trip to the Soviet Union for furth[er] talks.

However, in 1960, a U. S. U-2 spy plane w[as] shot down over the Soviet Union. Eisenhow[er] admitted he had known that spy flights had been goi[ng] on for some four years. His invitation to the Sov[iet] Union was withdrawn.

In January, 1961, during the last weeks [of] Eisenhower's administration, the United States a[nd] Cuba broke all diplomatic relations. Tensions betwe[en] the United States, Cuba and the Soviet Uni[on] continued on into President Kennedy's administrati[on] in the early 1960s.

Prairie Spirit

One of the most popular senators of the early 20th century was **Frank Carlson** of Concordia. Calson spent more than 40 years as a politician including being a governor, U.S. Senator and U.S. representative. He was one of several Kansas Republicans who convinced Dwight D. Eisenhower to run for president.

Questions Turn to Conflicts

In the months and years after the Eisenhow[er] presidency, January 1961, many of the questions t[hat] came up during the quiet time when nothing w[as] happening would give way to open conflict. Kan[sas] and the rest of the nation tried to find answers.

The stage was set for an era of turbulence a[nd] change.

ABILENE KANSAS

on the grounds of the Eisenhower Center, the
lower Chapel, Place of Meditation, is the final
ng place for President Dwight D. Eisenhower, his wife
mie and a son, Doug Dwight. The bronze sculpture by
obert Dean was dedicated in 1985.

post car

You have GOT to
visit the Eisenhower
Center in Abilene. Ike
Eisenhower was a great
leader in World War II,
and later became
president. The museum
is awesome!

Avery postcards, P.O. Box 20346, Wichita, KS 67208

© 1991 Photos by John Avery A-24
L-5045-E Printed in Canada

Another Great War and its Aftermath   249

Historical Events

1960 - Jim Ryun breaks track records

1961 - John Kennedy elected President

1963 - John Kennedy assassinated

1966 - Topeka Tornado

1968 - Robert Kennedy speaks at KS University

1969 - Man lands on the Moon

1970s - The Energy Crisis hits Kansas

1971 - Bob Dole chosen as Republican National
Committee Chairman

1976 - Dole runs for Vice-President

1977 - Tractorcades to Washington for farm aid

1978 - Whippoorwill goes down

1985 - Wolf Creek Generating Station goes online

CRUZPAGAN 99

Chapter 11

Decades of Change

Chapter 11

Decades of Change: The 60s, 70s & 80s

> *"Let the word go forth from this time and place, to friend and foe alike, that the torch is passed to a new generation of Americans -- born in this century, tempered by war, disciplined by a hard and bitter peace and unwilling to witness or permit the slow undoing of those human rights to which this nation has always been committed and to which we are committed today at home and around the world.*
>
> *"Let every nation know, whether it wishes us well or ill, that we shall pay any price, bear any burden, meet any hardship, support any friend, oppose any foe to assure the survival and the success of liberty.*
>
> *"Let both sides unite to heed in all corners of the earth the command of Isaiah - 'to undo the heavy burdens...and let the oppressed go free.'*
>
> *"All this will not be finished in the first hundred days, nor will it be finished in the first thousand days, nor in the life of this administration, nor even perhaps in our lifetime on this planet.*
>
> *"But let us begin..."*
>
> ***John Kennedy Inaugural Address, January 20, 1961***

A Bold Challenge

President John F. Kennedy's inaugural address was a stirring challenge. It was to get about the business of building a world that came with the new decade of the 1960s.

This challenge is about catching and passing the Soviets in the space race, about putting a man on the moon, about owning a home and about moving up the corporate ladder.

This world of the new decade is

Cedar Crest was built in 1928 and bequeathed to the state in 1955. It became the residence for Kansas Governors in 1962.
Photo courtesy of Avery Postcards

also about equal opportunity for Black people and other racial or ethnic minorities. Its about smashing the glass ceiling that has kept women from rising to top-level jobs. It is about enjoying the success of capitalism.

In the 1960 election, Kansas chose a war hero of its own to go to Washington. Republican Bob Dole of Russell was elected to his first term in the United States House of Representatives.

Setbacks Are There

Despite the fact that America was riding high on a wave of certainty, there were challenges in the early 1960s.

A communist government in Cuba, just 90 miles away from Florida, was a huge threat. In the 1950s, President Dwight Eisenhower had approved a CIA plan for American air support for a Cuban Refugee Army from America to invade Cuba. This was to drive the Communists out of Cuba.

Kennedy tried, with humbling failure, to execute the plan. The new president hesitated to commit American air support.

The invasion of April 17, 1961 failed. Hundreds more refugees from Communist Cuba then came to the United States.

Among them were Carlos and Idalia Ruiz, who came first to Miami and then to Kansas. Ruiz, a doctor, had been jailed by the Castro regime for activities against the government.

Republican women of Kansas attending the 1960 Republican National Convention are shown with Pat Nixon (wife of presidential candidate Richard M. Nixon.)
Photo courtesy of Wichita State University Special Collections

Ruiz came to Kansas to take a job at the La[
State Hospital. He later returned to school at
University of Kansas to study psychiatry. He op[
the first, private psychiatric clinic in western Ka[
and both he and his wife became Unites States citi[
in 1970.

A Fallen Hero

Most older Kansans, maybe your parents
for sure your grandparents, are old enoug[
remember November 22, 1963. Some can describe
where they were and what they were doing when
heard the news. Just as their parents remembered [
Harbor, they remember the murder of a president.

John F. Kennedy was shot and killed in D[
Texas that day in November. The assassin, Lee Ha[
Oswald, had connections to Cuba. When Oswald
shot and killed, just three days later, questions
conspiracy arose. Despite official reports that Os[
was a lone assassin, many Americans re[
convinced that the whole story is still unknown.

What is known is this: In one shattering mi[
an era of innocent optimism ended and an era of sh[
faith, distrust, violence and bloodshed began.

Kansas sunflower pin worn to the
1960 Republican National Convention.
Photo courtesy of Wichita State University
Special Collections

A Kansan Understands

During the summer of 1965, the worst ri[
America had ever seen took place in the Watts Se[
of Los Angeles, California.

In Kansas, it was hard for many peop[
understand the rage that boiled over into those rio[

However, there was one Kansan, watchin[
television in his Kansas City, Kansas home,
understood perfectly.

In 1965, Newton native Joe Sears had been
porter on the Atchison, Topeka and Santa Fe railr[
for 29 years. At one time, long ago, he had told a
worker that he'd like to be a brakeman some day.

e still remembers the answer he got: *"... you can't become a brakeman until your skin changes color."*

In all his years of work, he'd never gotten a promotion. In July of 1965, when the new Civil Rights legislation went into effect, he applied again to be a brakeman.

This time, he was told he was too old for the job. He was 53; the maximum age for a brakemen was 5. In May of 1966, he filed a complaint with the Commission on Civil Rights in Topeka.

It was 1993 before his case was finally resolved. Mr. Sears was 81 when a court awarded him and 273 other black employees of the Santa Fe Railroad $24.7 million in lost wages and damages resulting from illegal discrimination. Sears was happy with the money. But, he said, his case was never about money. He said: *"The only thing I wanted was a job that paid good enough that I could take care of my family. That's all there was to it."*

It seemed to many blacks, especially young people, that Joe Sears' choice to follow the legal process was just too slow.

During the summer of 1967, protests swept across the state. There were sit-ins in Emporia. There were demonstrations in Topeka. And at Wichita East High School students walked out of classes.

Other Means of Expression

Some Kansans found a way to express their feelings about social strife, racial conflict and war through the arts and music.

Fort Scott native, Gordon Parks taught himself photography and eventually got a job on *Life* magazine. In 1962, Harper & Row publishing company offered him money to write a book about his Kansas childhood memories.

Gordon Parks *by artist Jose Cruzpagan.*
Artwork courtesy of The Dangberg Foundation

Eva Jessye, from Coffeyville, Caney, Iola and Pittsburgh.
Photo courtesy of The Wichita Eagle and Beacon Publishing Company

The *Learning Tree* wa made into a movie. He ha directed movies. Mr. Parks live in New York City and continu to take photos, write and compo music.

Hutchinson's own, Mik Love is lead singer and one of th original members of *The Bea Boys*.

The band, *Kansas* wa formed in Topeka and recorded best-selling hit, *Dust in the Win*

Eva Jessye, was a singer, actress, compose choral director, author, and a poet. She became the fir African-American woman to succeed as a profession choir director. She was choral director of th Broadway show, *Porgy and Bess*. She died in 1992.

When Americans sat down to enjoy the levity some of television's first sit-coms, they watched Vivi Vance portray Ethel Mertz in *I Love Lucy*. Or, the watched *Leave it to Beaver* with Hugh Beaumont Lawrence portraying Beaver's father, Ward Cleaver.

The long-running western hit *Gunsmoke* ma Dodge City a cowtown icon. Milburn Stone of Burrt and Larned, portrayed Dr. Adams. He won an Emm for a 1968 episode of the show.

At the movies, they watched Dennis Hopp from Dodge City appear in *Rebel Without a Caus Giant, Easy Rider* and *Hoosiers*.

Elizabeth Layton of Wellsville became know for artwork that detailed the issues of the da women's rights, racism, hunger, and the problems the elderly.

Kansas Athletes Go Far

Vivian Vance was born in Cherryvale but grew up in Independence. Her contract as Ethel required her to wear "frompy" housedresses and remain 10-20 pounds overweight - so as not to take the spotlight away from Lucille Ball.
Photo courtesy of The Kansas State Historical Society

Wilt "The Stilt" Chamberlin, fro Lawrence, turned down offers from more than 2(colleges in 1955 to accept "Phog" Allen's invitation attend the University of Kansas. He played on the tea for two years and averaged 30 points per game. He le the Jayhawks to victory in 42 out of 50 games.

Chamberlin was twice named an All-American. He played a season for the Harlem Globetrotters before signing with the Philadelphia Warriors in 1959. He ended his career with the Los Angles Lakers in 1973. Wilt was named the NBA's most valuable player four times.

Jim Ryun at a high school track meet breaking a record.
Photo courtesy of The Wichita Eagle and Beacon Publishing Company

In the 1960s, Jim Ryun became the first high school student to run a mile in less than four minutes. In 1966, he was named Sports Illustrated's Sportsman of the Year and a Sullivan Award winner. In the 1968 Olympics, held in Mexico City, he won a silver medal in the 1,500 meter race.

In the late 1990s, Jim Ryun has been serving as Kansas State Representative.

John Riggins grew up in Centralia and went to college at the University of Kansas during the 1960s. He was chosen to play for the New York Jets in 1971. In 1976, he signed with the Washington Redskins. Two years later he rushed for over 1,000 yards and was called the comeback player of the year. In 1982, he helped the Redskins beat the Miami Dolphins in the Super Bowl. He retired from football in 1985.

Although he was born in Wichita, Gale Sayer grew up in Speed. Nicknamed " The Kansas Comet" he went to college at the University of Kansas where he played football. During his junior and senior year was named an All-American. In 1965, he was picked by the Chicago Bears and went on to become the Rookie of the Year. He retired in 1977.

During the late 1960s, Lynn Dickey of Osawatomie and Lenexa threw passes as a quarterback at Kansas State University totaling 6,028, a K-State record. When he graduated in 1971, he played professional football.

Topeka's Mike Torrez was the pitcher for the New York Yankees, when they beat the Los Angeles Dodgers in the 1977 World Series.

Barry Sanders set football records in the 1980s. He was the 1988 Heisman Trophy winner. In 1989, he was picked by the Detroit Lions. Then, in 1991 he was named the Pro Football Player of the Year.

Golfer Tom Watson began his career when he caddied for his father at the Kansas City Country Club in Shawnee Mission. By the age of 15, he had been invited to play an exhibition match with pro-golfer Arnold Palmer.

Nature's Demolition, The Topeka Tornado

In the late spring of 1966, Kansan's thought were turned to a tragedy at home.

A massive tornado struck downtown Topeka on June 8, 1966. Until that time, it had been widely believed that tornadoes did not hit cities.

Sixteen people were killed in the tornado and 550 were injured. There was more than $100 million dollars in property damage and 800 homes received some damage.

It was on the campus of Washburn University that the storm took its worst toll. Every large building on campus was destroyed as the twister moved along a path which was half a mile wide and almost 22 miles long.

Emmett Kelly was born in Sedan in 1898. He was one of the greatest clowns of all time. From the 1930s-1950s he appeared as the sad-faced clown with the Ringling Brothers and Barnum & Bailey Circus. He died in 1979.
Photo courtesy of Avery Postcards

Found untouched in the remains of MacVicar Hall, the music department building, was a harp, donated to the University by Theo Landon, the wife of governor, Alf Landon.

Also on campus that night a career path was changed. Bill Kurtis, an Independence native and KU graduate, was trying to decide between a career in journalism or a career in law. He was working at WIBW radio station. After broadcasting the tornado news, he decided to go into journalism.

Today, Bill Kurtis is the anchor of many programs on the popular cable station, Arts and Entertainment.

Almost before Washburn had finished picking up the pieces, there came more news that affected students over the nation. The need for troops to fight the ever-widening war in Southeast Asia, Vietnam, was growing. There would be no more student deferments from the draft. More regular military troops were being transported to Vietnam. Once again, America and Kansas were involved in a conflict that almost split the nation wide open. National Guard troops would be called to active duty.

Prairie Spirit

Wichita's **Lynette Woodard** is known as the first lady of basketball. Beginning in the 1970s, she set records for women. She attended college at the University of Kansas and led the Jayhawks in three Big Eight championships. She was named to the All-American team four years and scored a total of 2,649 points — the most by a woman in the history of the NCAA. In 1984, she made the Olympic team — and as the captain led the team to a gold medal. She then became the first woman to play on the Harlem Globetrotters. She played for the Globetrotters two years and then went on to play professionally for teams in Italy, Spain and Japan.

The Vietnam War Escalates

By July of 1967, American troops in Vietnam totaled 389,000.

Protests were growing at home as young people felt America should not be involved in the Southeast Asia war.

In January of 1968, the Chinese New Year or Tet, was marked by a huge Communist offensive. It was the most extensive fighting of the war. When it was over, Americans realized that there would be no easy victory.

In May of 1968, 4,600 citizen-soldiers of the Kansas Army National Guard's 69th Infantry Brigade were called to active duty. Almost 2,400 of them were sent to combat companies in Vietnam.

President Lyndon B. Johnson greets American troops in Vietnam in 1966.
Photo courtesy of National Archives

*Senator Robert Francis Kennedy
speaking at Kansas State University
on March 18, 1968.*
Photo courtesy of Kansas State University,
Department of Special Collections

A Fateful Election Year

It was a presidential election year in 196
Lyndon johnson had refused to seek or accept
party's nomination for another them as president.

Robert Kennedy, brother of the slain preside
announced his plans to run for the Presidency just tw
days before he arrived at Kansas State University
Manhattan to give a speech.

When he announced his candidacy, Kenne
told reporters:

*"I do not lightly dismiss the dangers and
difficulties of challenging an incumbent president
(Lyndon Johnson), but these are not ordinary times,
and this is not an ordinary election."*

His speech at Kansas State focused on t
Vietnam War.

*"I am concerned -- as I believe most Americans
are concerned -- that our present course will not
bring victory, will not bring peace, will not stop the
bloodshed,"* Kennedy told the students.

In June of 1968, just before the Democra
convention was to open in Chicago, Robert Kenne
was appearing at a rally in Los Angeles. As he left t
auditorium, he was gunned down by assassin, Sirh
Sirhan.

President Johnson appointed a commission to study the causes of violence. Its chairman was Milton Eisenhower, brother of Dwight Eisenhower. Milton Eisenhower had served as the president of Kansas State University from 1943 to 1950.

In November of 1968, Americans elected Richard Nixon president of the United States. In Kansas, Bob Dole, an outspoken supporter of the war in Vietnam, was elected to the U. S. Senate.

Man On the Moon

Apollo, a program to land a man on the moon, began in 1961. One major setback occurred when Apollo 6, the first planned manned flight, caught fire on the launch pad during a rehearsal and Astronauts Grissom, White, and Chaffee burned to death.

There were 10 steps to the program before the eventual landing of Apollo 13 July 20, 1969. Neil Armstrong then took *"one step for man, one giant leap for mankind."*

Today, the command module from Apollo 13, along with other memorabilia from the program, are on display at the Kansas Cosmosphere in Hutchinson.

Kansan Ron Evans was on the crew of Apollo XVII.
Photo courtesy of The Kansas State Historical Society

Conflict at Home

In 1970, with peace talks dragging on in Paris, the United States and South Vietnam widened the conflict by invading Cambodia.

Student protests were widespread. On the campus of the University of Kansas, demonstrations caused concern.

At the time, Jim Slattery was a young lieutenant in the Kansas National Guard. He, like many other young men, had joined the Guard to avoid the war. Now, he was concerned with what his alternate duty might require.

"We were in training for riot control. It appeared at one point that we were going to be called up to defend the KU campus," he said.

The Guard was never called out to mainta[in] campus order in Kansas but there were more protest[s].

Jim Slattery later went into politics and serv[ed] Kansas as a four-term Congressman.

In 1971, Kansas hero, Bob Dole, was chosen chairman of the Republican National Committee. H[is] fierce attacks on opponents of the war made even som[e] of his fellow U. S. Senators back away.

There were even some questions at high leve[ls] of the Republican leadership with presidential advis[or] J. R. Halderman opposing the Kansan.

Another Election

In 1972, Richard Nixon campaigned for r[e-] election on a platform that promised "peace wi[th] honor."

President Nixon was re-elected. The Republica[n] leadership promptly dumped Senator Dole, an eve[nt] that turned out to be a blessing in disguise for Dole.

Soon, the Nixon administration was in troubl[e.] The Washington Post had reported a story abo[ut] members of the Committee to Re-Elect the Preside[nt] breaking into the Watergate office complex. They we[re] trying to steal information that might help the[e] campaign. President Nixon came under investigatio[n.]

Two years later, Richard Nixon became the fir[st] president in American history to resign. Gerald Fo[rd] became President and later issued a pardon for Nixo[n.]

Kansan Bob Dole's ouster from the Republica[n] party leadership placed him outside the scandal.

When Gerald Ford made a bid for t[he] presidency, in his own campaign, in 1976, he cho[se] Bob Dole as his running mate. They were unsuccessf[ul] and Jimmy Carter of Plains, Georgia became Preside[nt.]

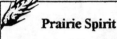

Prairie Spirit

Kansas City born **Ed Asner** is a seven-time Emmy winner. He played Lou Grant in the *Mary Tyler Moore* show of the 1970s. He also starred in the drama *Lou Grant*. During the late 1970s and early 1980s, he was president of the Screen Actors Guild.

Peace Comes

In January of 1973, there was agreement at the Paris peace talks. The United States would leave Vietnam. By the end of the year, most of the troops had come home.

Finally, in early April of 1975, Communist insurgents moved in and occupied Saigon. The remaining American forces were airlifted out.

In the United States, the "Great Society" had been halted by the expense of an unpopular war. America was left with the burden of a $200 billion price tag.

In Kansas, the economic mainstay of agriculture was headed into a downward spiral.

The Whippoorwill Goes Down

On June 17, 1978 with about 60 people aboard the Whippoorwill, a double-decker excursion boat on Lake Pomona, set off for the evening dinner cruise. It was just a few minutes before 7 p.m., and the skies were clear, though there had been an earlier storm.

At 7:31 p.m., a wall of water churned up by a tornado funnel crossing the lake, raced towards the boat. Winds behind it were gusting up to 65 miles per hour. The Whippoorwill rolled over, dropping most of the passengers on board into the water, trapping many of them beneath the boat.

The word was out almost instantly and rescuers came ready to help.

Marina operator, Lawrence Stadel was one of the rescuers who donned scuba gear. Underneath the sinking boat, he rescued two men who had been trapped for almost 45 minutes.

For 16 people aboard the ill-fated boat, help did not come in time. The sinking of the Whippoorwill was Kansas worst water disaster and its third deadliest tornado.

Dust and Tractorcades

The mid-1970s brought Kansas more reminders of nature's fury. Drought struck and dust storms rolled through parts of the state, reminding Kansas that the battle for soil conservation had not been won.

In Kansas, soaring interest rates compounded the troubles farmers already faced. Crop prices were falling and crops were lost to the drought.

Inflation was out of control as money was worthless. Farmland lost its value and farmers found themselves with property worth half the value of five years before.

Banks held mortgages on land now worthless than the loan against it. Foreclosures and bankruptcy sales were the result. Hundreds of Kansas farmers were forced out of business by the poor economy and bank foreclosures.

In 1977, the American Agriculture Movement began in eastern Colorado and picked up membership across Kansas and beyond. Farmers would take their case to Washington.

In January of 1979, more than 2,000 farmers climbed on their tractors and headed for Washington. They drove right onto the capital mall, calling attention to the need for something to be done.

The President responded with disaster emergency aid. But it was not enough. In the 70s many Kansas farms were lost. The land was quickly gobbled up by larger farms or corporations that thought more land and bigger farming operations were the answer to staying in business. The loss to America was the small farms, the independent farmers, and the single family farms.

Prairie Spirit

The Maytag repairman in television commercials is played by actor and filmmaker, **Gordon Jump** of Fort Riley, Manhattan and Topeka. During the 1970s, he played the radio station manager Arthur Carlson on the comedy series *WKRP in Cincinnati*. He also has produced, directed and acted in several movies.

Farm Crisis in the 1980s

The farm crisis deepened in the 1980s and prices of farm products continued to plummet downward.

By 1986, the President of the Kansas American Agriculture Movement, Stephan Anderson, a Wabaunsee County farmer, said it was unlikely there would be a tractorcade to Washington that year.

The farm economy had been so bad for so long that few farmers could afford the expense of the drive across the country.

Not that there weren't other protests.

He was one of 14 farmers arrested outside the Chicago Board of Trade after staging a protest there about the influence of commodity exchanges on farm prices.

Eventually, prices did improve for Kansas farmers and other food producers across the country. But not before hundreds more farms were lost.

In their wake, came bigger farms. Single owners made more by growing more. Rural towns lost businesses as families moved away and the population that had once supported grocery stores, theaters, hardware stores, and lumberyards was no longer there.

Prairie Spirit

Beginning in the late 1970s and early 1980s, **Stan Herd** of Protection, Dodge City and Lawrence gained national attention for his field art. Using the earth as his canvas and farm equipment as his brush, Herd has created artwork that literally covers acres. Some of his "paintings" have included portraits of Amelia Earhart and Van Gogh's sunflowers in a vase.

The Energy Crisis

One thing that helped Kansas farmers survive the downturn of the 1970s was a nationwide event that cost other consumers thousands of dollars. It raised a new doubt about the future.

In 1967, war had broken out between Israel and her Middle Eastern neighbors.

In the wake of that war, Middle Eastern Oil Producing Countries formed an alliance: The Organization of Oil Producing countries or OPEC.

Gas lines *were not an uncommon sight when the "Energy Crisis" struck.* *Notice the gasoline prices!*
Photo courtesy of The Wichita Eagle and Beacon Publishing Company

That event reminded the United States of ju[st] how dependent it was on Middle Eastern oil resource[s]. This was done by OPEC by restricting the supply of [oil] and by increasing the price.

This in turn caused what has been popular[ly] called the "Energy Crisis" of the 1970s. This was [a] time when Kansans took a hard look at the preservati[on] and the conservation of its natural resources.

Kansas Oil Producers Do Well

For Kansas, the energy crisis was a two-edg[ed] sword. While consumers worried about higher pric[es] at the pump for gasoline, Kansas oil producers ma[de] record profits.

America was looking hard at ways to reduce [its] dependency on foreign oil. Consumers considered t[he] conservation and alternative energy sources that wou[ld] help the Kansas oil and natural gas resources l[ast] longer.

Thus began a drive that has lasted to this day [to] find other ways to generate the power Kansans need[.]

Wolf Creek Generating Station

On September 3, 1985 Kansas entered t[he] atomic age when its only nuclear powered generati[ng] plant began producing electricity. The station, locat[ed] near Burlington, took 8 years to build at a cost of [3] billion dollars. Wolf Creek generates electricity [by] heating water to produce steam. Steam turns gia[nt] turbines that spin a magnet inside an electric[al] generator, thus producing electricity. Wolf Cre[ek] produces heat by splitting or "fissioning" atoms [of] uranium fuel. The plant produces 1230 megawatts [of] power, enough to supply about 800,000 homes.

The plant site is about 10,500 acres, including [a] 5,090 acre lake available for fishing and recreation.

From its beginning, the plant has fostered a deep commitment to the Kansas environment. More than one third of the land is leased to local farmers and ranchers for crops and cattle grazing. Another 1,500 acres are dedicated solely to area wildlife.

The plant also operates an Environmental Education Area that is open to the public and visited by hundreds of Kansas school children each year.

About 1,000 Kansans work around the clock at Wolf Creek to ensure you have safe, reliable, cost-effective power.

Wolf Creek Generating Station, Coffey County, 1999.
Photo courtesy of Wolf Creek Nuclear Operating Corporation

Power Alternatives

The problems of oil shortage made it clear how dependent on foreign oil America had become.

Heat for their homes and gas for their automobile were two things Kansans had never expected to worr about.

Now, Kansans began to realize, resources coul simply be used up. This realization had caused search for new ways to generate electricity withou burning coal. Not only was there a limited amount c coal. Burning it also polluted the air.

In 1999, still concerned about alternative fuel Western Resources, the major private electrical utilit company in the state, opened a "wind farm," nea Topeka and began generating electricity with two hug wind driven turbines.

For the most part, however, the state continue to get most of its power, 62% from coal-burning, an from natural gas or fuel oil plants.

End of The Cold War

The 1980s brought a dramatic and differer twist to world politics and U. S. military standing Communism in the Soviet Union, after years c economic struggle, failed.

The end of the Vietnam War caused slashes i military budgets that had cut deep into the revenue c Kansas companies like Boeing Aircraft. Boeing wa heavily dependent on military contracts.

Countries controlled by the Communist Sovie Union after WWII, satellite countries, were declare independent shortly after economic collapse of th Soviet Union. The Berlin Wall was then dismantled.

At the beginning of the new decade of the 90: America stood alone as a super-power, a circumstanc that brought new challenges to both military an civilian leaders.

BIG BRUTUS©

POST CARD

October 1984, the P & M Coal Company deeded Big Brutus and 16.7 acres of land to Big Brutus, Inc., to be used as a museum dedicated to the coal mining industry. Big Brutus is 160 feet or 16 stories tall and weighs 11 million pounds. Brutus could scoop up 150 tons of rock and soil in a single bite of its single bucket. Near West Mineral, Kansas, located 6 miles west of K7 and K102 Jct., then one-half mile south.

The Kansas Postcard Co., P.O. Box 122., Lawrence, KS 66044

I was dwarfed by the Big Brutus in South Eastern Kansas. All I can say is that it is H-U-G-E !!!

© Design by Zachary Norris Snipe
© Photo by Big Brutus
© KPC 1997
K23317

Historical Events

1988 - KS Cosmosphere forms Space Works

1990 - Iraq invades Kuwait

1990 - Hesston Tornado

1991 - Kansas Troops sent to Iraq

1991 - Andover Tornado

1992-1997 - Kansas Farms decreasing

1993 - Starbase comes to Kansas

1995-1996 - Drought hits Kansas

1997-1999 - Crash in farm prices

1999 - KS Board of Regents receives new
education responsibilities

1999 - Wichita and Haysville Tornado

1999 - Steve Hawley launches Chandra from
Shuttle Columbia

CRUZPAGAN 99

Chapter 12

The 1990s and A New Century

Chapter 12

The 1990s and A New Century

Kansas is now into a new century. The industrial economy is booming. Agriculture is better but still struggling. Unemployment is low, however, full-time jobs with good pay and good benefits still are hard to find. The military is growing smaller. Corporations are growing bigger. The Internet is booming into corporate business, many of which are on the stock market.

This new century has caused much reflection about what has happened to Kansas over the last 200 years. There should be some thought about what might be taking place over the next 100 to 200 years.

This chapter is a look at Kansas and how some of its important institutions and industries are poised just into the new millennium and the future.

The Military

Early in its history, Kansas was called the "Soldier State" because of its ability to muster troops. Kansas did this for the Civil War, Spanish American War, Philippine Insurrection, World War I, World War II, Korea, Vietnam, Desert Storm, and Bosnia-Kosovo action.

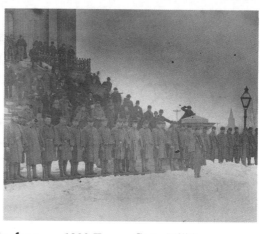

1893 Kansas State Militia.
Photo courtesy of The Kansas State Historical Society

In the 1990s, Kansas ranked in the top 10 states for generating the men and women who answered the call to military duty. The decade has been one of the great challenges for our military forces.

In 1998, Kansas's three active duty military bases brought in, from the government and elsewhere, more than $1.3 billion for the state's economy. In addition, National Guard and Reserve units generated another $150 million to $200 million.

Its geographic position in the center of the 48 United States is one mile north and one mile west of Lebanon in Smith County. Thus, making Kansas a logical choice for the location of aircraft refueling units and "superwing." McConnell Air Force Base near Wichita is one of three such wings in the nation.

Military forts, like this restoration of *Ft.Larned served many purposes throughout the history of Kansas.*
Photo courtesy of Avery Postcards

Kansas' history of community and employer support for the "citizen soldier" (National Guard) likewise made it a choice for the headquarters of one of the nation's largest Army Reserve headquarters. The 89th Regional Support Command, headquarters for reservists from Kansas, Iowa, Nebraska, Oklahoma, and Missouri, is at Wichita.

Kansas' wide open spaces, well-maintained training grounds and long Army tradition has made it home for hard-fighting, first-response infantry and artillery forces at Fort Riley. Also, a reputation for devotion to excellence has made it the home of the most prestigious military college in the world. That Command and General Staff College at Fort Leavenworth.

In the 1990s, the military had been called upon to assume a new role in maintaining world peace. The result has been a rapid increase in the numbers of deployments to foreign countries.

In all the years from 1953 to 1990, the United States sent military forces on 11 missions to help other countries. These were for their own defense or to perform humanitarian aid. Such as the Turkey Earthquake of August, 1999. Between 1991 and 1999 there were more than 46 such missions, not counting major operations such as the Gulf War and the 1999 bombing of Kosovo.

A Shield and A Storm

In August 2nd of 1990, Saddam Hussein of Iraq invaded neighboring Kuwait a small oil producing country. Saddam's attack posed a direct threat to the flow of oil coming out of the Middle East to the United States. The U. S. military and other nations began an immediate response in an action called, "Desert Shield."

It was Kansas Air Force reserve planes from Topeka who were the first to touch down on Saudi Arabian airfields to begin their mission.

Those planes were flown by Air Force Reservists from the 190th Air Refueling Wing at Forbes Field. They volunteered for the mission.

When ground troops were called to fight in the battle to free Kuwait in "Desert Storm," an action that began in January 21, 1991, it was soldiers from Junction City, who were the first to breach the Iraqi defenses. The men and women of the Big Red One then headquartered at Fort Riley, pushed deep through enemy territory in just under 100 hours and defeated elements of 11 Iraqi Divisions.

During the months of The Gulf War, called the "100 days war," also called "The Persian Gulf War," Kansas men and women served in combat or combat support roles. Almost 30 percent of them were reservists who left their full-time civilian jobs for military service.

Fort Riley

One brigade of the "Big Red One" is still stationed at Fort Riley, however, the headquarters of the famous battle unit has been moved to Germany.

Fort Riley, now called "The Home of America's Army," is still integral to national defense and to the modern military mission. The post is home to 10,256 active duty soldiers and an additional 3,312 civilian workers. Soldiers at Fort Riley drive tanks, Bradley fighting vehicles and trucks. They also fly helicopters used for medical evacuation as well as helping civilian rescue crews in times of emergency.

The Fort is the headquarters for Army Reserve and National Guard training exercises and home to Irwin Army Community Hospital.

In 1998, construction began on a regional simulated battlefield training complex. In 1999, the 24th Infantry Division was activated with Fort Riley as its headquarters.

Each year, more than 27,500 reserve soldiers train at the post and the number is expected to increase significantly when the new simulator complex has been completed in 2002.

The post also serves an important historic purpose. The main post has many of its original limestone buildings, dating back to the mid-1880s. Museums, tours of historic homes, including the 1860s era "Custer House" and the grave of "Chief" the last U. S. Cavalry Horse that died in 1956. All are open to the public.

Fort Leavenworth

The oldest fort in Kansas is well-known to many top military officials of every country in the free world and to a number of heads of states as well.

Fort Leavenworth houses the U. S. Army Command and General Staff College. Every officer above the rank of Major in the U. S. military is required to attend either that college or the "war-college" of his or her branch of the service.

Many officers come to Ft. Leavenworth for the year long school. Others take its classes by mail while st on duty elsewhere.

The college was founded in May of 1881 General William Tecumseh Sherman, the famous Ci War general. He was then Commanding General of t Army. Sherman's connection to Kansas was throu his wife, the daughter of U. S. Senator Thomas Ewin She had two brothers, both of whom were lawye practicing in Leavenworth.

In 1894, Swiss Army Lieutenant Hen LeComte attended classes there, and began a traditi of international, as well as national, education f military officers.

By the end of the 90s, more than 6,000 office from 122 countries were "Leavenworth graduates."

The post has an annual military payroll of mo than $120 million.

Leavenworth is also home to, although le prestigious, another well-known institution, t Federal Disciplinary Barracks, better known as t prison.

Military personnel ordered to serve prison term as a result of a court-martial are confined in th (prison) barracks.

McConnell Air Force Base

In the 1990's, McConnell Air Force Bas located in Wichita, housed one of three KC-135 Stratotanker superwings in the Air Force. The bas had 48 tanker aircraft and enough active duty airme to fly and maintain them. There was also enoug personnel to provide security and support to the bas and the flying crews.

The KC-135 was built by Boeing in the 1950 but has been upgraded several times. Boeing has wo the contracts for several modernizations including nev more powerful engines.

In 1998, two modifications were begun. On would allow two airplanes to be refueled at the sam time. Those modifications were tested at McConnel

Kansas National Guard In The 1990s

The Kansas National Guard troops, both Air and Army, respond to such disasters as floods and tornadoes. Guard troops were called out when tornadoes struck in Hesston in 1990, Wichita, Haysville, Andover in 1991 and in Haysville and Wichita in 1999.

The most visible military presence across the state is the National Army Guard which maintains 60 armories in 52 counties. The Army Guard trains its members in Field Artillery and artillery support, combat and combat support, engineering, aviation and other skills. The Army Guard payroll is almost $115 million.

There are Two Air Guard wings based in Kansas.

The 190th Air Refueling Wing (AFR) was transferred to Forbes AFB near Topeka in 1967 and, it became the only military unit in the world equipped with day/night capable bombers. The arrival of the first KC-135 Stratotanker in 1978 herald the still-current air refueling mission.

In 1990, the 190th was the first unit to arrive at Jeddah, Saudi Arabia for service during operations Desert Shield/Desert Storm. During 1999, the 190th was deployed twice to Turkey in support of Operation Northern Watch, refueling Allied aircraft over the northern No-Fly Zone in Iraq.

The 184th Bomb Wing is based at McConnell Air Force Base. In 1995, it became the first National Guard unit in the United States to be assigned a combat bomber mission. The McConnell unit, nicknamed the "Fighting Jayhawks" had been a fighter pilot training base.

The 184th has 10 B-1B bombers and one air control squadron whose members can assemble an entire radar control station complete with its own phone service, radar, communications systems and power generators.

The annual payroll of the Kansas Air National Guard is almost $124 million.

Colonel Floyd Dennis Parry, *Chief of Staff, Kansas Army National Guard*
Photo courtesy of KS ARNG

STARBASE began in 1991 at Selfridge Air National Guard Base in Michigan.

Kansas STARBASE is the nation's largest National Guard Youth Program, which covers more than 53 counties and 192 Kansas school districts.

The program is to spark the interest of at-risk fifth and sixth grade youths in science, math, technology, goal setting and positive life choices. The one day a week class is during the school year and STARBASE offers one-week camps during the summer.

The program reinforces their purpose by introducing positive role models into the children's lives.

In a partnership with the National Guard 34,904 Kansas children were served since 1993.

STARBASE is an anagram of Science and Technology Academics Reinforcing Basic Aviation and Space Exploration.

89th Regional Support Command

The Army Reserve 89th Regional Support Command, is another Wichita based military segment of Kansas.

The 89th includes troops from Iowa, Missouri, Nebraska, Oklahoma, and Kansas.

The Army Reserve has soldiers based in 1 communities: Topeka, Olathe, Kansas City, Fort Riley, Hays, Manhattan, Salina, Great Bend, Arkansas City, Lawrence, Hutchinson, Parsons, Osage City, Dodge City, Independence, Pittsburg, and Wichita.

Army Reservists fly and maintain helicopters, drive trucks, run hospital units, handle administrative duties, organize supplies, provide security police, and even supply band music for ceremonies and public events.

The annual economic impact of the Army Reserve in Kansas is estimated at more than $3(million.

Business Giants

Aviation companies continue to be the business giants of Kansas beyond agriculture and petroleum.

Oil in Kansas decreased in importance as well were depleted and prices fell in the late 1990s, but natural gas and helium production continue to be major industries.

Most economists are watching with interest to see how some new developments might effect the agriculture industry and especially the lifestyles of the more than 61,000 families who live on farms.

Those new developments are corporate farms and farmer-owned cooperatives there is also specialty crops engineered for specific markets.

Leading Kansas Companies
(average # of employees)

Telecommunications: Sprint/United Telephone - 20,000 employees
Southwestern Bell - 3,566 employees

Aircraft Production: The Boeing Company - 18,300 employees
Raytheon Aircraft Co. - 7,000 employees
Cessna Aircraft Co. - 4,840 employees
Learjet, Inc. - 2,800 employees

Health Care: Via Christi Medical Services - 3,500 employees
HCA Health Services of Ks. Inc. - 3,080 employees
Stormont-Vail Health Services - 2,950 employees
BCross & BShield of Ks. Inc. - 2,400 employees
Univ. of Ks Medical Ctr. - 2,300 employees
Sister of Charity - 1,794 employees

Meat Packing: IBP, Inc. - 6,000 employees
National Beef Packing Co. - 2,400 employees
Idle Wild Foods - 1,975 employees
Excel Corporation - 1,800 employees

Railroad: Burlington No. Santa Fe Corp. - 5,600 employees

Automotive: General Motors - 4,200 employees

Equipment:
Search/Navigation Allied Signal, Inc. - 3,245 employees
& Chemicals

Greeting Cards: Hallmark Cards, Inc. - 2,700 employees

Petrochemical: Koch Industries - 2,450 employees

Credit Center: Montgomery Ward Credit - 2,100 employees

Tire Manufacturing: Goodyear Tire & Rubber - 2,000 employees

Frozen Specialities: Schwan's Sales Enter. Inc. -2,000 employees

Information complied by Kansas Dept. of Commerce & Housing

The Colleges and Universities of Kansas

During the 1999 legislative session, the state of Kansas made sweeping changes in the way higher education is governed.

University of Kansas in Lawrence, an aerial view. National Geographic magazine has called the Lawrence campus one of the nation's most beautiful.
Photo courtesy of The University of Kansas, University Relations

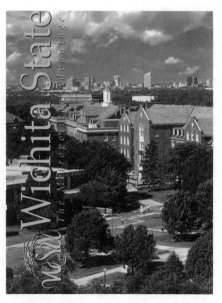

Wichita State University.
Photo courtesy Wichita State University Special Collections

Under the new law, which went into effect Ju 1, 1999, the Kansas Board of Regents received th responsibility of the supervision of the state's community colleges and 11 vocational-technic schools. This in addition to the state's six publ universities. The public universities are: Th University of Kansas including the Medical Center Kansas City, Kansas State University, Emporia Sta University, Pittsburg State University, Fort Hays Sta University, and Wichita State University. Washburn the only municipal college in the United States.

In addition to the public universities, Kansas h a number of private colleges, both large and small.

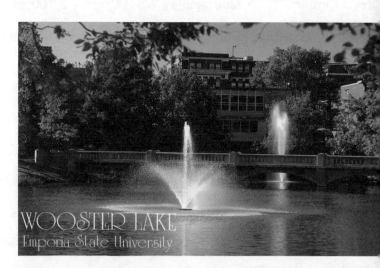

Wooster Lake, Emporia State University.
Photo courtesy Avery Postcards

Agriculture Is Changing

While not listed in the Kansas Companies as a corporation, agriculture as a whole remains central to the business base of Kansas. Especially if all the supporting and related industries, such as milling and shipping grain, processing and marketing beef and other livestock, manufacturing and distributing machinery, fertilizer, chemicals, and other products are taken into account.

Enormous changes in farming have occurred in Kansas in the 90s. Experts say those changes are likely to continue, or even speed up in the next century.

For one thing, there are fewer Kansans living on farms and depending on farming for their main income. Farming and its related industries, however, still have an enormous impact on Kansas.

The number of farms in the state decreased by some 1,700 farms from 1992 to 1997. The number of producing acres, however, only decreased by 1.3% of the states 46 million acres of farmland.

While there were fewer farmers, the value of the products they produced increased. The market value of agricultural products sold in 1992 was $8.3 billion. By 1997, it had increased to $9.2 billion. The number of farms reporting more than $100,000 in sales income also increased.

Among with bigger farms, there has been an increase in the number of specialized farming operations. Huge beef cattle feedlots, some with associated packing plants, are located in Dodge City, Garden City, and the Liberal area.

Grain Elevator
Photo courtesy of Kansas State University Special Collections

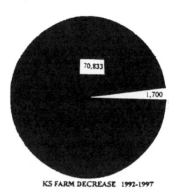

70,833
1,700

KS FARM DECREASE 1992-1997

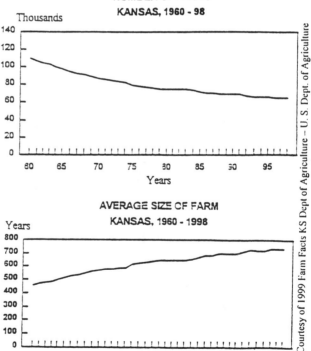

**NUMBER OF FARMS
KANSAS, 1960 - 98**

Thousands

Years

**AVERAGE SIZE OF FARM
KANSAS, 1960 - 1998**

Years

Acres

Courtesy of 1999 Farm Facts KS Dept of Agriculture – U. S. Dept. of Agriculture

KS DAIRY FARM DECREASE 1992-1997

Dairy farmers became more concentrated as well, with huge operations of thousands of cows taking the place of hundreds of small, family-owned dairies which went out of business in the 1990s.

The number of dairy farms dropped from 2,165 in 1992 to 1,466 in 1997.

During the 1990s, Seaboard Farms introduced corporate hog farming to the state. At times, local opposition to the big hog farms prevented some other companies from locating in Kansas.

Freedom To Farm

The biggest change in laws pertaining to agriculture since the Great Depression of the 1930s also came in 1995 when the U.S. Congress passed reform popularly called the Freedom to Farm Bill.

It did away with many of the government programs that restricted farm production. It was welcomed by Kansas farmers.

In the first years of the new law, farmers thrived. But in 1997, 1998, and 1999 a combination of things, including weather disasters, and economic problems in other countries caused a crash in farm prices.

Most farmers in Kansas found themselves facing a tremendous drop in income in 1998 with prospects not much improved for 1999.

Farm economy experts are working to improve crop insurance that will allow farmers to protect themselves against drought, hailstorms, floods, and disasters in the future.

Weather Disasters

As you have learned, weather has always been a challenge in Kansas. In fact, Kansans have come to think of surviving nature's whims as one of their defining qualities.

*A **tornado** roaring towards a Kansas highway.*
Photo courtesy of The Wichita Eagle and Beacon Publishing Company

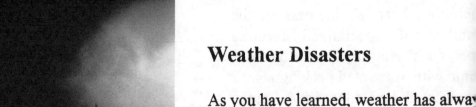

But the decade of the 1990s brought Kansas more of its usual share of natural disasters.

The decade began with a deadly tornado which ripped apart the small Harvey County town of Hesston in March of 1990. In June of the same year, an "inland hurricane" struck Wichita with sustained winds of more than 110 miles per hour. Hundreds of trees in the cities oldest neighborhoods were destroyed and thousands of people were left without power.

The destruction of a tornado is hard to imagine. *This 1991 photo shows people sorting through what was their homes.*
Photo courtesy of The Wichita Eagle and Beacon Publishing Company

In 1991, another of nature's more powerful tornadoes struck first in Clearwater, then Haysville, and South Wichita and then moved on into Andover.

1992 brought no massive tornadoes to the state. But one of the costliest storms in history struck Wichita on June 19, 1992 when hail the size of softballs, driven by 100 mph winds moved through a large portion of the city. Damage totaled about $553 million.

In 1993, it was floods. Some of the worst floods ever to hit the Mississippi and Missouri River basins, struck Kansas. The floodwaters caused millions of dollars which washed away railroads, businesses, homes, and farms on thousands of acres of bottomland.

The storm season of 1994 was quiet, but floods struck again in 1995, more devastating than the ones of 1993. Wide areas of the Arkansas, Whitewater, and Walnut basins flooded as did the Kansas, Missouri, Neosho, and Verdigris in the eastern part of the state.

After the flooding in 1995, the rains stopped. From August of 1995 to May of 1996, almost no rain fell over a major portion of southern Kansas. The 1996 wheat crop, planted in dust in September with the hope of rain, did not come up.

The deadliest tornado since 1991 struck in 1999, hitting south Wichita and Haysville. Some of the same areas wiped out in 1991 were hit again. Five people were killed outright and two others died in the following weeks.

The Question of Water

KANSAS PRECIPITATION - 1998
Upper figure, 1998 Total; Lower Figure, 1961-90 Average;
Inches of Water

County	1998 Total	1961-90 Avg.
Cheyenne	22.02	17.71
Rawlins	24.27	21.58
Decatur	18.22	22.26
Norton	22.47	23.36
Phillips	26.36	23.73
Smith	26.85	23.84
Jewell	29.21	28.68
Republic	26.70	31.04
Washington	43.11	31.80
Marshall	41.09	31.04
Nemaha	37.76	34.89
Brown	41.06	36.40
Doniphan	41.59	36.83
Atchison	47.49	36.90
Sherman	20.84	18.20
Thomas	22.39	19.14
Sheridan	20.37	20.42
Graham	23.48	21.05
Rooks	24.88	23.20
Osborne	28.86	25.31
Mitchell	32.66	26.68
Cloud	34.43	28.78
Clay	40.75	30.48
Riley	40.08	33.82
Pottawatomie	40.12	34.03
Jackson	48.98	38.84
Jefferson	51.39	
Leavenworth	na	40.54
Wyandotte	na	37.62
Wallace	18.09	19.11
Logan	21.44	19.50
Gove	23.76	23.60
Trego	26.22	22.28
Ellis	25.41	21.80
Russell	32.28	26.45
Lincoln	36.15	27.89
Ottawa	39.35	29.82
Saline	40.33	30.36
Dickinson	38.49	
Morris	38.27	31.98
Wabaunsee	42.16	35.61
Shawnee	39.03	
Osage	43.90	35.50
Douglas	48.34	39.28
Johnson	51.87	39.56
Franklin	49.89	38.86
Miami	48.63	40.80
Greeley	17.37	15.96
Wichita	18.96	17.12
Scott	18.41	20.30
Lane	24.44	20.26
Ness	18.16	20.99
Rush	19.69	23.51
Barton	26.12	25.96
Ellsworth	na	
Rice	31.97	27.96
McPherson	40.17	29.85
Marion	32.68	
Morris	31.87	32.44
Chase	44.80	34.04
Lyon	49.29	38.68
Coffey	51.24	34.82
Anderson	61.32	
Linn	53.67	41.00
Hamilton	19.87	15.81
Kearny	20.46	17.10
Finney	22.19	19.39
Hodgeman	22.22	19.74
Edwards	23.61	26.69
Pawnee	29.97	
Stafford	27.99	24.46
Reno	34.10	29.22
Harvey	37.75	
Sedgwick	31.15	34.66
Butler	42.72	34.75
Greenwood	50.70	38.16
Woodson	49.35	41.67
Allen	47.37	39.78
Bourbon	62.90	41.49
Gray	18.15	22.88
Ford	21.77	21.49
Kiowa	23.14	23.60
Pratt	24.00	25.84
Kingman	33.23	28.84
Elk	43.99	37.08
Wilson	48.50	38.78
Neosho	42.13	41.90
Crawford	55.16	43.05
Stanton	na	14.70
Grant	16.08	16.86
Haskell	18.74	19.27
Morton	20.99	16.54
Stevens	15.58	18.54
Seward	25.85	19.14
Meade	27.42	21.69
Clark	20.17	21.99
Comanche	23.01	24.96
Barber	25.86	26.21
Harper	36.38	29.00
Sumner	35.77	32.26
Cowley	46.28	33.85
Chautauqua	46.56	38.67
Montgomery	51.45	40.67
Labette	49.84	40.02
Cherokee	40.54	41.81

Courtesy of 1999 Farm Facts KS Dept. of Agriculture - U. S. Dept. of Agriculture

In Kansas, how to live [with] the shortage of water [is a] question, when answered, [will] contribute to the future [of] agriculture, business and ind[ustry.]

Increases in irrig[ated] farmland have caused g[rowing] concerns about depletion o[f the] underground water suppl[y in] western Kansas, where the O[gallala] Aquifer is being drained a[t an] alarming rate.

A further concern is [that] waste from livestock operat[ions,] especially huge beef and [hog] feedlots, will pollute the [water] supply, making it unsafe for people to drink. [The last] decade of the 1990s saw the increased concer[n for] clean water. New rules were needed for pollutio[n and] sewage disposal by cities. Runoff from farms [and] feedlots has become another area for new rules.

The hard question of who gets to use the [water] when the supply becomes threatened is one that f[uture] generations may well be required to answer.

Other Social Questions

Kansas in the 1990s looked for ways to fin[d an] answer to one of the largest problems plaguing soc[iety.] That problem is how to reduce the number of pe[ople] living on welfare.

The late 1990s brought Cessna Aircraft nat[ional] recognition for its program of training we[lfare] recipients to join the workforce.

The program provides on-the-job trainin[g for] people trying to get off welfare, then follows up [with] mentors to help them succeed in the workforce.

At the same time, it provides on-site daycar[e for] working parents and offers free medical care and [?] time off for parents when their children are sick.

Cessna's success in the program caught the attention of President Bill Clinton, who visited the training center and the aircraft factory in Wichita. He talked with company officials and meet with some of the people who had benefitted from the program.

Clinton called the program a national model of excellence.

The Sternberg Museum

This section has some information based in part upon the Theory of Evolution.

Photo courtesy of The Sternberg Museum

The Sternberg Museum in Hays, houses much of Sternberg's collection of prehistoric fossils. These include inland-sea monsters, pteranadons, and other fossils. The famous fossil, 'Fish within a Fish,' is housed there.

The hypothesis and theories of scientists, in an effort to explain the fossils and how they came to be in Kansas, tell us that the earth cooled from its heated beginnings more than 3 billion years ago.

Torrential rains caused a great sea to cover mo of the earth.

Scientists tell us that about 350 million yea ago, for reasons not known or possibly the continue cooling of the earth, massive rock plates beneath th sea cracked and moved. The pieces bumped togethe and some were tipped up. They formed what woul later be the platforms upon which the continents of th earth would rest. New land formed as terribl earthquakes continued and violent lava flows poure from the constant eruptions of volcanoes.

Over a long period of time (two billion years more) the land rose and the sea receded. Strang creatures came to life in the shallow ocean that covere the land that is now Kansas. Large sea creature looking much like todays lizards and turtles, thrive there, although they are miniatures in comparison.

Ancient mosasaurs are depicted at battle in the undersea world they once ruled.
Artwork by Jose Cruzpagan commissioned by The Dangberg Foundation

One group, named mosasaurs by the foss finders, were longer than a railroad engine. There wer giant clams more than four feet across, great shark with razor-sharp teeth, leatherback turtles as big as car and fish that were 20 feet long.

About 270 million years ago, along the shores of the ocean, many types of dinosaurs ruled the land. Above the ocean, flew pterasaurs, creatures with wingspans of more than 25 feet.

They often swooped down to swallow whole an unwary fish.

People today know what the mosasaurs looked like. They know how big they were, when they lived, and died. Their stories and their history in our state are preserved in their bones which now have been fossilized, turned into rock. Scientists call these remains fossils.

It has been estimated that there are more of these fossils in Kansas than in most other states. This is because so much of the land was once covered by an ocean and because there were so many of these creatures living in the ocean.

Through time, there have been hundreds of kinds of animals and plants - elephants, long-legged camels, 600 pound wolves, and saber-tooth tigers. Scientists tell us that all of their stories are in the fossils that can still be found all over Kansas.

What the Sea Left Behind

You've probably heard people say Kansas is as flat as a tabletop. If you've ever stood and looked across the landscape in many parts of Kansas, you would know it looks flat. However, think of Kansas as a table having much longer legs on one end than on the other. Because that's just the kind of table it is - a very slanted one. The southeast corner of the state is only 700 feet above sea level. The northwest corner is more than 4,000 feet above sea level. You could feel this steady rise in elevation if you started pedaling a bicycle westward across what looks like very flat land, such as in Finney or Johnson counties.

Across the state, there is a variety of terrains, hills, valleys, and long washed-out gullies where layers of limestone with jagged edges stick out from the sides. There are also huge standing rocks that became markers, monuments, and landmarks for native people and the first white travelers who crossed the plains.

Workers use small pick hammers *to break rock and brushes to clean off the rock they find.*
Photo courtesy of Mike Everhart

All of the terrains are the legacy of the ocea
that covered Kansas for millions of years.

Today, Kansas is almost as far away from
ocean as you can get. But beneath the surface of t
waving fields of wheat and grass, under the cities, t
interstate highways, are still layers upon layers of ro
filled with fossilized plants and animals. These
covered over by sand, soil, and silt. Geologists stu
the layers of rock and minerals to determine how lo
a certain period of history lasted, what the weather w
like, what kind of animals lived then, and what th
ate.

Today's legacy of those ancient times are fiel
of oil and natural gas and rich veins of coal. The qu
of people for Kansas's natural resources have caus
new industry and many conflicts.

A Catastrophe and
Lasting Change

What happened to the ocean?

Most scientists believe a great catastroph
perhaps a huge meteorite or asteroid colliding with t
Earth, throwing dust and other debris into the air
massive amounts, blocking out sunlight around t
earth caused a catastrophic change for living thing
Many scientists believe that less sunlight caused dea
of plants and other food sources which in turn wip
out the dinosaurs and the large marine reptiles. The
is evidence that some groups of animals died o
disappeared, suddenly or gradually declined.

Millions of years later, huge moving sheets
ice called glaciers slowly scraped the land. T
glaciers pushed mountains of rocks and dirt and le
mounds of it as they melted. The huge granite boulde
around Wamego originally were pushed from Canac
and were left as the glaciers melted. Water from t
melting ice carved valleys and became rivers. Some
the water became trapped in the layers of rock ar
covered over by sand and dirt. Today, we call the
huge pools of underground water, aquifers.

There is evidence that glaciers crossed northeastern Kansas at least twice, melting less than 15,000 years ago. The last glacier moved south to the Kansas River and west to the Blue River, wearing away the terrain. Shifting sands blew with the wind, piling up into dunes across the western part of the state. Today, these are covered with sparse clumps of thick, wiry grass.

The constant winds created a different terrain. Some of the finest and richest soils in the world are found in Kansas, deposited here by the winds. Geologists estimate that more than 90 percent of the soil in Thomas, Sherman, Cheyenne, Greeley, Hamilton, Wichita, Scott, Lane, and other western counties are from these deposits.

Below the Earth in Hutchison

About 650 feet below the earth in Hutchison, history is being preserved.

It is a world where there is no sunlight and fresh air is forcibly pumped down a shaft. In it, workers zip from one cavern to another by riding three-wheeled bicycles.

Bright florescent lights can reveal anything from top-secret government records to 19th century buggies.

Welcome to the Underground Vault and Storage, a company started during the height of the Cold War in the quarried caverns of the salt mines by Wichita businessmen.

Kansas is far removed from earthquakes and hurricanes and the mines are deep enough that they aren't affected by floods, tornadoes, or even fires. Both east and west coast film companies feel comfortable storing movies and television films in the spacious caverns.

Security is one of the selling points in these Hutchison salt mines because the only people who have access are the people who work there. People can't just drop in and see the records, they have to arrange in advance, going thru the company officials in order to get an escorted tour of the mines.

An elevator shaft used to get to the mines limits the size of articles to no wider than 44 inches, 58 inches tall and 60 inches long. Anything larger has to be taken apart and reassembled down below.

Another selling point is the natural climate. Temperatures of the mines average between 68 and 7_ degrees with a relative humidity between 45 and 50 percent.

Various countries store government records in the Hutchinson salt mines. Those that are top secret are sectioned off and have panels built around them, making them inaccessible except to authorized people.

Most of the records are shelved. In fact, the archives look much like the ending scene in *"Raiders of the Lost Ark,"* where the ark is stored in the midst of rows upon rows of government records.

But the place is a historian's dream. People store rare wedding dresses, classic, and not-so classic Hollywood movies, medical and business records, and just about anything else you can imagine.

The movies that are stored include the originals of *"The Wizard of Oz"* and *"Gone With The Wind."* Almost each week, another truckload of films arrives from Hollywood for storage.

One customer has stored a vintage McDonald's sign. Another has stored a 1930s dentist's chair. Still another has stored 19th century government records.

Because the temperature and humidity are constant and there is little dust, the artifacts stored have a much longer life than they would in other, more conventional storage places.

The Cosmosphere

A unique Kansas institution offers a blend of looking at the past and seeking answers for the future. It is perhaps fitting that the center of America's aviation industry would also be the state where space exploration is in the spotlight.

Morton Salt Company, *Hutchinson.*
Photo courtesy of The Reno County Historical Society

Prairie Spirit

Annette Bening was born in Topeka and lived in Wichita before she became an actress, starring in the 1991 movie *"Bugsy"* with, Warren Beatty, whom she latter married.

The actual Apollo 13 command module, "Odyssey" is housed at the Cosmosphere.
Photo courtesy of Kansas Cosmosphere and Space Center

The Cosmosphere in Hutchison provides both education for future generations and a museum where visitors can examine artifacts of the space industry.

Every summer the Cosmosphere offers an astronaut camp called the "Future Astronaut Training Program" for middle school students. Kansas's three astronauts, Steve Hawley, Joe Engle, and Ron Evans have all helped teach classes at the Cosmosphere.

In 1988, the Cosmosphere formed Space Works, a private subsidiary whose sole purpose is the restoration of space artifacts.

Spaceworks skill is highlighted in the Academy Award winning movie, Apollo 13 Command module "Odyssey", an SR-71 Blackbird aircraft, a full-scale shuttle replica, WWII German V-1 and V-2 rockets, a Northrop T-38 Talon, and a full-scale Apollo-Soyuz space docking exhibit.

The Cosmosphere is the only museum in Kans. to be affiliated with the Smithsonian. It has 105,0(square feet of exhibit space, rivaling some of t nation's other air and space museums.

In 1999, NASA raised Gus Grissom's spa capsule from the Atlantic Ocean. Its permanent hor eventually, will be the Cosmosphere.

The Cosmosphere will also have the largest ar most significant collection of Russian space hardwa outside of Russia, The Cosmosphere will have t country's largest exhibit of spacesuits and a full set actual Mercury, Gemini and Apollo spacecraft.

At the year 2000, the Cosmosphere has becon one of the top Kansas tourist destinations.

A Kansas Astronaut's View - A March 3, 1999 Interview with Steve Hawley

The Cosmosphere wasn't around when Shuttle Astronaut Steve Hawley was growing up in Salina. But if it had been, he says he'd liked to have gone to Space Camp there.

As it is, the astronaut who was part of the July, 1999 mission of the shuttle, Columbia, likes to be involved in the programs that are presented there.

He said that he didn't know he wanted to be an astronaut when he was young. He wanted to study the stars. The people who were flying space flights when he was a young person were all military test pilots and he didn't want to be a test pilot. He wanted to be an astronomer.

"When I was a kid, I actually envisioned the day that we would have big telescopes in space. I thought they would want astronomers who would be willing to go into space and operate those observatories, much like astronomers do on earth," Hawley said in an interview for this book, with the Dangberg Foundation's Director.

Steven A. Hawley, 1999.
Photo courtesy of NASA

Hawley has lived to see part of his childhood dream come true. He helped launch the Hubbell telescope in 1990. And in July, 1999 he was part of the mission that launched the Chandra X-ray Observatory.

"Kansas kids in classrooms today may be the people who get a chance to go back to the moon or to visit other planets," Hawley said.

But there is no way of knowing what other challenges there may be for today's students so his advice to Kansas students is to be as prepared as possible for anything that happens.

"Get as much education as you can and develop good work habits, good study habits, and of course work hard in school. It's those sorts of building blocks that you get from your teachers, from your parents, from your counselors as you go through school that are going to position you to be competitive when opportunities come up."

Hawley said he didn't know he'd ever have a chance to apply to the National Space and Aeronautics Administration (NASA) to be an astronaut.

"It was because of the training I had gotten and the hard work I had done in school and the good grades and all that other stuff that allowed me to be competitive," he said.

Hawley said, *"He can envision a time when there will be mines on asteroids or on the moon and when vast amounts of power for things on Earth will come from using the power of the sun."*

But first he said, *"students will have to learn the basics. And the basics tomorrow will definitely include computers."*

"My dad told me when I was in junior high that the single most important class I would ever take would be typing," he said. *"I said it's crazy, I'm not going to grow up to be a secretary. But I took typing anyway. It turns out I spend half my day typing and working on a computer. I'm so lucky my father made me do that."*

When ask about any exciting event that happened on a flight, Hawley replied:

"Well, it's all very interesting. A couple come to mind. When I was in orbit, I saw a meteor burn up in the atmosphere. From the ground, we can see that at night sometimes and I had seen it before but this was the first time I'd ever seen it underneath me."

"I don't care if they (kids) become astronauts and I don't care if they become astronomers, but if they are interested in math, they are going to become better citizens and that's going to help everybody."

When ask if there will be women on the July 9, 1999 flight Hawley replied, *"Yes, as a matter of fact. Two of the five are women and the Commander is a woman, Eileen Collins. It is the first time a space shuttle has been commanded by a woman."*

Hawley also spoke of his Kansas background graduating from Salina High School (now called Central High). He obtained his undergraduate degree from the University of Kansas and he completed his doctoral program at the University of California at Santa Cruz. He and his wife and dog, now live in Houston, Texas.

Land of Diversity

Kansas has been and is a land of diverse people.

As of the 1990 census, almost three million people live in Kansas. Of that number, 2.2 million are of European or Caucasian descent; 143,000 are black; 22,000 are American Indian; 31,000 are Asian and another 49,000 are of other races.

In some ways, the Kansans of today are no different than the settlers of 100 years ago or the explorers of centuries past. They came to seek land and to establish their version of wealth: a home, a good job, and a better life for their children.

On into the next 100 years and beyond, the same will probably be true of those who come to Kansas.

What The 21st Century May Mean to Kansans

Kansas's best times have been marked by resourcefulness.

But it will take more than that for Kansas to thrive in the 21st century.

For more than a hundred years, Kansans have prided themselves on the state's natural resources: the land, the rivers, and the physical resources, the ingenuity of business leaders and its people's work ethic.

But with the year 2000, 21st century, some things we Kansans have traditionally held as assets may be diminished or need to be redefined.

The globalization of business and the Internet has already had a huge impact on redefining Kansas business. The neighborhood store is capable of having and doing computer sales around the world for example.

Transportation is another area that has had to be redefined. While Kansas towns at the turn of the 20th century competed to lure the railroad and to build roads, the issues now have more to do with redefined air travel.

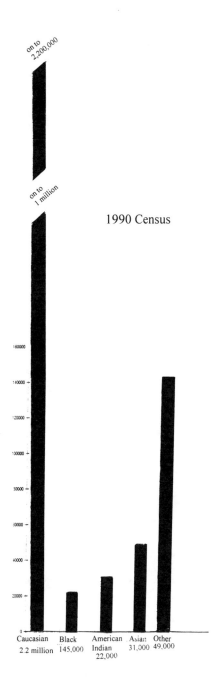

1990 Census

Transportation is also a key link to bringin people to the Midwest and the giant corporatior centrally located in Kansas. Transportation is also key to discovering the other things Kansas has to offe

One bit of news on the last day of the 20 century (Dec. 31, 1999) related to building railroad A Kansas company, Neosho Construction of Topek was awarded a 26 1/2 million dollar contract to build railroad alongside the Panama Canal. This 52 mi railroad will haul goods across the isthmus of Panam from the ships that are too large to use the canal. On again, as in the past, a Kansas company will build railroad transportation system.

There are thriving businesses, cities, and gia farms in Kansas today. But also, there is a landscape yesterday, still visible in the Gyp Hills aroun Medicine Lodge, the rolling prairies of the Flint Hill and the marshlands of Cheyenne Bottoms.

Just as it was more than a century ago.

Cattle Grazing in the Flint Hills.
Photo courtesy of Kansas State University
Special Collections

We visited the Cosmosphere again today
It's one place I've been a whole bunch of
times with my class from school. The
IMAX theater is my favorite part.
But I like looking at all the clothes
the astronauts have to wear to go to
space. Someday they'll have the space
capsule that got pulled up out of the
ocean on display here. Gus Grissom
was the astronaut on that one.

KANSAS FACTS PAGE

Date Admitted to the Union – January 29, 1861 ranking the 34th state

State Animal – American Buffalo or Bison
State Reptile – Ornate Box Turtle
State Amphibian – The Salamander
State Bird – West Meadowlark
State Tree – Cottonwood
State Insect – Honeybee
State Flower – Sunflower

State Song – Home on the Range
State Motto – "ad astra per aspera" Latin for "To the Stars Through Difficulties

State Nicknames – Wheat State, Jayhawker State, and Sunflower State

State Capital - Topeka

State Flag – Dark blue with a sunflower on top of the state seal. The word
        Kansas in gold letters, inside the seal is the state motto above
        34 stars

Total Square Miles – 82,277 Ranking 14th in the United States in size
Lebanon, in Smith County is the geographic center of the 48 United States

Major cities – Topeka, Kansas City, Overland Park, Wichita

Principal Lakes – Natural: none
        Man-made – John Redmond, Milford, Tuttle Creek, Glen
        Elder, Perry, Wilson

Highest & Lowest elevations – Highest: Mt. Sunflower at 4,039 feet
        Lowest: Verdigris River at 680 feet

Principal Rivers – Kansas River, Smoky Hill River, Solomon River,
        Arkansas River, Marais des Cygnes River, Neosho River

KANSAS GOVERNMENT

GOVERNORS OF KANSAS, 1861-2000

1861-1863	Charles Robinson	1925-1929	Ben S. Paulen
1863-1865	Thomas Carney	1929-1931	Clyde M. Reed
1865-1868	Samuel J. Crawford	1931-1933	Harry H. Woodring
1868-1869	Nehemiah Green	1933-1937	Alfred M. Landon
1869-1873	James M. Harvey	1937-1939	Walter A. Huxman
1873-1877	Thomas A. Osborn	1939-1943	Payne Ratner
1877-1879	George T. Anthony	1943-1947	Andrew F. Schoeppel
1879-1883	John P. St. John	1947-1950	Frank Carlson
1883-1885	George W. Glick	1950-1951	Frank L. Hagaman
1885-1889	John A. Martin	1951-1955	Edward F. Arn
1889-1893	Lyman U. Humphrey	1955-1957	Fred Hall
1893-1895	Lorenzo D. Lewelling	1957	John McCuish
1895-1897	Edmund N. Morrill	1957-1961	George Docking
1897-1899	John w. Leedy	1961-1965	John Anderson, Jr.
1899-1903	William E. Stanley	1965-1967	William H. Avery
1903-1905	Willis J. Bailey	1967-1975	Robert B. Docking
1905-1909	Edward W. Hoch	1975-1979	Robert F. Bennett
1909-1913	Walter R. Stubbs	1979-1987	John Carlin
1913-1915	George H. Hodges	1987-1991	Mike Hayden
1915-1919	Arthur Capper	1991-1995	Joan Finney
1919-1923	Henry J. Allen	1995-present	Bill Graves
1923-1925	Jonathan M. Davis		

Kansas has 2 branches of government: The Executive and The Legislative.

Executive Branch:

Governor: Bill Graves   State Treasurer: Tim Shallenburger
Lt. Governor: Gary Sherrer   Sec. of State: Ron Thornburger
Attorney General: Carla Stovall   Ins. Commissioner: Kathleen Sebelius

The above are all elected officials in the Executive Branch. Also in the Executive Branch are 10 elected members of the State Board of Education. All serve terms of four years.

Legislative Branch:

There are 40 State Senate Districts and 125 State Representative Districts. Senators serve four-year terms and the Representatives serve two-year terms.

The Legislature meets yearly from January to April.

U. S. Senators:
Sam Brownback
Pat Roberts

U. S. Representatives:
1st District: Jerry Moran
2nd District: Jim Ryun
3rd District: Dennis Moore
4th District: Todd Tiahrt

The Kansas Judicial:

A Chief Justice and 6 Justices serve on the Kansas Supreme Court. The Court of Appeals has nine Judges and a Chief Justice.

Throughout the state, there are 31 districts with a district court in each county. Many judicial districts also have District Magistrate Judges.

KANSAS COUNTIES AND COUNTY SEATS

CHEYENNE	RAWLINS	DECATUR	NORTON	PHILLIPS	SMITH	JEWELL	REPUBLIC	WASHINGTON	MARSHALL	NEMAHA	BROWN
St. Francis	Atwood	Oberlin	Norton	Phillipsburg	Smith Center	Mankato	Belleville	Washington	Marysville	Seneca	Hiawatha

Map courtesy of The Dangberg Foundation

Glossary

African-American – Black or partly black Americans whose ancestors came to America from Africa.

a-mouldering – To crumble or falling apart.

archaeology – The scientific study of remains of ancient peoples and buried artifacts.

arsenal – A collection of many weapons.

astronomers – People who study the universe, the planets, and the solar system.

Australian Ballot – A ballot given out only at the polling place and marked in private.

backfires – A fire started to meet an alarming forest fire or range fire by burning an area so it cannot burn.

barnstormer – One who travels from place to place to take people on sight-seeing flights in an airplane. Or one who does stunts at an airshow.

bigotry – Intolerant of another's beliefs or being devoted to one's own beliefs.

bogus – Not the real thing, counterfeit or a sham.

Bootlegger – One who sells alcohol or drugs when or where it is against the law.

carbine – A lightweight firearm originally used by cavalry.

cattle chips – A piece of dried cow manure formed into a flat disc.

combine – To unite or join. A harvesting machine which cuts and threshes grain while traveling across a field.

Communism – A government that eliminates the ownership of private property. Everything belongs to everyone, all of it supposed to be shared equally.

conquistador – An early Spanish leader who conquered Spanish America.

dauerrlotype – A photograph produced on a tin, silver, or copper plate.

devout – To vow or dedicate by a solemn act.

divan – A large sofa designed so it can be used as a bed. Or a council.

dragoons – A group of heavily armed mounted troops that commit violent acts.

drought – A very dry season which lacks of rain.

dugouts – A shelter made in the side of hill.

engraving – Cutting figures or letters onto metal, stone or wood.

epidemic – The outbreak of a disease.

erosion – The slow destruction of soil or rock by water or weather wearing it away.

fugitive – One who flees from the law.

gattling guns – A gun which operates by cranking it

guerrilla – A member of an underground unit that does irregular warfare.

gypsum – A mineral used to make plasterboard and plaster of Paris.

Helium – A light colored gas that is lighter than air. Used to lift passenger balloons and airships.

heyday – The time of greatest strength or of great prosperity.

hoarding – Keeping a hidden supply of something stored up.

homelands – A place where a person was born or where he chooses to live for the rest of his life. A native land for people.

homestead – A parcel of land given by the government to settlers who agree to live on the land and develop it.

Howitzer – A short gun firing a heavy shell fired with low velocity, at a high angle, reaching objects not able to be reached with a regular gun.

jayhawker – A member of a band of anti-slavery guerrillas in Kansas and Missouri before and during the Civil War. Nickname for a person from Kansas.

martyr – One who suffers death or persecution to defend any cause.

massacre – Killing of helpless peoples or people who could not resist.

monument – A structure or stone or other material to mark the place where something happened.

motherland – The country regarded as the place of origin for a race or group of people.

mustered – To bring together. As gathering soldiers for service.

newcomer – A person who just arrived.

nomadic- Moves around as a way of life. Nomad- one who travels all the time.

parched – Dry or scorched

Populist – A political party who practices a program of national control and proprietorship of all natural means of production.

projection – Picturing a curved surface on to a flat page.

Socialist – A person who practices the system in which the government owns and controls the means of production and distribution.

smallpox – An acute contagious disease that causes fever, sores, and scarring.

synagogue – A Jewish place of worship.

suffrage – The right to vote.

surrendered – Yielded power, or control, or possession of something to someone else.

surveyor – A person who examines a condition or state of anything.

taboo – Something forbidden. The setting of something apart and away from human contact.

tepee – A cone-shaped tent of poles covered with skins. Used by some tribes of the American Indians.

ticks – An small bug that burrows into an animals skin, sometimes carrying disease.

toll bridge – A bridge that requires payment for the right to travel across.

tornado – A violent, destructive whirling wind accompanied by a whirling cloud, violent wind, lightening, and rains moving across the land destroying things in its path.

trivet – A three-legged support used for placing hot items on.

Utopian – A perfect condition or community.

watershed – A region that drains out into a river or a lake.

wranglers – A cowboy or herdsman who round up or takes care of cattle or horses.

Index

A

Abilene – 94
Adair Cabin – 45
Adair, Samuel – 52
Adams, John Quincy – 11
Adams-Onis Treaty – 11
Air Refueling Wing 190th – 274, 277
Allen, Henry J. – 182, 200, 212
Alma Farmers Cooperative – 200
American Agriculture Movement – 264
Anderson, "Bloody" Bill – 59
Anderson, Walter – 154
Apache Indians – 82
Apollo program – 261, 291
Arapaho Indians – 82, 130
Archaic Period – 3,
Asner, Ed – 262
Atchison, David – 50, 51
Atchison, Topeka & Santa Fe – 87, 88,
   90, 99
Aurora Oil Well – 162

B

Baldwin, Curtis – 159
Ballard, Robert D. – 268
Battle of Mine Creek – 66, 67
Battle of Westport – 66
Baum, Lyman Frank – 163
Baxter Springs Massacre – 65
Beaumont, Hugh – 256
Beach Boys – 256
Beech Travel Air 6000 – 199
Beech, Olive – 169
Beech, Walter – 168, 169, 199
Beecher's Bibles - 41
Bellamy, Frank E. – 170, 171
Bening, Annette - 290
Bethany College – 113, 213
Big Timber – 79
Bleckley, Erwin – 181
Blue River – 14

Blunt, James G. – 65
Boeing Aircraft Company –223, 279
Bogus Laws – 37
Border Ruffians – 39
Bosin, Blackbear – 234
Bossi, Joe – 231
Bourgmont, Ethienne – 8
Branson, Jacob – 40
Branson, John F. – 233
Bremyer, Lt. John – 234
Browder, Earl – 181
Brown vs. Kansas Board of Ed. - 246
Brown, John – 42-46
Brown, John Henry – 97
Buffalo (bison) – 2, 84

C

Caldwell – 97
California – 30, 254
Capper, Arthur – 179, 185, 191, 221
Capper Foundation – 191
Carlsen, Frank – 240, 248
Carlson, Marshall – 233
Carson, Christopher "Kit" – 30
Carver, George Washington – 156, 157
Central Pacific – 88
Cessna Aircraft Company – 198, 223
Cessna, Clyde – 168
Chamberlin, Wilt – 256
Chanute, Octave – 88
Chase, Mabel – 139
Cherokee Strip – 130, 132
Cheyenne Indians – 2, 82, 130
Chief Black Kettle – 82, 83
Chief White Hair – 17
Chief White Plume – 18, 23
Chisholm Trail – 84, 93, 131
Cholera – 79, 81
Chrysler, Walter P. – 164
Civil War – 30, 84
Clark, William – 12
Cloud, Henry Roe – 189
Cody, Wm. "Buffalo Bill" - 80, 84, 85
Coffeyville – 100
Coleman, William – 226